PRAISE FOR

SAYING NO TO GOD

"Far from being antithetical to faith, the struggle against God has a long and hallowed history within the 'religions of the book.' Indeed, the very name given to God's people in the Hebrew Scriptures testifies to this truth. Yet today, this type of sacred conflict is largely rejected on all sides. Those inside the religious camp defend their position doggishly, while those on the outside critique it unrelentingly. Fidelity to religion on one side, betrayal on the other. In contrast to this, Matthew Korpman carefully excavates the noble tradition of faithful betrayal. In this much needed book, Korpman not only reveals a more healthy and mature faith, but also shows us how it can help us moves beyond both the Conservative and Progressive forms of faith."

PETER ROLLINS
Author of *The Idolatry of God* and *The Orthodox Heretic*

"More people are finally waking up to the reality that conventional approaches to the Bible and faith ('God said it, I believe it, and that settles it') have done much harm and must be re-examined. In this insightful work, Korpman invites readers to do what Abraham, Moses, and many other biblical characters did: to dare to argue with God. This book is not only interesting, it's needed."

BRIAN D. MCLAREN
Author of *A New Kind of Christian* and *A Generous Orthodoxy*

"*Saying No to God* offers a powerful statement of the case against bibliolatry and the sin of treating the Bible as though it were God. Korpman brings into focus the Bible's depiction of a God that not only can be but *wants* to be argued with and at times disobeyed. There is a long and theologically rich tradition of talking back to God and of arguing with the Bible and with orthodoxy, however defined. Korpman invites today's readers and people of faith to join that conversation and discover the positive transformational impact on religious faith when one accepts the Bible's invitation to talk back to its authors, as well as to the God that they themselves wrestled and argued with."

JAMES F. MCGRATH
Clarence L. Goodwin Chair in New Testament
Language and Literature at Butler University

"'God told me...' I sometimes hear said to start a sentence. Really? Such phrases make me want to debate the divine! In this remarkable book, Korpman gives good reasons we ought sometimes to disobey, disagree with, and argue against God's voice. Saying 'no' to God may be the most holy thing we can do. Reading this book may be the second most!"

THOMAS JAY OORD
Author of *God Can't: How to Believe in God and Love
after Tragedy, Abuse, and Other Evils*

"This is a well-thought, well-written and well-researched book by an author whose voice is a very welcome and much-needed one in today's theological climate. Read it and prepare to be amazed. Simply put, this book is freaking awesome."

KEITH GILES
Author of the *Jesus Unbound* and *Jesus Undefeated* and
Co-host of the Heretic Happy Hour podcast

"Love is not submission, but passionate engagement. No one loves the Bible more than the one who has wrestled with it. No one loves God more than the one who has argued, questioned, and talked back. *Saying No to God* is a work of profound love—and I loved every passionately engaged word. A book that will change your life."

DONNA BOWMAN
Author of *The Homebrewed Christianity Guide to Being Human: Becoming the Best Bag of Bones You Can Be*

"In *Saying No to God*, we discover the inspired *No* of God's most faithful friends, modeled in the Scriptures by characters who were closest to God and by the test itself as a work of polyphonic genius. I see in Korpman's work the maturity of spiritual individuation—a kind of growing up that emulates the great saints and illuminates the path ahead. I'm grateful for the good minds and hearts willing to dust off the Bible and take it so seriously."

BRAD JERSAK (PHD)
Author of *A More Christlike Way* and
IN: Incarnation & Inclusion

"Matthew Korpman has thoughtfully compiled stories from Scripture that tell an often-hidden story: sometimes, God wants us to disagree. And not only can the Bible handle our disagreements; it's designed for it. *Saying No to God* reminds us that our firmly held beliefs can be empty, and our doubts can be holy. These stories and insights remind us that the goal of faith isn't certainty but trust. And that will always require doubt in the process."

DANIELLE SHROYER
Spiritual Director, Speaker,
and Author of *Original Blessing*

"Absolutely beautiful and life giving. I've often said that a 'yes' means very little if it is not preceded by a 'no.' We are born into a world that thrusts its affirmations and orthodoxies upon us, demanding we take them on as our own, but the Spirit of Christ within will never allow us to mindlessly shout 'amen' to things we 1.) aren't convinced are true, and that, 2.) may very well be horrendous mischaracterizations of the God of Grace he ever lives to make known. And so, at some point in the sincere seeker's journey, a 'no' will begin to form in their souls. Some push it down, and refuse to look at or come to terms with what it implies, but some let it grow, emerge, and begin to articulate itself. In this timely work, Matthew J. Korpman's 'no' emerges, finds articulation, and calls a generation of discontented disciples to bravely join him in saying no to the 'god' who would refuse us the right to do so. With the skill of a scholar and a surgeon, the author takes a scalpel to the malignant views of God that have spread throughout our creeds, pulpits and pews, and points us instead to that of which only an 'amen,' and a 'yes' can be spoken. These are the sorts of books that this generation and those that will follow are in desperate need of. Were such a book around when I was in the throes of my own existential crisis and theological unraveling, I would have felt not quite so alone, and as though someone else out there understood me, the journey I was on, and the God I was coming to know, who was not threatened by my questions or my 'no's. Get this book. Read it. Throw it across the room a few times. Tear out a page or two, and, by all means, say a few 'no's.' But in the process, may you experience and discover the one concerning whom your soul longs to say 'yes.'"

JEFF TURNER
Author of *The Atheistic Theist: Why There Is
No God and You Should Follow Him*

"Are we supposed to say no to God? Most Christians would scoff at such a notion. However, in *Saying No to God*, Matthew J. Korpman argues—convincingly, I might add—that it's not only permissible, but encouraged… by none other than the Bible even! Admittedly, this will ruffle some feathers, but for those willing to put aside their theological presuppositions for a moment, they will assuredly find biblical warrant for such an idea. All in all, this book is a theological and literary tour de force, and one that should be placed in the hands of everyone who calls themselves a Christian."

MATTHEW J. DISTEFANO
Author of *From the Blood of Abel* and *Heretic!* and
Co-host of the Heretic Happy Hour podcast

"Matthew Korpman's *Saying No to God* is a paradigm-shifting and theological masterpiece! His ability to see the biblical text with fresh, creative, and imaginative eyes is bound to stir the heart and beautifully confound the mind—in a profoundly transformative and vital manner. Korpman's work gives us permission to say no to an oppressive, violent, misogynistic, authoritarian, narrow-minded, and Hell-condemning God and opens us up to a God, that while cannot be boxed in, is also at the very least a God who looks like Jesus. I highly recommend this life-changing book!"

MARK GREGORY KARRIS
Author of *Divine Echoes: Reconciling Prayer
With the Uncontrolling Love of God*

All rights reserved. No part of this book may be used or reproduced, stored in a retrieval system, or transmitted in any form or by any means, electronic, mechanical, photocopying, recording, scanning, or otherwise, without written permission from the publisher except in the case of brief quotations embodied in critical articles and reviews. Permission for wider usage of this material can be obtained through Quoir by emailing permission@quoir.com.

Copyright © 2019 by Matthew J. Korpman.

First Edition

Cover design and layout by Rafael Polendo (polendo.net)

Unless otherwise identified, all Scripture quotations in this publication are taken from the New Revised Standard Version Bible, copyright © 1989 National Council of the Churches of Christ in the United States of America. Used by permission. All rights reserved worldwide.

ISBN 978-1-938480-51-5

This volume is printed on acid free paper and meets ANSI Z39.48 standards.

Printed in the United States of America

Published by Quoir
Orange, California

www.quoir.com

SAYING TO GOD

A Radical Approach to
Reading the Bible Faithfully

MATTHEW J. KORPMAN

DEDICATION

To my dear aunt, Kathleen Marlin, whose faith helped lead to this book and whose words of wisdom and humor will always be cherished; and to my dear friend, Christian Batchelor, whose faith was far too deep for his life to be cut so short. I miss you both more than words can say and wait for that promised day when we will meet again.

TABLE OF CONTENTS

Foreword 13
A Parable 21

PART 1 – CONFRONTATION
Introduction 25
1. Doubt Everything 35
2. Abraham Didn't Believe God 49
3. Did God Say That? 63
4. Saying No to God 77
5. Job's Lawsuit Against God 93
6. Did God Say It or Moses? 109
7. Becoming Like God 127

INTERMISSION – REALIZATION
8. Pyrotheology 149

PART 2 – INCARNATION
9. Saying No to Orthodoxy 157
10. Saying No to Prejudice 177
11. Saying No to Patriarchy 195
12. Saying No to Homophobia 215
13. Saying No to Divine Violence 233
14. Saying No to Hell 253
15. Saying No to Exclusivity 283
16. We Aren't Always Right 309
17. Adam and Eve's Failure 333
Concluding Parable 343

Citations 347
Acknowledgments 355

FOREWORD

I was just eighteen years old when I packed up my new bright yellow Sunfire to head over two-thousand miles to Dallas, Texas. There I would begin my journey as an official "Bible school student." I had sensed a strong spiritual compelling into what they used to call "full-time ministry" five years prior.

I was so "on fire" for Jesus in my public high school that my friends and I were labeled the "Church Girls," a group of radical teenage Christian girls that I naturally led. The label was meant to be an insult at first, but we quickly embraced the name, making it lose its sting.

Since I was thirteen years old, I had one mission on my mind, and that was to serve God in ministry for the rest of my life. It was clearly my purpose. I was interested in almost nothing else and I also happened to have the gifts to do to the job of pastoring my family and friends. The Gospel has been at the center of my entire existence. I was born with this one sense of calling and purpose, and if I refused to fulfill it, I would "explode."

As the radical and moody Old Testament prophet Jeremiah put it:

> But if I say, "I will not remember Him or speak anymore in His name,"
> Then in my heart it becomes like a burning fire shut up in my bones;
> And I am weary of holding it in, And I cannot endure it.
> (JEREMIAH 20:9, NASB)

I could not imagine doing anything else with my life except becoming a preacher, Bible teacher, Christian leader, or all of the above. That was simply who I was, and apparently who I always was. When my dearest grandmother was still alive, she would continually remind me of when I used to preach to my baby dolls as a little girl. When she was dying, she would tell me this same story over and over again, as if to say "you know who you are; don't forget." As she was passing away into Heaven, she spoke with an angel-like awareness and a divine "wink" in her eye.

I came from a supportive egalitarian family and my dad was a minister, which was awesome as a teenage girl who felt destined to become a minister herself; however, I also had no idea that there were people out there who did not support women in ministry. You can imagine my shock and dismay when I received my education in this patriarchal belief system from guess who? Christian guys in Bible school who did not believe in having women involved in ministry.

I remember the day well. I was walking out of my Bible School's cafeteria at eighteen years old when several of the older "cool" guys called me over to have a chat with them in the front lounge of the building. I sat down thinking that they wanted to include me in a conversation as a peer. Boy, was I wrong!

They opened up their Bibles and began to point out Bible verses that they interpreted as "women should not be preachers and pastors; especially over men." I had seriously never heard of such a concept and my heart was absolutely shattered by the entire experience.

Of course, I sucked it up like a big girl in the moment; never would I have allowed those "Bible Bullies" to behold my tears. I politely tolerated the conversation and even listened to their points with an open mind and heart; something I would not tolerate today because I now see this whole scenario as spiritual harassment and abuse. The traumatic event happened almost two decades ago and it still hurts my heart to recall and retell it.

That was the first moment in my life that I was confronted with the question, "*Are you going to say no to what appears to be God, or are you going to keep saying yes to the God you know?*"

I walked to my dorm alone fighting back the tears. Not only was I now questioning my entire life purpose, but I also felt utterly used and rejected by those young men. They made a fool out of me and I knew it, but I did not yet know how to stick up for myself or defend my calling. I was so young, so passionate about Jesus, so involved in serving the church already, so naive about the sexist realities woven into our church cultures and doctrines, and so utterly unaware that some Christian men reject women's voices and leadership under the guise of religion.

When I arrived at my dorm, I called my dad immediately, bursting into tears the moment he picked up the phone. I told him about my chat with those young men and asked, "If God does not call women into ministry, why am I here in Bible School?" My dad was prepared, as if he had always been waiting for me to run into this problem. He said with calm authority and clarity, "those guys don't know what they are talking about" and went on to reassure me and my calling with Scripture.

Just a few days later, I received a box in the mail from my dad. It was filled with egalitarian theology books. The days of being naïve about gender inequalities and injustices in the church were over. It was no time to give up on my mission, but it was time to hit the books and study hard. As a woman minister it became evident that I would not only have to defend the Gospel of Jesus Christ, but I would also have to defend the very act of "preaching the Gospel" as a woman.

At eighteen years old I had the blessed opportunity to "say no to God" when I was confronted by "Bible-School-Bullies" who wanted me to say "yes" to *their* interpretation of Scripture and God. In having the opportunity to "say no" to their version of God, I became wiser, stronger and keener on hearing the actual voice of God.

That day, when those young men were "cherry-picking" the Scriptures in order to convince me to not follow my ministerial calling due to my being a woman, I zoned out for a few seconds and happened to glance outside. There was a young brown-skinned man in a beanie walking by. He was very "hipster" and way cooler looking than the guys who were talking down to me.

I imagined he was Jesus, outside of the religious institutional walls, saying, "Hey, what are you doing hanging out with those dudes when you could stand up, walk out those doors and come follow me?" It was the first time I ever saw that guy on campus and now that I think about it, it was also the last.

In *Saying No to God*, Matthew does not challenge the woman preacher simply trying to spread "the good news," or the woman pastor simply trying to care for her congregation, or the LGBTQ+ person simply trying to live out their existence and faith in peace, or the poor simply trying to get by, or the sick simply trying to survive, or the person of color simply asking for genuine equality, or the single person simply asking to be included, or the abuse victim simply trying to overcome trauma and be heard, or the grieved simply trying to heal. Instead, Matthew challenges the broken system, the legalistic culture and the toxic theology that allows Christians to continue to defend the powerful in Christ's name, while dismissing those who are experiencing oppression, exclusion, marginalization, injustices and inequalities in Jesus' name every single day.

Saying No to God will be one of the most eye-opening books you have ever read and every Christian should reserve the opportunity to read this book! Korpman has done his theological homework and challenges us to know the depths of God's character; even to the point of God being pleased with those who have serious spiritual doubts and questions. This book will both challenge and revolutionize your faith.

Jory Micah
Upcoming Author of *Breaking the Glass Steeple*
and Blogger at JoryMicah.com

TRADITIONAL RELIGION

Never say no to God. God must always be obeyed, no matter what he commands. What God says, we should do. God's word is an unquestioning law. If we disobey it for any reason, we are unfaithful sinners.

THE BIBLE

Always be ready to say no to God. God should not always be obeyed, depending on what he commands. What God says, we shouldn't always do. God's Word is an instructive guide. If we disobey it for the right reasons, we are faithful saints.

A PARABLE

I would like to tell you the story of a small town filled with believers who sought to act always in obedience to the voice of God. When faced with difficult situations, the leaders of the community would often be found deep in prayer, or searching the scripture for guidance and wisdom. Late one evening, in the middle of winter, a young man from the neighboring city arrived at the gates of the town's little church seeking refuge. The caretaker immediately let him in and, seeing that he was hungry and cold, provided a meal and some warm clothes. After he had eaten, the young man explained how he had fled the city because the authorities had labeled him a political dissident. It turned out that the man had been critical of both the government and the church in his work as a journalist. The caretaker brought the young man back to his home and allowed him to stay until a plan had been worked out concerning what to do next.

When the priest was informed of what had happened, he called the leaders of the town together in order to work out what ought to be done. After two days of discussion, it was agreed that the man should be handed over to the authorities in order to face up to the crimes he had committed. But the caretaker protested, saying, "This man has committed no crimes; he has merely criticized what he believes to be the injustices perpetrated by authorities in the name of God."

"What you say may be true," replied the priest, "but his presence puts the whole of this town in danger. What if the authorities work out where he is and learn that we protected him?"

But the caretaker refused to hand him over to the priest, saying, "He is my guest, and while under my roof I will ensure that no harm comes to him. If you take him from me by force, then I will publicly attest to having helped him and suffer the same injustice as my guest."

The caretaker was well loved by the people and the priest had no intention of letting something happen to him. So the leaders went away again and this time searched the scriptures for an answer, for they knew that the caretaker was a man of deep faith. After a whole night of poring over the scriptures the leaders came back to the caretaker saying, "We have read the sacred book all through the night seeking guidance and found that it tells us that we must respect the authorities of this land and witness to the truth of faith through submission to them."

But the caretaker also knew the sacred words of scripture and told them that the Bible also asked that we care for those who suffer and are persecuted. There and then the leaders began to pray fervently. They beseeched God to speak to them, not as a still small voice in their conscience, but in the way that He had spoken to Abraham and Moses. They begged that God would communicate directly to them and to the caretaker so that the issue could finally be resolved. Sure enough, the sky began to darken and God descended from heaven, saying, "The priest and the elders speak the truth, my friend. In order to protect the town, this man must be handed over to the authorities."

But the caretaker, a man of deep faith, looked up to heaven and replied, "If you want me to remain faithful to you, my God, then I can do nothing but refuse your advice. For I do not need the scriptures or your words to tell me what I ought to do. You have already demanded that I look after this man. You have written that I must protect him at all costs. Your words of love have been spelled out by the lines of this man's face; your text is found in the texture of his flesh. And so my God, I defy you precisely so as to remain faithful to you."

With this God withdrew with a smile, knowing that the matter had finally been settled.

(PETER ROLLINS)[1]

PART ONE
CONFRONTATION

INTRODUCTION

"The place of theology is direct confrontation with this Word, a situation in which theology finds itself placed, and must again and again place itself."

KARL BARTH[1]

When was the last time that you said *no* to God? That's a strange question, I'm sure. But even so, allow me to ask it anyway. Essentially, have you had times in your life in which you've felt that God was leading you in a certain direction that you didn't want to go or even chose not to? If you're like many countless people (both past and present), the answer probably is *many* times. And more than likely, you may feel regret for those decisions, for not trusting a higher power to guide your limited perspective on life. Likewise, you may even, in retrospect, now sing that famous hymn: "I was blind but now I see."

Many sermons are preached quite passionately each year, not only in America but across the world, emphasizing how we need to trust God with our pain and shortcomings, allowing him to lead us in ways only our Creator can. And it makes complete sense. Two proverbs from Israel's early history warn that "whoever trusts in his own mind is a fool" (Prov. 28:26) and that we should "trust in the LORD" with all our hearts, not leaning on our "own understanding" (3:5). One of the Psalmists remarks that it is better to trust God "than to trust in man" (118:8). And the prophet Jeremiah goes so far as to curse anyone who "trusts in man and makes flesh his strength" (Jer. 17:5–6, ESV). Paul, much later in Israel's history, explicitly points out that the "sentence of death" they believed had been given to them since Eden, that which Christ redeemed, was given so that they would not trust themselves (2 Cor. 1:9).

However, in spite of these oft-quoted texts, I want to ask the earlier question again, but this time a bit different. When was the last time that you were *glad* that you disagreed with God? When did you last tell God no and felt relieved, perhaps even blessed, that you did? When, if ever, have you felt that it was the morally right thing to do? This probably sounds like one of the strangest questions you've ever had to read in a book on the Christian faith. Is it a trick question? If you answer yes, would it be heresy?

For most Christians, the idea of resisting God is understood to be a universal negative. There is no debate for the average believer that God knows more than we do, and well, that's that. If we are merely dirtlings, as Genesis calls us, then who are we to disagree with the Almighty, the creator of dirt? Who are we to make judgments on the judge of all? And yet, there's a truth to this that could shock you. There's a foundation behind the questions that could shake your very concepts of religious faith. What is it? Simply this:

God *wants* us, sometimes, to say no.

This is *not* something to avoid.

In fact, this is exactly what God invites us to do… *in* the Bible.

That's a lot to swallow, I realize. It's probably a radically new idea for you. God wants you to fight with him? The answer is yes. As surprising and unexpected as it might seem, the God of Abraham, Jacob and Moses—yes, *that* God—wants you to resist him. While I realize your skepticism about my claim, I invite you to open up your own

Bible (or app), grab some popcorn (or a crunchy haystack*) and join me for what may well be the ride of your spiritual life. But in order to get us moving forward, allow me to briefly take you back in time, four years ago to when the birth of this realization started.

EUTHYPHRO WHO?

It was a Monday night in February and the weather outside was exactly what you'd expect from Southern California: clear skies, plenty of stars, and warm temperatures. In other words, perfection. That evening, I was sitting in what was quickly becoming one of my favorite courses during my time in college. My professor was Maury Jackson, assistant professor of Practical Theology at La Sierra University's Divinity School, and a longtime friend and mentor during my academic and spiritual journey. He also happened to be a gifted teacher and, arguably, one of the most popular in the school. When I say that he never taught a boring class, I undersell his countless accomplishments.

In this particular class that night, we were surveying the origins of ethics in ancient Greece. While that in itself may not sound riveting, the main topic at one point in the lecture was what has become known as *Euthyphro's Dilemma*. If you haven't heard of it, there's no shame in admitting it. The name alone is a mouthful. It comes from one of Plato's dialogues, in which Socrates asks Euthyphro: "Is the good loved by the gods because it is good, or is it good because it is loved by the gods?"

It's a fundamental question: what makes something good? In the context of religion, the question broadens: is what God does always

---

* A "haystack" is the name of a common potluck dish served in Seventh-day Adventist churches. It consists of a number of chips which are covered in beans, salad, and other toppings.

27

good because God does it or is something good and because it is good, God does it? In short, is "good" as a concept separate from God (so that God chooses it), or defined by God (so that whatever God chooses is automatically made good)?

Lest we assume that such an idea is just philosophical mumbo jumbo that doesn't relate to the real, concrete, and tangible reality we live in, I must give a warning: the way we answer that question has serious consequences for how we understand God and morality. It also largely defines how we as humans *relate* to God in our experience of faith. How we answer Socrates' challenge determines whether it's possible for us to ever *challenge God*. In short, it makes it either possible or impossible to say *no* to God.

To illustrate this: if you claim that the good is whatever God does, then that means that when God decides to murder everyone in a city one day, there can be no judgment given against God for doing so. No one would have the right to object. One must, in this view, admit that whatever God does is good only because he did it. There is no logic about it from which we can judge. It also means that God can tell us not to commit murder and yet do so himself, because although it would not be good for us to do it, whatever God did would be good if he did it. This view is often called *Divine Command Theory*, because what is good is ultimately what is commanded by the divine.

The other option is to believe that whatever makes something good is separate from God and that God does what he does because he recognizes that it is good. However, in this view, the idea of "goodness" becomes an almost equal power to God, something which God must answer to just as we do. It means that as far back in time as you can go, there was always God and the idea of *the Good*, with one being the master of the other. For a polytheistic Greek, that might not be such a problem. For a monotheistic Christian like myself, that idea doesn't sound quite right, even if it avoids the problem of approving arbitrary divine homicide.

And yet, there's also an alternative to the two that has been proposed by those who don't like either of the two options. A third possibility is to believe that because the good and God are inseparable, and that God always acts according to the good, that the entire dilemma that Socrates creates is a false choice to begin with. This view argues that God wouldn't murder a city, not merely because that isn't good, but because God *is goodness*, and as such, such an act is unthinkable to him. That has been the standard answer from Christians and Jewish philosophers for ages, including Augustine, Anselm and Aquinas. But the idea has its flaw too: if God is the same as goodness, then doesn't that still mean that a *Divine Command Theory* is right? We may think that genocide is wrong, but if God did it, we would have to conclude even according to this third theory that God's acts were good because he is goodness. So in the end, all three possibilities still leave us lost without a satisfying answer.

And yet, I still remember sitting there in that class, front row and center, thinking to myself: *this doesn't make any sense*. As I stared at the blackboard with the options spelled out in white chalk, I grew increasingly uncomfortable. Now, I'm not alone in feeling discontent with the answers provided. Countless individuals have agonized over this question for centuries, recognizing that none of the solutions appears to solve all the problems that they create. However, my frustration was, admittedly, a bit unique compared to others. I had a nagging thought in the back of my head, something that wouldn't stop annoying me.

I kept thinking: wasn't there some story in the Bible that talked about a character who disagreed with God? The details were fuzzy in my mind, but I remembered that there was some story somewhere in which God said one thing, a human called him out on it, and God in response "changed his mind." I definitely remembered that last part, because it was something most pastors had spent time attempting to explain away. If you're anything like me, you too probably can vaguely recall those same details. And so, with just that little bit of knowledge, I found myself squirming in my chair.

If a human in the Bible could disagree with God, didn't that mean that, at the very least, that character in the Bible believed that the idea of goodness was separate from God? By disagreeing with God, by saying no to the Almighty, was he not affirming that God was going against what was good? And didn't God's choice to "change his mind" confirm this idea? At first glance, this seemed to lend credibility to the first response: the good is separate from God and something which God himself admires.

Yet, I also knew that God was proclaimed in Scripture as the creator of all that ever was (including the principle of morality). So, if God was affirmed within the Bible to both be the creator of the good and to be one who humans could disagree with about the good, where in the world did the biblical God fit in Socrates' question? It was, in short, a massive paradox.

Little did I realize that beginning that night, the spark of this book's origin would be born and with it, the beginning of a theological journey so grand, that I might have been terrified to undertake it had I known all that it would have entailed. That night, consciously and unconsciously, I set out to discover the answer to Socrates question as it related to the God of the Bible. In short, just what sort of God was I worshipping? What sort of sacred text was I deriving my morality from? What did it mean to call the Bible Scripture and in what sense was it inspired? And perhaps foremost, but certainly underlining all the other questions: was it ever acceptable to reject something God said? Or to be more audacious: is it ever *the morally right thing* to tell the Almighty no?

When I began these thoughts, I was an hour south of Los Angeles, California. As I write about them now, I'm twelve minutes north of New Haven, Connecticut, still studying the Bible, only this time at Yale University's Divinity School. Life clearly takes some interesting twists and turns and I'd be lying if I didn't admit to enjoying the ride. I'm newly married, considerably colder, increasingly exhausted, and neverendingly excited by what I learn. And yet, the questions remain after all these years, as they always have. I knew then, as I know now, that whatever was happening in the Bible didn't neatly fit either the dichotomy that Socrates proposed or the negation of it that other Christians philosophers had surmised. The God of the Bible was doing something different, something Socrates or Anselm had never imagined, and I've remained determined to find out what that is.

THE JOURNEY AHEAD

This book is modeled as a journey, an expedition into the mystery of what sort of relationship God is seeking with his creation. Is it one of servitude? Does God seek our obedience and unilateral agreement? Or is it one of struggle and challenge? Does God perhaps seek wrestling partners who are more apt to argue than to obey? And most important of all, this is a journey to discover what role Jesus plays in all of this. In what way does he, as the revelation of God, reveal God's desire for our relationship with him?

Inevitably, in journeying to understand this divine mystery, we will need to travel into the heart of what contains, for us as Christians, our witness to God: the Bible. In so doing, we will be placing a spotlight on all the parts of the Bible that most ministers try deeply to avoid. Every dark crag and dusty crevice of Scripture will need to be examined, no matter how painful, confusing and disturbing. One of the purposes of this book is in part to reorient us in how we read and approach the Bible as both an *ancient* book and as *living* Scripture. And while this is by no means an original goal or a unique project, this book will attempt to approach the issue and tackle it in ways that are *very* different from how they have been done before.

As a conservative Christian who was raised to read the Bible as the very words (or at least, the *thoughts*) of God, I struggled in my young adult life to make sense of both what the Bible was and how it could be authoritative. In some ways, that struggle has never ended and honestly, it likely won't. Perhaps you can relate to me in that struggle, or perhaps not. Either way, we can both agree that there are things in Scripture that defy our sense of morality and reality. These things challenge us, and require a careful response.

Endless confusion plagues sincere believers and skeptics who find a plethora of books either warning them that the Bible is hopelessly human or unrealistically divine. Both of these typical approaches struggle to acknowledge the real human qualities of the Bible and abysmally fail to challenge the biblical text in any way that comes close to the way that many of the biblical heroes of faith challenged God to his face.

That's where I hope this work is able to break the odd dichotomy of an either/or scenario, where it is often argued by certain conservative leaders that either "you accept the Bible as fully authoritative and put your human reasoning away" or "you place your human reasoning above God and the Bible no longer bears the divine imprint." Stuck in the dichotomy between either accepting the Bible as if it were verbally inspired like the Qur'an or choosing human reasoning as a tool that makes Scripture outdated, we have large swaths of Christians in both liberal and conservative communities who look on either side of them and wonder where they are supposed to go when they seem to be on neither the right or left path.

INTRODUCTION

This book is for you if you are one of them. It comes from the heart of a young scholar and minister (in training) who loves Scripture with a deep passion, but feels that the current conflicts over interpretation have threatened to rob the Bible of its power. In short, I'm trying to write a book for the rest of us. By avoiding this fork in the road, I'm walking a path not only less traveled, but one that doesn't exactly exist, even if many of us are unaware that we are already walking on it.

In particular, what this book does differently than most others, is that it seeks to recover, polish, and remind us of a very specific and overlooked root of our faith that lays at the very foundation of not only the stories of Abraham, Jacob, and Moses, but reaches back to the beginning of Genesis with Adam and Eve. And this root, as one discovers, is so radically different from what many think of as their origin, that it can seem as if it is the root to an entirely different faith. What is that paradoxical root? *God's personal invitation, in Scripture, for us to fight and ultimately, to say "No!" ... to God.*

To explore this radical idea, we will travel through three sections that make up this journey. The first part will be to explore the idea of *confrontation* with the Divine, looking at the Bible for examples of those who embodied this idea best: heroes of faith such as Abraham, Jacob and Moses, to say nothing of Jesus himself! The next part will be a very brief, but necessary *intermission* for us to catch our breath, giving time to reassess where we stand in the midst of this deconstructive process. The second large section will be an exploration of the idea of *incarnation*, where the practical application of these ideas will be examined with regard to modern theological issues, topics that include Orthodoxy, Women's Ordination, Hell, and Salvation.

By the end of the book, you will be able to evaluate my central argument: that in order to faithfully say *Yes* to God, we must first learn when to radically say *No*.

1
DOUBT EVERYTHING

"If doubt appears, it should not be considered as the negation of faith, but as an element which was always and will always be present in the act of faith."

PAUL TILLICH[1]

Let me start this chapter by asking a trick question: which disciple doubted Jesus' resurrection? If you're like most, you'll probably shout "Thomas!" Most would. Many preachers do. Of course, depending on where you are reading this, shouting may not be advisable. Anyway, the point is that you'd be partially wrong. The question was a trick because "disciple" should be in the plural. While it is true that Thomas doubted Jesus' resurrection (and we'll get to him in a bit), he wasn't the only one who did. In fact, a great number of Jesus' disciples doubted Christianity's central event! In the Gospel of Matthew, at the close of his story, we read the following stunning and baffling account:

> Now the eleven disciples went to Galilee, to the mountain to which Jesus had directed them. *When they saw him, they worshiped him; but some doubted.* And Jesus came and said to them, "All authority in heaven and on earth has been given to me. Go therefore and make disciples of all nations, baptizing them in the name of the Father and

of the Son and of the Holy Spirit, and teaching them to obey everything that I have commanded you. And remember, I am with you always, to the end of the age."

(MATTHEW 28:16–20)*

This is supposed to be the greatest moment of Christianity, in which the disciples behold Jesus rising with the angels to his heavenly throne, fully alive and having conquered death. And what does Matthew's Gospel tell us about this powerful moment of faith? *Some doubted.* Watching their master and rabbi ascend into the sky, those closest to Christ doubted. What did they doubt? Apparently, everything. I'm certain that this is shocking for some of you to imagine, especially if you have been brought up believing that such behavior is wrong to have as a person of faith.

But, *here's the rub* (as John Collins is fond of saying in his classes at Yale): regardless of the doubts of the disciples, Jesus still commissions and empowers them. Their doubts about his resurrection, even as the ascending Jesus stares down at them, do not prevent them from being Christ's apostles. Their doubts are not said to be solved or dealt with, and yet, even so, Jesus sends them out on his behalf, promising to be with them "to the end of the age." In the midst of their doubting, Jesus commissions them to be his disciples. In other words, he accepts them and commissions them to take those doubts and utilize them in service toward the one they doubt. If that was powerful two thousand years ago to Jewish and Gentile readers, it is certainly just as powerful in today's *post*-postmodern society.

---

* As a general note, all quotations from the Bible will be drawn from the New Revised Standard Version (NRSV), unless otherwise noted. All italics within biblical quotes are added by me for emphasis.

GOD WANTS YOU TO DOUBT

Which leads us to another biblical bombshell: God doesn't just overlook our doubts, he encourages them. Paul once wrote in 1 Thess. 5:21 that the early Christians should *"doubt everything, and keep what is good."* It's a verse that seems perfect for our postmodern age, yet most Christians never hear it in church. The Greek word δοκιμάζω (*dokimazo*) is often translated in Bibles as "test," but the meaning is given variously by biblical dictionaries as "to try and determine the genuineness of," to determine its "acceptance as trustworthy," to "discern" or to "verify." All of which ultimately means that in order to test everything, you must also test things that you already believed were proven. And that inevitably means that you must question certain things, things that you never had reason to doubt before, with a healthy dose of skepticism. And like a series of links in a chain, one realizes that in order to question whether your legs can lift your weight (something most take for granted), one must be willing to consider the possibility that your legs might not be able to. To test means *to question*, and to question means *to doubt* (if done sincerely, rather than jestingly).

Paul's advice is not for Christians to simply become skeptics who throw their hands up in the air (enough people today already do that), but it is a cautious warning to realize that all of our beliefs and ideas (even about the Bible) require testing (which begins with doubting) in order to throw away what is no longer needed and "keep what is good." That last statement by Paul is important as well, since he affirms that we will often find good things mixed with not-so-good things. We are not advised to throw away the good just because of the bad. And while this is certainly true of many things in life, I especially believe the same is true of Scripture, which is why Paul affirms that we "should *try* to find out what is pleasing to the Lord," but stops short of saying that it is something we can easily do even when reading our scriptures (Eph. 5:10). And in Romans 14 he goes so far as to state that if Christians cannot come to one interpretation, God isn't ultimately concerned with whether they do or don't (vss. 22–23).

It's a shocking idea for some. Does God really leave room for us to question and to doubt? Does the Bible encourage questions rather than quickly attempt to solve them? The answer is yes! Rather than being a sin, it is God's delight for us to question what he says. And moreover, I firmly believe that once we have this principle in our minds, we can begin to move forward and become (re)introduced to the Bible that we either are learning about for the first time or are falling back in love with once again.

CERTAINTY IS A PROBLEM

It's fascinating to note that in the Gospel of Luke, the disciples are said to doubt even earlier than Matthew's account had alluded. In fact, in Luke's account, not just *some*, but *all* of the disciples doubt Jesus' resurrection.

> While they were talking about this, Jesus himself stood among them and said to them, "Peace be with you." They were startled and terrified, and thought that they were seeing a ghost. *He said to them, "Why are you frightened, and why do doubts arise in your hearts?* Look at my hands and my feet; see that it is I myself. Touch me and see; for a ghost does not have flesh and bones as you see that I have." And when he had said this, he showed them his hands and his feet. While in their joy they were disbelieving and still wondering, he said to them, "Have you anything here to eat?" They gave him a piece of broiled fish, and he took it and ate in their presence.
>
> (LUKE 24:36–43)

Gathered together, Jesus' inner circle of eleven (minus Judas), come face to face with the risen Christ. Unlike the previous account, this one gives more details about the questions on their minds. According to Luke, the object of all the disciples' doubts was whether Jesus was a ghost (and indeed dead), or whether he was resurrected (and indeed alive). They cannot bring themselves to believe that he not only *appeared* to them, but that he is physically present among them.

Again though, Jesus does not judge them, nor does he reprimand their disbelief. Instead, he asks for food to demonstrate that he is alive and physically with them. He understands his followers' questions and willingly attempts to provide what they desire and need. Their very doubts lead them into a better understanding of the risen Jesus.

It is within *this* context that we find John's account of Thomas, and it is only within this context that we can start to appreciate what John is doing in his narrative.

> But Thomas (who was called the Twin), one of the twelve, was not with them when Jesus came. So, the other disciples told him, "We have seen the Lord." But he said to them, "Unless I see the mark of the nails in his hands, and put my finger in the mark of the nails and my hand in his side, I will not believe." A week later his disciples were again in the house, and Thomas was with them. Although the doors were shut, Jesus came and stood among them and said, "Peace be with you." Then he said to Thomas, "Put your finger here and see my hands. Reach out your hand and put it in my side. Do not doubt but believe." Thomas answered him, "My Lord and my God!" Jesus said to him, "Have you believed because you have seen me? Blessed are those who have not seen and yet have come to believe."
> (John 20:24–29)

If you're like me, you've probably heard this story told from the pulpit a thousand times. "Remember Jesus' words," preachers remind their congregants, "Don't be a doubting Thomas. Believe!" The entire story is transformed into a condemnation of questioning and doubt. Yet, these sermons do a great disservice to this story, distorting its meaning. For the message of this story in John neither condemns Thomas for his doubt nor does it present Thomas as the only doubter.

The event in John's story is the same as Luke's. They are both attempting to narrate the same thing. So, it is with great interest that we can note that when these two accounts are placed together, it becomes clear that not only Thomas, but *all* the disciples doubted Jesus. His words then are not directed to Thomas, but all the disciples as a whole. However, we don't actually need Luke's account to show this to be true. Even John's Gospel reveals the same set of facts all on its own terms.

To begin, the story in John 20 opens with the note in verse 18 that Mary had told the fearful disciples that she had seen Jesus and that he was ascending to his reign in heaven. Yet what does the text tell us next? We are informed that the disciples are still hiding in fear within the room. Does this sound like the reaction of those who believe Mary? No, certainly not. Only a few verses earlier, it mentions in John's Gospel that the disciples doubted Mary's initial report that the tomb was empty. In short, the disciples doubt Mary's word until they see Jesus themselves, and all John has added is that Thomas doubts the disciple's words until he sees Jesus himself.

With that in mind, let us look at the words of Jesus to Thomas. Again and again, many ministers claim that Jesus is reprimanding Thomas' doubt. But is he? Jesus' questioning words to Thomas are profound, "Have you believed because you have seen me? Blessed are those who have not seen and yet have come to believe" (John 20:29). As we already pointed out earlier, these words are not directed only to Thomas. Christ's words bless those who have not needed to "see" to believe, something that Mary required, something which the other disciples required (who doubted Mary), and something that Thomas needed (when he doubted the disciples).

Yet, aside from who it was directed to, what exactly is Jesus' rebuke? It is not, as so many have claimed, a rebuke of doubt itself. Far from it. Jesus never once condemns Thomas or the disciples *because of* doubting, but rather rebukes their personal requirement (stated explicitly by Thomas) to never believe unless they first see. In other words, Jesus accepts doubt's healthy role in our faith, but rejects an unhealthy requirement for the eradication of doubt. His warning is not that doubt is wrong, but that our desire for its removal is! A requirement for certainty, the opposite of doubt, is what Jesus condemns. Ironically, rather than rebuking a skeptical mindset, Jesus actually condemns the need for a faith based on certainty, the sort of faith that so many who condemn Thomas from the pulpit promote.

Jesus implores Thomas to believe. But what exactly does that mean? Biblical scholar Marcus Borg notes that our familiar English word carries a forgotten meaning. "Prior to the seventeenth century," he wrote, "the word 'believe' did not mean believing in the truth of statements or propositions." In fact, "grammatically, the object of believing was not statements, but a person." So what did it mean in English to say that you believed something?

> Most simply, "to believe" meant "to love." Indeed, the English words "believe" and "belove" are related. What we believe is what we belove.[2]

We can note something else too: to love something is to trust it. Trust is not the same thing as certainty. Far from it! For example, when I love my wife, I place my trust in her. That does not mean that I can never question anything regarding her, but rather that I am certain that my trust is well placed in her. It means that because of my trust, my doubts are either directed at myself (do I know her as well as I should?) or toward something abnormal in her own actions (why is she acting the opposite of how she normally does?). As such, there is always a careful balance between trust and doubt in any bond. The same is true of our faith and relationship with Jesus. Doubt is a healthy part of our walk with God. We need doubt to help us to evaluate the Bible, to grow deeper in our understanding of Christ, and even to recognize the Holy Spirit (as opposed to any other rival spirit).

Because biblical scholars, theologians, and scientists often deal in matters of doubt, Thomas has sometimes been called the "academic's apostle." While that has a nice ring to it, I would disagree only because I know that doubt is not special to those of us who study in the halls of schools. It is a constant friend or enemy to many in the Christian faith, professional and ordinary alike. The sad reality is that so many have felt and are continued to be made to feel ashamed of such things. Doubt, they hear, is the enemy of faith, when the opposite is true: it is a great ally.

Even before the crucifixion, we find Jesus showing a positive attitude toward those who doubt. For example, take John the Baptist. He is remembered and immortalized at the beginning of every Gospel account as the prophetic voice declaring the way for Jesus' future ministry. He's as much a symbol of true and sure faith as any that can be imagined. And so, it is surprising how few remember that every Gospel account also records that shortly before John's death (beheaded at the request of King Herod's dancing daughter), John came to *doubt* whether Jesus really was the Messiah after all.

> When John heard in prison what the Messiah was doing, he sent word by his disciples and said to him, "Are you the one who is to come, or are we to wait for another?" Jesus answered them, "Go and tell John what you hear and see: the blind receive their sight, the lame walk, the lepers are cleansed, the deaf hear, the dead are raised, and the poor have good news brought to them…"
>
> (MATTHEW 11:2–6)

According to the stories, John sent messengers to Jesus asking him (with perhaps a hint of sarcasm), whether he was the promised one or they should continue to wait for another. The last major prophet before Jesus, the one who Jesus himself said there was "no one greater," and who was like Elijah... *doubted* Jesus' ministry. He *doubted* Christ. And guess what? As theologian Fritz Guy notes: "Jesus did not reject the question as improper, criticize John for a lack of faith, appeal to his own self-authenticating authority, or exhort John to believe." Instead, "Jesus both respected and appealed to John's intelligence and rationality by pointing to evidence."[3] Just like with his disciples, Jesus routinely shows an open and encouraging response to the questions and doubts that are directed toward him. Moreover, in each of these narratives, the people doubting grow in their faith *because* of their doubts.

A HUMBLE FAITH

But some may wonder: how can doubt be a good thing if our faith is built on certainty? The answer: it's not. That's why Jesus, although welcoming Thomas' doubt, discouraged his demand for certainty. Because in truth, our faith is actually built on humility.

> For *we* know *only in part*, and *we* prophesy *only in part*; but when the complete comes, the partial will come to an end. When I was a child, I spoke like a child, I thought like a child, I reasoned like a child; when I became an adult, I put an end to childish ways. For *now* we see in a mirror, *dimly*, but then we will see face to face. *Now* I know *only in part*; then I will know fully, even as I have been fully known.
> (1 CORINTHIANS 13:9–12)

This is a famous text in Christianity, which makes it all the more surprising that so few actually recognize the curious and slightly unorthodox message that it contains. Paul is speaking *as* a Christian *about* Christians. In other words, he is not saying that "the world" knows only dimly, but we as Christians know in full. He is not saying that we were children before Christ, but have now become adults *in* Christ. No, he isn't saying that at all. Instead, he's describing what Christians are *after* Jesus.

According to Paul, it is *because* of Jesus that we know as much as a child does. *Because* of Jesus, we know only in part. *Because* of Jesus, we now see dimly. So what does that mean about *before* Jesus? It means that before the incarnation of Christ, we knew almost nothing (not even "in part"). Before Jesus, we were blind (we couldn't even see "dimly"). In short, it means that before Jesus, we weren't even born yet!

The great news of Paul in 1 Cor. 13:9–12 is that because of Jesus, we can finally see… something (but not much). Talk about humility! But it's even more humble than you imagine. The Greek word translated as "dimly" isn't what it sounds like in English. The Greek word is αἰνίγματι (*ainigmati*), where we get the word "enigma" from; and it means the same thing as it sounds like: it refers to something that is itself *a riddle*, something indirect, difficult, obscure, and very perplexing. So, Paul literally says in that verse that "now we see an enigma," or to better get the sense: "now we see an obscure perplexing riddle." Crowd stirring, isn't it? And mind you, he's describing the Christian faith.

What does an "obscure perplexing riddle" tell us? Well, it tells us that Paul has a sense that what Jesus revealed was only a small taste of the *real* truth. There is something bigger coming, something so incomprehensible that everything we already think we know is similar to a child imagining there's nothing left to experience in adulthood. Paul is inviting Christians to recognize that far from having all the answers, they are but children beginning the journey. The promise, not the present reality, is that we will eventually meet "face to face."

Jesus, although revealing God in the incarnation, scarcely scratched the surface of the divine. The fact that we often feel as if we received so much light and revelation already, Paul would likely say, is just evidence of how deeply we were in the dark before. Even an obscure and riddling *enigma* seems like a stunning vision of clarity when compared to pitch-black blindness.

So now, maybe we can better understand why Paul urged the church at Thessalonica to "test/question/doubt everything; and keep all that is good." Because at the end of the day, Christianity for Paul was never about claiming to have the answers and reciting them, but was always an admission of humility and the beginning of a search for them, a search Paul likely believed was only now possible thanks to Jesus.

STANDING WITH JESUS

But was Paul crazy? Sure, we've seen the disciples doubt. Yes, we've even seen Paul encourage doubt and undermine any idea that Christianity is a religion built on certainty and clarity. Yet, could they all just be wrong? Could perhaps their doubt simply be evidence of their own blindness? Should we really be drawing these lessons from them? The answer is a resounding yes. Why? Because Jesus did it too.

> When it was noon, darkness came over the whole land until three in the afternoon. At three o'clock Jesus cried out with a loud voice, "Eloi, Eloi, lema sabachthani?" which means, "My God, my God, why have you forsaken me?"... Then Jesus gave a loud cry and breathed his last. And the curtain of the temple was torn in two, from top to bottom.
> (MARK 15:33–38)

Though often ignored and explained away, Jesus himself is the poster child of doubt in the Gospels of Mark and Matthew. Here, we find a vision of Christ so striking and challenging that it remains haunting for many who read his words. The very epitome of human existence is encapsulated in this one moment by Jesus during his incarnation. It is here that some would argue Jesus demonstrates his true humanity.

Peter Rollins, a philosopher and theologian from Ireland, describes Jesus' cry of doubt as "the true scandal of the cross." What is that scandal? That Jesus experienced an "existential atheism" on Calvary's hill.[4] It is not that Jesus actually stops believing in God (a rational atheism), but rather that Jesus stops sensing God (existential). "On the cross, Christ undergoes the deepest, most radical form of divine loss, one that is experienced." He argues that "it is only when we see the crucifixion as the moment where God loses everything that we begin to glimpse the true theological significance of the event."[5]

In his book *Insurrection*, he writes that:

> While various religious systems provide a place for this painful experience of unknowing (as a test, as something to endure, or something to overcome), in Christianity when one is crushed by a deep, existential loss of certainty, one finds oneself in Christ… we find the staggering message of the Cross: *Radical doubt, suffering, and the sense of divine forsakenness are central aspects of Christ's experience and thus a central part of what it means to participate in Christ's death*. The moment we feel the loss of all that once gave us meaning is not a time in which we are set free from Christ, nor is a moment where we fall short of Christ: *It is the time when we stand side by side with Christ*.[6]

The subtitle of his book sums up well the implication of this understanding of the cross: "to believe is human, to doubt, divine." Rather than the enemy of faith, Rollins argues that the experience of doubt is the moment in which man and God unite in the most intimate of ways. Anyone can believe an intellectual truth. Or to quote the letter of James: "Even the demons believe!" (James 2:19). Doubting, on the other hand, is something that as far as Scripture witnesses to, only humans and God have ever shared.

Jesus' doubt on the cross sends an important message to all who are willing to listen: if Christ could undergo and experience such deep and piercing doubts, he can relate to your own. If he could doubt God while hanging on the cross, he can sympathize with your own piercing cries as you limp to your own crucifix. As Rob Bell writes in his classic book *Velvet Elvis*, that "…the kind of faith Jesus invites us into doesn't skirt the big questions… but takes us deep into the heart of them." Because in the end, there is, after all, "no question that Jesus cannot handle, no discussion too volatile, no issue too dangerous."[7]

And yet, if Jesus can handle any question that we come to him with, then why are so many Christians convinced that there are some questions that aren't acceptable to bring up in church? Why are so many in conservative denominations taught to bury their "doubts"? Why has Paul's vision of stark Christian humility transformed for many into a narcissistic and self-congratulatory pride? People have deep-seated questions and almost nowhere to take them. And this has grave consequences for some. As Austin Fischer, a pastor in Texas, wisely put it: "People don't abandon their faith because they have doubts so much as people abandon their faith because they think they're not allowed to have doubts."[8]

It is an unavoidable truth that we inhabit a post-modern and post-certain world, and many find themselves fighting the forces of skepticism and doubt. Yet, this is a losing battle. For no matter how much one tells you to believe, doubt will not magically disappear unless one is intellectually dishonest. We all cry, just as the father did to Jesus: "I believe! Help my unbelief!" (Mark 9:24). Yet, we mistake the unbelief as a problem to solve rather than a tool to aid us in the Spirit's ministry. Doubt in other words is healthy. Or as biblical scholar Peter Enns writes: "Doubt is sacred."[9]

For far too long, the church has looked at Christians who doubt as either a threat or problem to solve, rather than what they have the potential to be: a blessing. In every church, just as with the disciples in Matthew, we as the body of Christ can report that "some doubted," and just as back then, Jesus still calls and commissions us to move forward not in spite of our doubts but alongside them. In a world and society that revels in its supposedly secular and post-modern age of skepticism, Christianity and Scripture offer untapped treasures for the church, if only it can listen to them and be brave enough to put them to good use.

And so, I want to suggest that if we are to rediscover the power of the Bible and the witness it bears, we must not be afraid to bring our nagging doubts and questions about it to the table. We must trust that Jesus is big enough to handle our "childish" thoughts. If we are to try and slowly grow to be adults (as Paul continually hoped), we must throw everything of ourselves into this endeavor. Moreover, we must recognize and be willing to accept that as Paul himself intimated, we will often find the truth encased and mixed with the false. Growing our faith to adulthood means recognizing that this is as true of Scripture as it is of the world at large.

2

ABRAHAM DIDN'T BELIEVE GOD

"Abraham's words convey disobedience, which is nothing but the true affirmation of his faith."

OMRI BOEHM[1]

Perhaps we can better frame both the topic of doubt and the central idea of this book by exploring a story that many people of faith struggle with. The story of Abraham and Isaac's fateful march up Mount Moriah is famous to the majority of Christians around the world, and certainly to Jews as well, who know it simply as "the Akedah" or "Binding of Isaac." Even if someone doesn't know the details, the paintings of the scene are familiar to even the most biblically unacquainted. In each of these, Abraham stands holding a knife in his hand, before an altar to which his only son is tied, prepared to kill him. It's a revolting image that strikes more than a few people as morally horrendous. Of course, the real horror is that the story in Genesis reveals that God ordered Abraham to do it.

During one of my summer vacations back home from college, I remember visiting my old home church in San Diego, California. My family had come to celebrate in an agape-feast and Communion (or what is called the *Eucharist* in the New Testament). The church had an adjacent building with a basement that had numerous large tables set out for members to sit at. As we did, the guest speaker who had come began to preach his homily to prepare us for accepting the bread and wine (grape juice). No sooner had he started than I began to regret that I had come. The message was focused on the story of Genesis 22 and the speaker had decided that the best way to prepare us for communion was to imagine Abraham, hand held high, ready to plunge a knife into the chest of his son.

Apparently, he had hoped that those present would see the angel stopping Abraham as a reminder that God himself would take Abraham's place and plunge the knife into Christ. Although the idea is certainly a common one amongst many churches and wasn't unique to that minister, and though I'd heard it many times prior growing up, I couldn't help but feel disturbed. Moreover, I couldn't help but think that although this was supposed to *prepare* me to accept the gift of Christ's death, it actually seemed to be teaching *against* it. My mind raced to a passage in the Gospel of John, one that far too many have sadly overlooked.

> They answered him, "Abraham is our father." Jesus said to them, "If you were Abraham's children, you would be doing what Abraham did, but now you are trying to kill me... This is not what Abraham did. You are indeed doing what your father does... You are from your father the devil, and you choose to do your father's desires. He was a murderer from the beginning...
>
> (JOHN 8:39–41, 44)

In the passage from John's Gospel, Jesus contrasted Abraham's actions with the Jewish leaders. Whereas Jesus' contemporaries sought to kill him (under the false belief that they were doing so for God's sake), imitating the original murderer Satan, Abraham was an example of one who rejected death and murder. Where, though, did Abraham reject murder? Only at Mt. Moriah with Isaac. Jesus, rather than predicting that his future death would somehow be analogous to Abraham's story (as the guest speaker at the church was trying to do), argued the opposite. Abraham had rejected the idea of murdering for the sake of God and as such, truly represented what God's children look like.

According to Jesus, the moral of the story wasn't that Abraham was willing to kill his only son (that actually comes from the devil!), but that Abraham stopped himself from killing (confirming God as his father). Yet, given how universally accepted and historically rooted the minister's message still is across Christianity, it may seem shocking to imagine why and how Jesus was able to speak of the story in the way that he did. Wasn't Abraham tested for his obedience? Wasn't Abraham faithful because he was willing to kill Isaac? For Jesus to have been right in his alternative interpretation, it must mean that something went terribly wrong in our own.

REJECTING ABRAHAM

If I surveyed Christians about the story of Abraham sacrificing Isaac, and asked whether they believed that it was morally right for Abraham to follow God's orders and prepare to kill his son, the majority (certainly of conservatives) would say yes, even if they themselves felt that the act itself was awful. They'd talk about what an amazing example of faith, trust, and *blind obedience* Abraham showed by being willing to kill his son. Yet, if I asked them whether people today who claim God told them to sacrifice their children were right to do so, they'd adamantly tell me *no*. This obviously invites a pressing question.

Why is something back *then* acceptable but that same thing *now* is not?

Strangely, my horror at the story is probably shocking to many Christians who have grown up with this biblical tale as a cornerstone of faith, an oft-cited example of godliness. Yet, I find it far more shocking (downright spooky) that if you asked these Christians whether *they* would do the same thing as Abraham, that if God came to them today and told them to sacrifice their child, many of them would give one of two responses: they'd either likely attempt to defend the idea that he wouldn't ask them that or they'd admit that they would, because they, like Abraham, *trust God*. To be clear: I find that latter answer horrifying. Sure, they don't believe God would ever ask that. Sure, they would only do it if they knew for sure, without a doubt, that it was God appearing to them and not an angel of darkness wrapped in light. But still… it's scary that they'd consider doing it at all.

But this of course opens up an even bigger concern: if I say no, that we wouldn't (shouldn't!) want to follow God's orders to kill, what does it mean for the story of Abraham and Isaac? If we say that it's wrong to follow such an order from God, what does that mean for everyone's favorite patriarch? How do we understand the story of the Akedah if we come to believe that what God asked Abraham to do was wrong? What happens when we believe that Abraham *should* have said *no*?

ABRAHAM'S ABOMINATION

Let's briefly look at the story of Abraham and Isaac, reflecting on the question I posed earlier. If we affirm that Abraham should not have done it; that it was, as we now believe, immoral, what does this mean? Or, to ask a more succinct question: did God, in fact, request something immoral? Though many might have a gut reaction to say no, the reality is that, yes, God *did* ask for something immoral. Not only immoral, God actually asked for something sickening... something which was evil. Yes, when God asked Abraham to commit the murder of his son, *it was evil.* If that idea is at all shocking, it shouldn't be. I'm actually just quoting Scripture.

God warns in Deuteronomy that "there shall not be found among you anyone who burns his son or his daughter as an offering... for whoever does these things is an abomination to the LORD" (18:10–12). The Deuteronomist warns that "you shall not worship the LORD your God in that way," because, he goes on to explain, that is the way in which the foreign nations worship their gods and Israel's God, Yahweh, "hates" it (12:31). Leviticus likewise bans child sacrifice as contrary to God's character (18:21).

The Psalmist exclaims that those who sacrifice their sons or daughters as an offering to God, actually do so to demons (for only demons ask for children to be killed). This act kindles "the anger of the LORD... against his people," to the extent that God "abhorred" his own people and ultimately caused their exile (106:37–41). God, speaking through Jeremiah, is even more clear on this point. Referring to some Israelites who had built shrines and offered their sons and daughters as sacrifices to him, God exclaims that he "did not command" these things, "nor did it come into my mind" (Jer. 7:31).

But wait... let's consider what this implies. Abraham, according to these texts, was asked by God to do something God believes is an abomination, something he banned, and moreover, something that he hates? He was asked to make a sacrifice that the biblical writers would later call an offering to demons? Abraham was asked by God to do something so abominable that God would reject his entire people for doing something similar? How can that happen? Further, what are we to make of this story as a result?

ABRAHAM DOUBTED

There's a number of odd and curious details in the story of Isaac and Abraham's journey, details that might help illuminate the questions that I have raised. These small details are easy to miss, especially if countless pastors have already helped to shape your imagination. Yet, they help reorient us in our understanding of this story tremendously.

According to one of the authors of Genesis, when Abraham was told in the night to sacrifice his son, he immediately rose early in the morning. Gathering wood for an offering and bringing two servants along with his son Isaac, the four set out on a journey to Mt. Moriah. Three days into the journey, the group finally reached their destination. It's at this point that Abraham says something very subtle and odd.

> Then Abraham said to his young men, "Stay here with the donkey; the boy and I will go over there; we will worship, and then we will come back to you."
>
> (Genesis 22:5)

People read that small bit of text all the time and yet never spot the hidden gem inside it. Did you catch it? He said "we." Let that sink in for a moment. Abraham, about to walk up the mountain to sacrifice his son's life just told his two servants that he and his son would go up *together* and come back down *together*. What in the world is Abraham saying?

Many have long attempted to suggest that Abraham trusts that God has the ability to resurrect Isaac back from the dead after he kills him. Ignoring how gruesome that idea is at face value, the historical reality is that this is simply not possible. The idea of resurrection, historians are aware, did not exist for either Abraham or the Israelite authors of Genesis. It was an idea that first appears in the prophet

Daniel and only became popular at the time of Jesus. Entire books exist to demonstrate why we know this with absolute precision. As such, scholars can confidently rest assured that whatever Abraham is doing when he suggests that he and Isaac are returning, it isn't due to resurrection. That then leaves us with two possibilities for what Abraham means.

It's possible that Abraham is lying to his servants. He may wish for them not to follow him, perhaps thinking to stop him. After all, Abraham had a history of lying in the past (Gen. 12) and there's no mention that he told his wife what his plans with Isaac were. Yet, this idea doesn't make sense at all, because *there's actually no reason* for the two servants to even think to stop Abraham. Child sacrifice, as hard as it might be to imagine now, was part of the religious *norm* then. While not everyone practiced it, some of the familiar religious groups of his world required it and even some later Israelites would practice it in honor of Yahweh. His servants would not have thought he was crazy for doing it as we now would. It would not make sense to think that they would have tried to stop him. So on its face, the idea of Abraham lying doesn't makes sense.

The other option then, is that Abraham means exactly what he says: they are both coming back. What does *that* mean? It means, in short, that Abraham didn't believe God. It means that he didn't believe that God, his God (Yahweh), would actually require the death of his son.

The other curious detail that follows in the story seems to corroborate this idea. In Gen. 22:6–8, the two travel up the mountain together. Isaac eventually asks his father what must have surely been a pressing question on his mind: where was the lamb to be offered as a sacrifice? Abraham's response, we would imagine, should be the solemn truth that he, Isaac, is the sacrifice. Instead, Abraham oddly tells his son that: "God himself will provide the lamb for a burnt offering, my son."

You might want to read that slowly a few times. If you're anything like me, you quickly noticed the problem with Abraham's words: they are categorically not true. If Abraham believes God and has taken his request seriously, then he knows full well that God said that Isaac was the sacrifice. His reply to Isaac, telling him that God will provide a lamb, is simply not true (at least, according to what God told Abraham). Abraham, not God, is the one providing one! Not only that, but his response also seems potentially deceptive. There is only one thing that Isaac can do when interpreting his father's words: rest assured that something *other than himself* could be the sacrifice, since God, and not Abraham, is providing the sacrificial materials. If Abraham believes that God really wants him to kill his son, then he is, unavoidably, lying to Isaac.

Yet, the question to ask is: *did* Abraham believe God? If we take Abraham's words to Isaac seriously (that is, we assume he's telling the truth), then the biblical text seems to point us to the idea that Abraham *didn't*. He's telling Isaac, even before revealing to him what God said, that God will not require a human sacrifice. His words to Isaac, combined with his promise to the two servants, would seem to tell us that Abraham, far from blindly following the will of a demanding God, does not actually believe that his God's words are true. In short, he doubts God's command to kill his son.

The passage describes how Abraham bound his son Isaac and placed him on the altar, and states that he "took the knife to kill his son." Read that very carefully. It only says that he took the knife. It doesn't say he even put it to his neck. The author doesn't want us to even assume that Abraham got that far. Instead, God stops Abraham at that very moment when the voice of an angel cries out.

But should this really surprise us? This is the same Abraham who questioned God's sense of justice to his face in Genesis 18, the same Abraham who bartered with God for lives. Is it strange to imagine that this same Abraham would question God's orders? What's fascinating to realize is what this means. For many of us, we have grown up with this image of a faithful Abraham who trusted God so deeply that he was willing to kill an innocent boy, and was rewarded as a result for his trust. Yet, if we take seriously what has just been discussed, this view *must* disappear.

Instead, we have an Abraham, much like his younger self, who tests God, who tests his justice. He obeyed the command to go and prepare a sacrifice, yet all the while believing that his God, the God who had led him his whole life, did not really intend to follow through with that command. He believed that his God wouldn't want the death of his son. Why though? How could Abraham be so certain? And why didn't he, like his younger self, argue with God about it?

This is where I believe the power of the story lies. As mentioned earlier, child sacrifice was not unheard of in the time of Abraham. In fact, it was more common than we might like to imagine. There would have been nothing theologically strange (or revolting) to Abraham about the idea of a god requiring the sacrifice of his child. Recognizing that ancient reality, though, forces us to understand that the question is properly not "why wouldn't Abraham protest?" The real question is "why *would* he ever doubt God's request?"

The story of Abraham's life seems to suggest over and over that God revealed himself to this new believer in stages, slowly and over time. Nowhere does it give us reason to think that God explained his ways in one big event, like when Moses received the law on Sinai. As a result, I believe we have good reason to imagine that God had never explained to Abraham on any previous occasion his views on child sacrifice (outlined elsewhere in the Old Testament).

If Abraham had known God's abhorrence of child sacrifice, then surely he would have affirmed what Psalm 108 claimed, that the one requesting was not God but a demon. Yet he didn't resist God, or like he did with Sodom, tell him: "far be it from you!" This is simple to understand when one realizes that Abraham did not know what the rest of the Bible writers knew. He had no specific reason to believe his God was any different than any other god with regard to sacrifices. It was possible for Abraham to believe at this time that maybe his God *did* require human sacrifice.

This then is the truly shocking thing: that Abraham for some reason, in spite of not raising an objection, believes that Yahweh will not have him do what he asked. This all points out what is the real question in all of this: Why on earth would Abraham *doubt* that his God would want a human sacrifice? Why doubt something like that when it was true for so many other gods around him?

He should have simply thought, "Oh, I guess he's like those other gods too. He demands blood like they do." But strangely, we discover much to our surprise that his own answer is no: Abraham doesn't believe that God is like those other gods. He doesn't believe that his God would want *that*. This gives us a tremendous insight into the relationship that Abraham and God had grown over the years together. Without ever having been told by God that this was something contrary to his character, Abraham already had come to know God so well that he knew instinctively that this was not the same kind of bloodthirsty god that he had grown up with. This god was different. This god was Yahweh.

God was, as the text said, *testing* Abraham's faith (Gen. 22:1). He was not, as most typically think, testing whether Abraham would blindly follow his orders. After all, if that had been the case, then the fact that Abraham began to travel to commit the sacrifice would have been proof enough for God that Abraham passed the test. No, rather, God was testing Abraham's knowledge of *his character*. Did Abraham know God well enough after a hundred years of journeying with him, to know what he would or would not desire? The answer in this case was that yes, Abraham knew God well enough not to believe his very words.

That is a lot of faith: faith in God's unspoken character, and even faith in father and son.* Abraham went so far as to lay his son on the altar. Why? Because, to use a modern analogy, it was all one big game of chicken. When Abraham reaches for the knife, he's daring God. He's calling God out. He's saying: "Are you really going to go through with this? When are you going to quit this game?" God's response was immediate: "Do not lay your hand on the boy or do anything to him." Game over. Abraham was right. Or as Søren Kierkegaard would put it, Abraham "conquered God."[2]

Abraham trusts God so well that he will go through the motions of an act that he believes full well that God won't do, all to prove to God that he knows that God won't do it. To prove that he "knows" God's heart. To prove that he knows that this act is more revolting to God than it even was to man. Abraham, in short, has come a long way from his confrontation with God over Sodom in Genesis 18 (which we will explore in a coming chapter).

But wait! I can hear the objections from some even as I write this. Didn't God say that Abraham would be blessed because he "obeyed my voice" (Gen. 22:18)? Doesn't that point us to the idea that it was

---

* The book of Judith (found in non-Protestant Bibles) has a curious statement. Speaking of God, Judith admonishes her people to: "Remember what he did with Abraham, and how he tested Isaac…" (8:26). Tested Isaac? It's an intriguing idea. In what way might have Isaac been tested during this tumultuous episode in Abraham's journey of faith? Simply put, Isaac had to trust his father's doubts. The text in Genesis never tells us when, how or if Abraham told Isaac about God's request. It simply says that he bound him and placed him on the altar. Yet, if Abraham really did believe that God would not do such a thing, I can't imagine that he didn't share such thoughts with his son. Isaac then had a test to be given: would he believe his father? Did Abraham really know God as well as he thought he did? Would Isaac believe that his father shared a relationship deep enough with God to know him as well as he claimed? Isaac's test was trusting that his father's knowledge of God's character truly was "that" deep.

because Abraham was willing to sacrifice his son that God blessed him? Doesn't that mean that the traditional explanation of this story is more accurate? Actually, no. The question to ask is this: *what* voice did Abraham obey? The voice at the beginning that commanded him to sacrifice Isaac or the voice at the end that cried out for him to not lay a hand on his son? It's the same voice but with two very different messages.

As Cesar Baez, a friend and fellow ministerial student, once wrote in response to an early draft of this chapter: "If Abraham had actually obeyed God's first voice then Isaac would have died. Any act not completed to the fullest is an incomplete act and ultimately unfulfilled." Abraham could only follow one voice or the other. They were both mutually exclusive. In the end, he chose the cry of the angel. That is the voice for whom God praises obedience to. And after all, it makes the most sense given the historical context. God knew that Abraham had no reason to expect differently than what God had originally requested. The victory God celebrates is that Abraham's faith is imitating God so well that he no longer must be *verbally* taught in order to *intuitively* learn.*

This is why Jesus can in the Gospel of John present Abraham as a child of God and the leaders of Jerusalem as children of the devil. Though they call themselves children of Abraham, they seek to kill

---

* As a last thought, note that God's final words to Abraham afterward affirmed that "now I know that you fear God, since you have not withheld your son, your only son, from me." So the question that we should answer is what did it mean for Abraham to "withhold" Isaac? Given what I've previously talked about, the traditional answer doesn't seem to make much sense. However, there is another possibility that could make sense, which I'll propose. If Abraham had killed Isaac, the boy would have to have gone to Sheol (the land of the dead spoken of in the Hebrew Bible). Sheol was the resting place of the wicked and righteous who died, and as the author of Ecclesiastes bemoaned, no matter how wicked or good you were, both groups ended up in the same place (Eccl. 9:2). Sheol is where the Hebrew Bible tells us that "there is no mention" of Yahweh (Psalm 6:5), where no one thanks God, praises God,

Jesus, fulfilling the original command of God unquestioningly. What defines the children of Abraham, Jesus reveals, is that they, like Abraham, know God's ways and so recognize that violence is from the demons, not God. Unfortunately, for far too long we have interpreted the story of Abraham through the same lens of those leaders, rather than the way Jesus taught it.

In the end, Abraham dared God with a knife and won. He knew God so well that he promised his son that God would provide a sacrifice, that he would not have to kill him, because he knew intuitively that God was not the same as the other gods, or as they would later be called by the Bible, the demons who demanded child sacrifice. And guess what? He was right. As a result, Genesis tells us, Abraham named the place *Jehovah Jireh*, otherwise translated as "the Lord will provide." This was the place where man proved he knew God's heart. This was where Abraham proved that he truly was a man of faith… and it had absolutely nothing to do with blind obedience.

---

and no one hope for God's faithfulness (Isa. 38:18), where ultimately those who go there are hidden from God (Job 14:13). This concept of Sheol, a timeless and forgotten place where "the dead know nothing" (Eccl. 9:5), where there the dead not only do not do anything, but do not think any thoughts (Eccl. 9:10), possibly provides the answer to this question. Although Christians have understood God's words to Abraham to mean that God was pleased Abraham didn't withhold Isaac as a sacrifice, in the context of what I have discussed in this section, it seems that it would be better to interpret that God is pleased that Abraham did not kill his son, hiding him in Sheol and withholding him from God's presence. As Jesus would later say, "He is not the God of the dead, but of the living" (Mark 12:27). God wanted a living sacrifice in Isaac, not a dead one.

3

DID GOD SAY THAT?

"[The Bible] itself places us into various situations where the God we read about is one whom we must question, not out of our weakness and selfishness but rather from out of the very depths of our faith."

PETER ROLLINS[1]

Although many people can affirm a belief in the Bible as a total product, it's an entirely different thing for many to begin to discuss, explore and affirm the actual *content* of that sacred collection. The reason is that this is by no means a simple task, and no sooner does one start than one realizes how many problems, obstacles and difficulties they can encounter in doing so. The one I wish to give particular focus to here—because I believe that it is the key to understanding the rest—is the uncomfortable fact that there are conflicting portraits of God that one can find between the pages of the Old and New Testaments.

When it comes to Scripture and our struggles with it, blind obedience is often the prescription of the day offered across the counter of many pulpits and conservative seminaries. As patients enter their steeple topped hospitals, injured or poisoned from their encounters with their sacred texts, their doctors, dressed in ministerial robes or suits and ties, all too often recite their hypocritical oath: Scripture can *never* be wrong. In the face of ignored verses that threaten to unravel many people's view of and relationship with God, they are told to simply swallow their doubts and accept the mystery of God.

The truth is that many Christians struggle with reading certain passages of Scripture that seem to contradict everything they believe about God. Within the various pages of their sacred text, they read of a God that at times seems both strangely foreign and oddly familiar to the God that they have primarily become acquainted with through the New Testament, or more specifically the Gospels. As a result, they find it difficult, if not impossible at times to reconcile some verses with others.

This is no truer than in mainline Protestant churches that follow a more structured worship service, sometimes called "high church." Congregations such as those of the Anglican and Episcopalian variety typically have four passages of Scripture read aloud during the worship service, and after each reading has finished the church as a whole affirms: "Thanks be to God for this Word." Those words can either be the song of your soul or its deepest chasm.

While it's easy to affirm verses such as John 3:16 that tell us that "God so loved the world that he gave his only begotten son that whoever believes in him will have everlasting life," it's not so comfortable or even possible for us to affirm others, such as Jer. 13:14. There we read God declare that "I will smash them one against the other, parents and children alike… I will allow no pity or mercy or compassion to keep me from destroying them." It's not until you're forced to affirm out loud in church that *this* is the Word of God and you are thankful, that you begin to question whether you truly are.

At the very least, it makes you pause and realize that perhaps you need to read that passage again. Perhaps you need to study it. Why? Because though you are supposed to affirm it as God's Word, there are some passages that you almost resent the fact that you have to affirm. Did God really say that? Do I really believe in a God that would do something like that?

In 1 Samuel, God is said to have ordered the destruction and murder of every man, woman, child and even infant within a city (15:3). Innocent children. Infants. Murdered by zealous invading Israelites? Ordered by God? A similar incident is found in Joshua, which records that all the children were killed by the edge of the sword, on the order of God, during the invasion of Jericho (Josh. 6:20–21). And Psalm 137:9 actually speaks of how happy the righteous shall be when they have the chance to take their enemies' "little ones and dash them against the rock!" It's not hard to see why so many Christians choose not to deal with such parts of Scripture and when they do, why they feel forced to excuse God for the violence, sometimes described on a genocidal level.

Other oft-avoided passages include God blessing people for murdering their family members, friends and fellow Israelite neighbors simply because God told them (Ex. 32:26–29), God claiming that he inspired the soldiers of foreign nations to beat little children to death, have wives raped, have no mercy on helpless babies, and "show no compassion for the children" (Isa. 13:15–18), as well as vindictive passages in which God warns that he will kill the children of those who refuse to obey him (Lev. 26:21–22). It takes a Christian with a strong stomach to hear the words of Ezek. 9:5–7, which declare: "Then I heard the LORD say… Show no mercy; have no pity! Kill them all—old and young, girls and women and little children." How do you stand by and hear such things read aloud and then, in good conscience, say: "Thanks be to God for this word"?

Most Christians do not believe in the God of Hos. 9:16 who promises the Israelites that "if they give birth, I will slaughter their beloved children." Most Christians do not have faith in a God who sends bears to tear apart children as described in 2 Kgs. 2:23–24. They do not affirm a God who judges a child for the sin of his father and condemns him to be "slaughtered" (Isa. 14:21).

Yet, didn't God say it? Well, the Bible certainly says God did. But if we accept this, we run into a problem. Isn't this the same God that Jesus said he came to reveal? The contrast between those two portraits of God is a tad too dramatic. How does a Christian maintain a reasonable faith in the God of the Bible and yet, not succumb to affirming that these things are God's doing?*

A REASONABLE FAITH

The issue of maintaining a reasonable faith and the question of biblical authority are tied together in ways that are sometimes unforeseen. In some sense, the dividing wall between what are labeled as Progressive and Conservative Christians is typically built of the issues relating to these two details. In short, Progressive Christians don't see how one can have a reasonable or logical faith and maintain biblical authority to a strong degree. They read certain (typically violent) passages in the Bible that they cannot accept in good faith reflect the God they believe in, and come to the inevitable conclusion that God could not have inspired those passages. As such, they conclude that the entire collection *cannot* be authoritative. On the opposite end of the spectrum are Evangelically-minded Christians who accept

---

* Inevitably, some misguided Christians have developed a disturbing habit of attempting to defend such actions or statements attributed to God. One website I found claimed that God killed the children so that they would be "saved" and go to heaven instead of growing older, sinning and sealing their fate to Hell. Yes, you read that right. Some Christians are defending infanticide as acceptable. Yet I have to wonder: has their desire to defend God blinded them from the evil that they are propagating? Do they not see how a faith built on God's early command to "love your neighbor as yourself" (Lev. 19:18) is being potentially disfigured by them?

the entire Bible as authoritative and as a result, force themselves to accept, explain, and uphold everything in the sacred collection, even those things that might revolt them in any other circumstance. In other words, if the Bible disagrees with their sense of God's character, then *they* are the ones who must change their ideas of morality, not the Bible.

This situation has inevitably led to internal divisions within the different Christian churches and has created distinct internal subcultures within both local and larger denominational structures. Each group views the other with a certain level of disdain and a sense of moral superiority that diminishes the other's humanity, as well as their shared salvation. For many watching, the disputes between these two groups has produced nothing more than strife and tension in a church that has already long been defined by its internal divisions.

The other unforeseen consequences of these disputes have been the increasing perception that certain Christians and their faith are unthinking, illogical and embattled. Progressive Christians look at Conservatives as willfully ignorant, ignoring what the Bible actually says and the context of the ancient world that created it. They see Conservatives as anti-intellectual and holding to a version of faith that is untenable in a modern and rational world. Conservatives, on the other hand, view Progressives as ignoring what they see as "the plain reading" of Scripture and accuse them of allowing culture to define how they should read and understand passages in the Bible. They argue that liberal Christians are falsely imagining a moral and intellectual superiority, one which will cost them their salvation when Jesus comes and disowns them.

The question that we must ask, when attempting to refine and possibly reform our understanding of the Christian faith, is whether this conflict is even warranted. Must the debate over biblical authority be so divided? Was the debate warranted at the level that it eventually rose to become? I want to propose that it isn't and didn't have to be. A reasonable faith and biblical authority can go together, but not necessarily in a way that either Progressive or Conservative Christians may have imagined. The Bible does not require us to choose one or the other.

It just requires us to do one thing: *have faith*.

A PERSISTENT WOMAN

In order to explore what sort of faith we need, and to even discover what faith itself may mean, we need to turn to the story of Jesus. That's not a radical suggestion, is it? In particular, we need to look at a very specific moment from the life of Jesus recorded in two of the four Gospels. Yet, it must be noted that this is not any ordinary story of the rabbi from Nazareth. Moreover, this story is in fact quite painful for many people who hear it and so, given this, we'll need to consciously put aside our predisposed opinions about it. We will need to listen to it as best we can, without necessarily assuming that we already know it.

The Gospel of Mark records the story of a woman, the first Gentile Jesus ever encounters, who has a daughter possessed by a demon. The woman is described as Syrophoenician, which in short means that she is a foreigner, a non-Israelite. She likely does not believe in the God of Abraham. The story ultimately reveals that she came to Jesus for her daughter's healing, but was turned away because of her national origins.

> From there he set out and went away to the region of Tyre. He entered a house and did not want anyone to know he was there. Yet he could not escape notice, but a woman whose little daughter had an unclean spirit immediately heard about him, and she came and bowed down at his feet. Now the woman was a Gentile, of Syrophoenician origin. She begged him to cast the demon out of her daughter. He said to her,

"Let the children be fed first, for it is not fair to take the children's food and throw it to the dogs." But she answered him, "Sir, even the dogs under the table eat the children's crumbs." Then he said to her, "For saying that, you may go—the demon has left your daughter." So she went home, found the child lying on the bed, and the demon gone.

(MARK 7:24–30)

At first glance, the story is incredibly uncomfortable. In fact, the Gospel of Luke doesn't include it. He purposefully rejects the story when editing Mark's Gospel, perhaps because he found it too offensive for his largely Gentile audience to understand or accept. In truth, many (if not most) readers of this story today find it similarly offensive. It may be one of Jesus' *only* unpopular stories. Part of the reason it carries such a stigma has to do with the fact that Jesus refers to the woman as a *dog*. Yes, Jesus, in British terminology, called the woman a *bitch*, literally. If you think that's too harsh to attribute to Jesus, it's actually not. He not only called the woman a *dog* in the practical sense, but he used the term in the sort of derogatory way that *bitch* is often meant today.

In Jesus' day, the term *dog* was used to describe and denigrate all Gentiles (male and female). Anyone who wasn't a Jew, in short, was an unclean and filthy *dog*. When Jesus uses the term, his Jewish audience immediately knows what he's saying. Yet, it's important to note that just like how the "N word" was once so widely used in Southern America that very few Southern Whites were even consciously aware that they were using it on such a regular basis, so too in Jesus' world did most Jews use the term constantly without much thought. It was just part of the culture of Jesus' day, a part of the culture that stigmatized and ostracized most of the outside world. This doesn't make it less negative, but simply helps us to understand how pervasive the idea was in the Jewish culture at the time.

In Matthew's editing of Mark's story (Matt. 15:21–28), he changes the woman to a "Canaanite," as if to truly emphasize her outsider status (Canaanites were the people, if you remember, that God was said in Joshua to want slaughtered indiscriminately). This makes the story particularly interesting, since part of this book has explored the question of what to do with stories such as the Canaanite slaughter and other seemingly divinely-ordained violence. When the Gospel of Matthew invokes the term Canaanite, it makes this woman not only a foreigner, but stereotypically one of the most hated people and enemies of God.

Additionally, Matthew makes other edits to heighten the tension. Instead of *immediately* coming to bow at Jesus' feet as in Mark's earlier version, Matthew states in his version that she began shouting for Jesus' attention in the beginning from afar. She is unable to approach him because of the disciples who block her. Jesus is not bothered by her inability. In fact, it states that Jesus "did not answer her *at all*" (vs. 23). He, in short, ignores her cries for help.

Furthermore, the Gospel of Matthew has Jesus state what was only implied in Mark's version:

> "I was sent *only* to the lost sheep of the house of Israel."
> (MATTHEW 15:24)

Up until this point in Matthew's version, Jesus is clear that he has no interest or need to help those who aren't Jewish. This woman, a Canaanite, is apparently of no interest to him. Yet, there is a curious and small detail that should not be missed. Jesus does *not* tell her to stop yelling or attempt to send her home. Why do we know this? Because the disciples later have to *ask* Jesus to "send her away, for she keeps shouting after us" (15:23). Why is Jesus ignoring her, but not trying to send her away? We'll return to that question shortly.

Somehow though, Matthew says that the woman breaks free and collapses near Jesus' feet, pleading with him. He repeats the words from Mark's version about dogs and children's food and the woman responds with her famous words about the crumbs. Jesus in the end praises her and grants her persistent request.

In both Mark's account and Matthew's, the story is clear: Jesus rejected the foreign woman's request of healing for her daughter. Moreover, Jesus uses a derogatory term (something similar to a racial epithet) to describe the woman in his explanation to her that she *should not* be granted her request. And finally, both agree nearly word for word, that the woman refused to agree with Jesus' explanation and instead *argued* with a counter proposition, one which Jesus surprisingly praises her for and then grants the request he said he wouldn't.

In Mark's account, Jesus says that the woman succeeds "for saying *that*" (7:29). Yet, in Matthew's account, Jesus gets more specific and proclaims "great is your faith!" (15:28).

Faith?

This is what *faith* looks like?

Think about the absurdity of it all: Mark says that Jesus praised her for rebutting him. We don't often think about it that way, but that's literally what she did. Jesus was emphatic that he shouldn't care about her, that she was a "dog," and that he was not sent by God to help people *like her*. And yet, she didn't care and argued that Jesus had forgotten that "even the dogs eat the crumbs." She literally tells Jesus that his argument is faulty. She points out that his logic is shaky and Jesus responds by praising her "for saying that."

Like Job, who God praised for speaking "right" of him, this woman is praised for her very act of resistance. Moreover, Matthew is clear that this fight she had with Jesus over her daughter's fate was "great faith." This, Matthew says, is great faith: that a woman wouldn't let God tell her no.

To return to what was earlier said, notice too that the Gospel of Matthew is clear that Jesus purposefully refused to send her away or tell her to stop yelling, in spite of him choosing to ignore her. That seems odd at face value. If he really wanted to ignore her, then why wouldn't he send her away? Some have thought that maybe this episode was a real moment in Jesus' life when he faced the prejudices he grew up with and recognized God's face in the *other* (Gentiles). Such a view has been seen as powerful as evidence of Jesus' incarnate full humanity. Others have been disturbed by the suggestion that Jesus was ever influenced by his culture's prejudice. However, *what if Jesus wasn't changing his mind at all?* What if something else, *something deeper,* was going on? Hold that thought, because we'll return to it in a later chapter.

MOTHER KNOWS BEST

If the incident with the Syrophoenician/Canaanite woman was the only example of Jesus praising someone for not obeying him, we could perhaps overlook it as an oddity, a singularity in the breadth of Scripture. However, as it turns out, it is not the only example. The Gospels contain a similar story about another woman who resisted Jesus, and not only him, but also God. The more comical of the two, this story features not just a woman, but one of the most revered and honored of all biblical women: Mary.

The mother of Jesus is presented as many things in the Gospels, but one of the least known depictions is her role in *fighting* her son. The fact that it's so little known is surprising when you consider that it's how one Gospel begins her and Jesus' life story! And yet, as ironic as this ignorance is, it is magnified by the fact that the story it is featured in just so happens to be one of the most beloved and well-known stories from the Gospels.

In the second chapter of John's Gospel, we read of a wedding at Cana, the location of Jesus' first miracle and the current modern-day site of a beautiful church (and many surrounding wine stalls).

> Jesus and his disciples had also been invited to the wedding. When the wine gave out, the mother of Jesus said to him, "They have no wine." And Jesus said to her, "Woman, what concern is that to you and to me? My hour has not yet come." His mother said to the servants, "Do whatever he tells you." Now standing there were six stone water jars for the Jewish rites of purification, each holding twenty or thirty gallons. Jesus said to them, "Fill the jars with water."
> (JOHN 2:2–7)

The story is sparse on details (as most biblical narratives seem to be), so some of the details have to be implied. It does not tell us the movements of the characters, but we would be safe to assume that the men and women sat separate, so that Mary had to stand and walk to approach Jesus. As a woman, even as his mother, it was etiquette for a woman to stay silent until spoken to. Her words as such, coming before his, are potentially provocative. Jesus' use of the word "woman" is not rude, even if it sounds that way to us now. However, his message to Mary is clearly negative: the answer is no. Jesus essentially says to his mother that it's "none of my concern."

For the perspective of John's Gospel (unlike say, Mark), Jesus is portrayed unequivocally as the full incarnation of God on earth. So this means that, for John, not only does Jesus say no to Mary in the story, so too does God himself directly reject her request. Jesus is very clear on the reason: "My hour has not yet come." Mary, however, does something that is startling: she doesn't obey his wishes. She doesn't obey God. Instead, she turns to several servants nearby and tells them to do whatever Jesus tells them to do when they approach him. Even though Jesus said no, even though God's plan was made expressly clear, Mary didn't care.

Instead of trusting Jesus' words and giving up, she seems convinced that he will do the opposite of what he said. She seems sure that if she sends the servants, Jesus will end up helping, despite his claim that he won't. And do you know what happened? Jesus did it anyway. God ended up doing something after he had literally just said he wasn't going to, and even after he said it wasn't the right time. And it was all because of a woman who was *faithful* enough not to care what he had said. For John, Mary's resistance to Jesus is not only an important role, but a defining one for her, since he introduces Mary as a character with this story. She fought God and paradoxically, unbelievably, won. Surely we are left wondering: why and how? Did Jesus change his mind, or was something much more profound occurring? Whatever was happening, we can rest assured about one thing: neither the story of Mary nor the Canaanite woman teach that obedience is what God sees as faithful. Rather, it is their resistance and obstinance to Christ that appears to be praised and highlighted.

FAITH ISN'T BLIND OR OBEDIENT

Faith is a big word. Obedience is too. They're probably among the most frequently used words by certain groups of Christians, right after the words Jesus, Christ, and of course, Christian. Yet, like with so many words that come to be widely used, they take on new meanings, some of which are helpful, while others prove less so. One of the biggest misconceptions that has arisen from these new meanings, and quite possibly one of the most dangerous, is the deceitfully simple idea that faith and obedience are both *blind*.

This popular belief, taught to many Christians from grade school onward, teaches that we must always have unwavering and unquestioning faith even if we do not have any evidence to believe in something. In order to have faith, so this logic goes, one must realize that reason and sense must step down so that an unshakable belief and foundation takes priority in a Christian's heart. We must "take it on faith" and trust in something entirely, without any real reason other than what is seen by others to be simply a claim.

This concept can be illustrated by a humorous ploy which some atheists use when debating biblical ideas with Christians. It starts with a relatively simple question: why do you believe the Bible contains God's truth? The stereotypical Christian typically answers: "Because God's word is in it." The atheist responds: how do you know that it's God's word? The Christian sighs and responds, "Because the Bible tells me so!" At this point, the atheist is chuckling. "So, what you're telling me is that you believe a book is God's word only because the book itself told you so?"

Perhaps you are laughing. Perhaps you are not.

The obvious but unspoken question in that atheist's probe is: Why do you believe this book and not another? Why not the Qur'an, which, unlike the Bible, actually claims every word is from God? In other words, it looks to an atheist like this sort of reasoning is as strong as a seven-year-old who says that Santa is real merely because his father told him so.

If I begin by claiming that a book is from God and then go on to use that book as my proof that it is God's word, then I am guilty of a logical fallacy known as Circular Reasoning. It's the sort of thing that scientists, philosophers, and just about everyone in thinking-oriented disciplines have been trained to avoid. What is so sad is that most Christians have been raised on this model of thinking and so it no longer sounds like *a way* of thinking (let alone a bad one) but has simply come to be seen as *the only way* to think.

Likewise, when it comes to obedience, Christians are taught that nothing matters more than obeying God. Fundamentalism is built on the foundation that God's will is absolute and that *fundamentally*, one must have one's house in order before God will walk inside. When God says drop and give him twenty, you don't ask questions but get on your knees and obey your heavenly drill sergeant. If God tells you to do something, you don't figure out why. You just do it!

As I said before, I believe that these ideas are not only dangerous and lie at the root of much religious intolerance and violence, but that they are deeply and importantly *unbiblical*. This may come as a surprise to some readers who have grown up with these concepts taught from the pulpits of their churches, pronounced on the lips of their parents, and perhaps even repeated by themselves on many occasions. After all, aren't there verses in the Bible that seem to point in this direction?

That is why, I want to point out, this idea is so *insidious*. We've become convinced of something that isn't necessarily true, and appears actually not to be, the *full* biblical picture of faith. Although this may come as a shock to many, the Bible *doesn't* expect you to believe the words within it *simply* because the book itself claims it to be from God (and mind you, it doesn't even claim that). In fact, and this might prove to be a hard pill for some to swallow at the moment, but as seen in the stories of the two women and Jesus, even when God speaks, it's not always the case that he himself wants you to accept what he says.

Am I really suggesting that sometimes God says things that he wants us *not* to accept? Yes, and no. Yes, because that *is* what I'm saying. No, because it's not my idea… *it's actually from the Bible itself.*

And Jesus is by no means the only example of it.

4

SAYING NO TO GOD

"The Scriptures... seem to suggest that one must wrestle with, disagree with, and even disobey God for the sake of retaining one's fidelity to God."

PETER ROLLINS[1]

Can we tell God no? Does God actually encourage us to do so? If so, why on earth would such a paradoxical idea be true? To explore this contentious issue, I'll return to the individual who the book of Genesis tells us laid the foundation for the Hebrew people. I am of course speaking of Abraham, a man from Ur (ancient Mesopotamia) who had no previous knowledge of Yahweh, the God of the Bible, and who one day heard a voice from Heaven speak to him so that the world, as a result, was forever changed. That's the story in a nutshell. For Protestants, he's considered one of the great heroes of faith. In Gen. 15:6, it tells us that Abraham believed in God and God in return credited it to him as righteousness. As Luther and others would proclaim: he was called righteous not because of something he did, but due to his *perfect faith*. Less known, however, is that this ancient bastion of faith, this central figure for three of the world's central monotheistic religions, also had a strange encounter with God a few chapters later than that infamous verse, an encounter that changes what it means for us to call this man an example of faith.

The story is found in Genesis 18, following a visitation from three strangers, one of which is revealed to be God himself. Though many Christians hear sermons preached on the exchange between Sarah and the Lord—during which God promises Abraham that Sarah will bear a son at the ripe old age of ninety-one—often little is said of the very curious (and heated) exchange between Abraham and God afterward when he and the other two men (i.e. angels) are leaving.

In this encounter, God tells Abraham that the sin of the nearby city of Sodom has come to his attention and that he has heard an outcry against them by those who have suffered from their abuses. He dispatches the two angels beside him to investigate the crimes, to see whether they are true or not. However, as the angels leave, Abraham does something bold: he comes near to God and tells the creator of the world that *he's wrong*. Actually, that's putting it too mildly. Abraham questions aloud God's very morality. "Will you," he says with either sincerity or agitation, "sweep away the righteous with the wicked?" (18:23).

Those aren't just questioning words, they're provocative. Abraham is doing something few, if any, Christians would feel comfortable even imagining: he's questioning God's sense of justice to God's very face. But just in case that wasn't enough, or he didn't get the point across, he admonishes God to not do what he is planning. "Far be it from you to do such a thing," he exclaims, "to slay the righteous with the wicked, so that the righteous fare as the wicked! Far be that from you! Shall not the Judge of all the earth do what is just?" (18:25).

Pay attention to the words that Abraham is said in Genesis to have chosen, because they have heavy implications. The first thing to notice is that they make clear that Abraham believes that he has a sense of morality that, much to his own disbelief, appears higher than the God he serves. That in itself is shocking. He, a mortal human, argues that he believes that God's divine plan to wipe out Sodom is morally reprehensible. When he says "far be it from you," he's essentially asking God to come back to his senses, implying that God is not speaking sensibly. In other words, Abraham is telling God that he's speaking as if he's crazy. Abraham believes that such a course of action is both immoral and not something that his God would do, and more importantly, something that he must speak out against.

But there's something even more shocking that Abraham said in that brief statement. He told God, "Shall not the judge of all the earth do what is just?" The implication is clear: what God is now planning to do is *not* just. That may sound bad enough even to our own twenty-first century ears, but it's much worse than you might even imagine. According to Psalm 82, the actual job description of a god is to give justice and be just. That's what they are required to do in order to still be considered a god. As hard as it might be to believe how brazen Abraham is acting, he appears to be suggesting that God is not fulfilling his job as a god. But this isn't just an irreverent and agitated suggestion by the man from Ur, it's actually a challenge.

Keep in mind that Abraham wasn't previously a believer in Yahweh. God had been, throughout his life, revealing himself to this man. Abraham had been discovering who this God was over time and learning, in that time, to trust him. By telling Yahweh that he's not acting just (which meant that God was failing to do what a god should do), Abraham is threatening that perhaps he should look for another god. In the aforementioned Psalm 82, the judgment against gods that fail to act as they should is *replacement*. This isn't simply a plea by Abraham to God, it's a veiled threat.

However, Abraham doesn't just speak out grievances, he also attempts to proposition God. "Suppose there are fifty righteous within the city," he asks, "will you then sweep away the place and not forgive it for the fifty righteous who are in it?" Given the way in which many are taught about God, one might imagine God ever ready to strike Abraham down for his lack of manners and complete lack of trust. Instead, God does something unexpected. He agrees. "If I find at Sodom fifty righteous in the city, I will forgive the whole place for their sake."

But Abraham isn't finished. This, he believes, is still not justice. This is still not morality. Yet, something *does* change. Abraham gains some humility. He begins to speak again, saying: "Let me take it upon myself to speak to the LORD, I who am but dust and ashes." Unlike his opening words that began with a rash accusation of God's injustice, now suddenly he shows an unexpected humility. Why? I would point out the obvious: God listened. God humbled himself before Abraham, heeding and even agreeing with his council. Stunning, isn't it? God was listening to the advice of his own creation?

If all of this seems to be more than you ever imagined, it gets even stranger. In Gen. 18:22, the text tells us that all of this began and continued while "Yahweh was still standing before Abraham." Yahweh, it tells us, was standing *before Abraham*. You won't actually find that translation in almost any Bible (except the NLT, Alter and maybe one other), but that's what the original Hebrew text appears to have said. In most Bibles, the text has been changed to "Abraham was still standing before Yahweh."

Why did it get changed? Why were ancient scribes uncomfortable with the original wording of the Bible? Because the question is this: who is teacher and who is disciple? To say that someone stands before another is to imply that the one standing before someone is in the position of a student. In other words, the original Hebrew of Gen. 18:22 appeared to suggest that as this story began, before Abraham began to vent his frustration at God, Yahweh "stood before Abraham" as a student would stand before a teacher. Basically, God humbled himself to be "taught" by Abraham.

With that in mind, let's continue the story. Abraham, after getting God to agree to fifty, continues to insist that God lower the number of righteous people needed in order to spare Sodom. Beginning with forty-five and working his way down, he continues to show an increasing humility as the number lowers, saying things such as "do not let the LORD be angry if I speak." He's testing the Almighty's morality. It's as if Abraham isn't quite sure anymore what to think about God's justice, as if he's discovering it all over again.

Finally, God settles on a much more reduced number. If ten righteous people exist in Sodom, he agrees, then he will spare it in spite of all of the guilty. With this said, before Abraham can even speak another word, God is said to turn and walk away, ending the conversation. Abraham might have pressed further, but God was no longer interested in listening.

So what are we to make of this? What in Heaven's name is going on here? Everything about this appears to be contrary to the way in which we think that a man of faith should have acted. And in other ways, this is everything opposite of how we imagine God *would* act in response to a situation like this. This is the man who, just earlier that same day, sincerely heeded God's promise that Sarah would give birth at around ninety, even though Sarah herself laughed. Abraham, at the time of the story, is around one hundred years old, having trusted and experienced God's presence for a long time. So, what gives? Is this the outcome of someone that old with that much faith?

If you pay very close attention to the story, you'll discover something curious (aside from everything else mentioned). Although Abraham attacks God for the injustice of a judgment that would wipe out the city of Sodom, God never actually claims he will do any such thing. He merely sends his angels to investigate, saying: "I must see whether they have done altogether according to the outcry that has come to me; and if not, I will know." God's statement, the words that Abraham initially heard, left room for Sodom's salvation. Perhaps they're *not guilty*! God would supposedly find out.

No mention is ever made by God of the consequences Sodom might suffer if they *are* guilty. If this is true, why did Abraham attack God as he did? Why did he speak out against God before God ever breathed a word about judgment? Because, strangely, Abraham already knows what God's not saying. Abraham isn't just telling God that his decision isn't just, he's also calling God out for not being honest to him. In the following chapter, Abraham's suspicion is confirmed by the two angels who tell Lot (his nephew) that God had already ordered them beforehand to destroy the city. God wasn't actually investigating anything. The judgment had already been given.

So why did God tell Abraham that he was still investigating? Why did God tell Abraham something… that *wasn't true*? Intriguingly, the story also tells us that God, prior to telling Abraham this, debated with the two angels as to whether he should tell Abraham his plans. He asks, "Shall I hide from Abraham what I am about to do?" Notice that once again, even before the angels reveal to Lot their mission, we see that God has already made up his mind that he was going to destroy the city. Yet, if this is true, why did he choose not to tell Abraham? And moreover, why did God, in the end, decide to tell Abraham something other than the truth?

The answer to this strange riddle, in my opinion, is that God was testing Abraham. *He was testing his faith.* He was testing if it was strong enough, secure enough and motivated enough to fight back, to fight against God. Abraham, after all, is not condemned, frowned upon or diminished as a man of faith because of his exchange with God. Rather, his faith is strengthened, not because he ultimately trusted God (he didn't), not because he accepted God's will (he didn't), but because he faced God's will, resisted, and in a sense, won. Although we will return to examine this story again much later, let's look at two other stories that appear to reveal a similar pattern throughout Scripture.

YOUR NAME WILL BE ISRAEL

Here's a pop quiz. What does Israel's name mean? I realize that some may be aware that Israel was the name given by God to a specific man in Genesis whose descendants became the nation we know both from the Bible and modern geography. But, the real question is, do we really know why that name was even given, who gave it, and what it means? Do we understand what it actually means to talk of the "people of Israel?" To find the answer, we need to quickly look back at that original story in Genesis.

> "Jacob was left alone; and a man wrestled with him until daybreak. When the man saw that he did not prevail against Jacob, he struck him on the hip socket; and Jacob's hip was put out of joint as he wrestled with him. Then he said, "Let me go, for the day is breaking." But Jacob said, "I will not let you go, unless you bless me." So he said to him, "What is your name?" And he said, "Jacob." Then the man said, "You shall no longer be called Jacob, but Israel, for you have striven with God and with humans, and have prevailed."
> (GENESIS 32:24–28)

The text as it stands is short on details, but what it does in fact detail is quite telling. The story does not tell us why this mysterious "man" came to Jacob or how the encounter began, but it does tell us that this *man* was fighting with him in the darkness of night. And interestingly, it appears from all indications that the *man* initiated the struggle, not Jacob. Although translations describe them as having "wrestled," the sense in Hebrew is that the *man* assaulted Jacob. In other words, this was not a WWE competition.

More importantly, the attacking man *wanted* to win. He intended to defeat Jacob, to prove him weaker. Only when "the man saw that he did not prevail against" Jacob, did he do something unexpected. Seeing that he had no other choice if he wanted to win, he struck Jacob at his hip and crippled his opponent. Foul play? Sure. Yet, that's not the point. Even with a dirty trick, even with his opponent at a huge disadvantage, somehow Jacob still manages not only to remain fighting, but capable of preventing his opponent from winning and, more importantly, leaving.

The *man* who initiated the fight with Jacob appears to have gotten more than he expected. He actually wants to stop! Now, at daybreak, the *man* seeks to leave. "Let me go," he pleads with the injured Jacob. What an irony! The disabled has proven stronger than the abled. "I will not let you go," Jacob jabs back. And then something is revealed in the story that we were not told before. "Unless you bless me," he tells the *man*, he won't let him go. Wait, who is it that he is wrestling with? Who is the *man*? The answer: no ordinary man.

One of the prophets of Israel, a man by the name of Hosea, living much later, comments on the story briefly in one of his oracles.

> ...in his manhood he strove with God. He strove with the angel and prevailed, he wept and sought his favor.
>
> (HOSEA 12:3–4)

Hosea clarifies for us what we suspected all along, that the man who fought with Jacob was none other than an angel. This helps us to begin to understand the circumstances of this encounter which Genesis vaguely alluded to. It turns out that God sent the angel to fight Jacob and it appears that the angel fully expected to win. Jacob, surprisingly, stands his ground, not truly fighting the man he perceived in front of him, but the God who *sent him*.

In the Genesis account, after asking him for his name, the angel informs Jacob that he will be Jacob no more. Israel, a new name, would be his, because "you have striven with God and with humans, and have prevailed." Notice the play on words by this writer of Genesis. We were told earlier that the man saw that he could "not prevail" against Jacob. Now we are told that Jacob prevailed against the man and not only him, but actually the one who he stood as a representative of: God.

The King James Version, perhaps stretching the meaning a bit, has more shocking language when it says, in the text of Hosea, that "he had power over him." Power over God? That's definitely not how we typically imagine a human/divine relationship. Either way, that's probably not what you were imagining the history of the name of God's people would be.

As Peter Rollins brilliantly summarizes this paradox:

> It is here, in this encounter between Jacob and God, that we discover why the Jewish community is marked out by the name "Israel." This title represents the spirit of a people who have "wrestled with God and with men and have overcome." This name illuminates the living dynamic of Hebraic faith. It magnifies a radical idea that marks out the Jewish people, describing something almost paradoxical about this faith: that absolute commitment to God involves a deep and sustained wrestling with God. In this story, we discover that the Israelites are to be marked out, not as a people who live out their faith through unquestioning submission but as a people who demonstrate their love and commitment to the source of their faith in a radical commitment to fighting with that source. This is a people to be marked out by struggling, by passion, by critical engagement. The name Israel is not some kind of curse, or dispassionate description, it is a blessing. Here God does not merely describe something that the Israelites do; the name describes what they ought to be... For the blessing that God bestowed upon Jacob brings us face to face with the fact that God wants a fight.[2]

This is the secret of Israel's name. This is the power of its meaning. Israel, as the name of both a man and a people signifies "the one who fights God." The people of Israel are those who withstand God and stand their ground. Israel is the one who *prevails against God* for the sake of achieving a blessing *from God*.

MOSES AND THE ANGRY GOD

Let's take a look at another story. We'll fast forward almost half a millennium and glance at a man who is credited in the Bible for leading a revolution: Moses. Like Abraham, Moses was known as a man of faith, "a man of God" (Psalm 90:1). And like Abraham, Moses also had a curious exchange with God. In Exodus 32, we read of how Moses, having spent time atop Mt. Sinai, is informed by Yahweh that the people he led in the Exodus from Egypt have made a golden calf and begun to worship it.

> The LORD said to Moses, "Go down at once! *Your* people, whom *you* brought up out of the land of Egypt, have acted perversely; they have been quick to turn aside from the way that I commanded them.
> (EXODUS 32:7–8)

God, angry at their disobedience, tells Moses: "Now then let Me alone, that My anger may burn against them and that I may destroy them; and I will make of you a great nation" (32:10). God essentially tells Moses: *I've decided to restart. The Exodus wasn't worth the effort I gave it. I will wipe them all out and like Noah, start things over with only your family.*

For many, that's a tough pill to swallow. God is describing a massive act of genocide. But then again, who's to argue with God's plan? If God wants to do something, who is to tell the Almighty otherwise? Apparently, Moses.

> But Moses implored the LORD his God, and said, "O LORD, why does your wrath burn hot against *your* people, whom *you* brought out of the land of Egypt with great power and with a mighty hand?
>
> (EXODUS 32:11)

The first thing to note is the play with words between Yahweh and Moses in this encounter. God began by putting the blame on Moses, calling the Hebrews "your people" which Moses "brought up out of the land of Egypt." Yet, now, in rebuttal, Moses shoots back that God is wrong and that these are "your people" who "you brought out of the land of Egypt." In other words, Moses won't let God off the hook.

He warns God that if he carries out his plan, it will mean that he brought them out with an evil intent to kill them in the mountains. Evil intent? Planned genocide? Heavy stuff. He states all of this and tries to get away with it by saying that it will be the Egyptians who say this. But it's pretty clear that *he's saying it*. It's clear that he's prodding God. He urges him, "Turn from Your burning anger and change Your mind about doing harm to Your people!" As a last-ditch effort, Moses appeals to God to remember his promise to Abraham, Isaac and Jacob (Ex. 32:11–13). If God won't do it for reasons of morality, Moses thinks, then maybe he'll do it for the sake of the covenant.

So what did God do? Did he get upset at Moses for not trusting his decisions? Did he punish Moses for his lack of trust in the divine plan? No. We are told that in response to Moses, "the LORD changed His mind about the harm which He said He would do to His people." Let that statement sink in for a moment. God changed his mind? Because of Moses? It's another shocking concept.

Yet the surprises continue. When Moses ascends the mountain a second time, Yahweh informs him that he will not forgive the Hebrew people and will ultimately blot their names out. He also tells Moses, more importantly, that he will not come with them to the promised land, because if he did, he would kill them all along the way. Yahweh has, in short, informed Moses that he has decided to abandon them (Ex. 32:34). But he does promise that he will at least send an angel to guide them.

> The LORD said to Moses, "Go, leave this place, you and the people whom *you* have brought up out of the land of Egypt.
>
> (EXODUS 33:1)

There God goes again. Yahweh continues the word game from before, placing the responsibility of the Hebrew people on Moses. Why is God intent on disowning the people he brought up from Egypt?

Moses, of course, responds.

> Moses said to the LORD, "See, you have said to me, 'Bring up this people'; but you have not let me know whom you will send with me... Now if I have found favor in your sight, show me your ways, so that I may know you and find favor in your sight. Consider too that this nation is *your* people."
>
> (EXODUS 33:12–14)

Notice Moses' request. He asks God to "show me your ways," which might sound at first glance to be a devoted and holy request, but is actually sarcastic. On his earlier trip up the mountain, he had already implied to God that God's decision to wipe out the Hebrew slaves would be seen as evil and would break the covenant he had made with their ancestors. When Moses now asks God to "show me your ways," he's asking God to live as a god should, to act as a god should. It's Moses' equivalent of when Abraham reprimanded God and said, "Far be it from you!" Moses is pleading for God to come back to his senses. He *already* knows God's ways and sees that God appears to be acting contrary to them.

Finally, Moses chides back that perhaps God could "consider too that this nation is *your* people." It wasn't his idea to save them. It was Yahweh's. And Moses is going to keep reminding God of that fact for as long as it takes. As if that were the key that unlocked the secret door, Yahweh breaks the deadlock battle with a new pronouncement that has the potential to change everything.

> He said, "My presence will go with you, and I will give you rest."
> (Exodus 33:14)

Finally, God agrees to accompany the Israelites after all. Or does he? Notice that God doesn't say that his presence will go with "them," but rather it will go with "you," a reference to Moses. The promise of rest is given to Moses. God's words are ambiguous, even if in context one would assume they applied everyone. Moses himself appears to catch this ambiguity and doesn't like it. He's not going to back down and so he continues to protest, ignoring Yahweh's new promise.

> And he [Moses] said to him, "If your presence will not go, do not carry us up from here. For how shall it be known that I have found favor in your sight, I and your people, unless you go with us? In this way, we shall be distinct, I and your people, from every people on the face of the earth."
> (Exodus 33:15–16)

Moses presses God further, telling him that if he won't promise and commit to remaining responsible for them, then he shouldn't have anything more to do with any of them, including Moses. Yet, he attempts to proposition God to stay with them and do something that has never happened with any other people on earth.

Finally, God agrees.

> The LORD said to Moses, "I will do the very thing that you have asked; for you have found favor in my sight, and I know you by name."
> (Exodus 33:15–17)

And so... God changed his mind... again? As much as the victory rings sweet for Moses, we are left wondering, what does this portrait of God do for us? It seems so contrary to what we expect. Why does

Moses have to fight God, like Abraham and Jacob did, in order to convince God that he should stick with his people and not wipe them all out?

So what, in the end, did all of this even lead up to? What was the point? Well, for one thing, God reveals his name as Yahweh to Moses again (a pretty significant event). Most important, God describes himself in the exact terms that Moses was prodding God for through the past two chapters of Exodus.

> "Yahweh, Yahweh,
> a God merciful and gracious,
> slow to anger,
> and abounding in steadfast love and faithfulness,
> keeping steadfast love for the thousandth generation…"
>
> (Exodus 34:6–7)

Now we see God's ways. Now we see the character of God that Moses fought to reign supreme. And what is the gift that God gives to Moses and the people following his argument with Moses? A new covenant with the Hebrew slaves bound by the Ten Commandments (34:28). Yes, all of this has somehow lead to God revealing to Moses the law of God.*

Truly then, this story creates more questions than it appears to answer. Why was God changing his mind so many times? Why was he intent on destroying the soon to be nation of Israel? How can a mere man, Moses, manage to change God's mind? Why didn't Moses trust God's divine will? More importantly, how can he face God directly, fight his will and actually prevail?

---

* For those who are Bible nerds, you might be interested to know that contrary to your Sunday school or Sabbath school teachers who taught you that there were two versions of the Ten Commandments preserved in the Bible (Ex. 20 and Deut. 5), there's actually a third list in Exodus 34 and most scholars consider this to be the oldest of the three. It's also, curiously, the only one out of the two given in Exodus that is actually called "The Ten Commandments."

The secret, I suggest, might be found in Ex. 33:11 which informs us, in the midst of their argument, that "the Lord used to speak to Moses face to face, as one speaks to a friend." This is a tough secret to crack. What does it mean that they used to speak like a friend to each other? Is this really how friends act? Is this the kind of relationship God is calling *us* to? To get closer to an answer to that, we'll need to take a trip outside of Israel.

5

JOB'S LAWSUIT AGAINST GOD

"The prospect of acknowledging that while one can be brought closer to God by scripture one can also be led astray, provokes profound religious anxiety. To say nothing of the anxiety that may accompany the realization that... following scripture may actually be a sin."

RABBI DONNIEL HARTMAN[1]

Let's turn to another famous story of someone who fought God: a man from the land of Edom named Job. Job's story is both similar and different to the stories of Abraham and Moses. It is similar in that, like them, Job argues that God is wrong. It is different in that, unlike them, God does not *directly* argue with him for most of the story.

Job is an interesting character, to say the least. A wealthy man blessed with plenty of land, livestock, slaves, and children, he is also a man of devout faith. He's also a foreigner, and it might be surprising for some to learn that he doesn't believe in the God of Israel the same way that other writers in the Bible would. He is an outsider. In this sense, he's like Abraham in that he doesn't have all the answers yet. He doesn't know all the ways of Yahweh. I doubt that I need to go over the entire story, as it is so well known, but in short: Job loses almost everything in his life and becomes covered in boils to such a degree that it brings him to wish for death. Unbeknownst to Job, this is all happening because Satan challenges God about his righteousness and God agrees to allow Job to be tested, asserting that Job could withstand these trials. Job's friends, unaware of these facts, assume that because God is cursing Job, he has sinned. Job, on the other hand, believes that the curses falling upon him are unjust and upholds his conviction that God has no right to do so.

It's not clear that Job knows exactly who God is. Neither Job nor his friends ever make reference to past events from Israel's history, and God is spoken of only in regard to his sovereignty over the world, not in regard to any special care of his for a country or people. Although Job only speaks of a single God with whom he has complaint, when God speaks to Job, God references the existence of other gods, implying that though Job recognizes Yahweh as the superior deity, he also accepts the existence of other gods (Job 41:9, 25, NRSV). Which honestly makes sense, since Job is from the land of Edom and is, as already mentioned, not an Israelite. He grew up in a polytheistic world. How do we know? One obvious clue is that Job mentions that he does not know where God's dwelling is (23:3). If he was an Israelite, he would know of either the temple or the ark of the covenant and the tent of meeting, all of which were connected with the dwelling place of God.

Although the book is clearly written by an Israelite who believes in Yahweh and uses his name in the Hebrew text, the story itself is about a foreigner who is discovering the God of Israel *apart from* the influence of the established Israelite cult. Like Abraham who grew up in polytheism and was called to follow a God he had never known, Job may have been modeled to be similar as a character. As a result, some later Jewish commentators came to assume that the book was written or set against the backdrop of the same time period of Abraham. Scholars today, however, realize that the book of Job was written sometime shortly before the Babylonian Exile, or soon after.

Job begins his series of lengthy speeches with what is the equivalent of raising the middle finger at the sky: "Let the day perish which I was born…" (3:3). Job's misery is so great that early on in his ordeal, he actually calls upon sorcerers and diviners to rouse up the monster Leviathan in order to swallow the sun and undo Creation (3:8). And it only goes downhill faster as he continues.

Job accuses God of giving the earth to the wicked and of perverting justice, proclaiming that he "covers the eyes of its judges" (9:24). He describes God as cruel and having sent evil to those who looked for good (30:21; 26). In even stronger condemnation, Job speaks of the "dying groan" of those in the city and the cry of the wounded who seek help, concluding that "God pays no attention to their prayer" (24:12). In graphic imagery, he paints a portrait of a god who "seized" him "by the neck" and "dashed him to pieces," who set him "up as a target," spilled out his gall and slashed his kidneys, ultimately showing "no mercy" (16:12–13). He sarcastically asks God, "Does it seem good to you to oppress… and favor the schemes of the wicked?" (10:3).

Job has not simply declared God to be morally ambivalent, nor has he proclaimed that God is simply callous toward the plight of men. Rather, Job accuses God of being *the reason* why the wicked prosper, and the force that oppresses those who suffer. At one point, he refers to God as "his adversary" and soon after proclaims that he himself is God's adversary (16:9; 19:11).

God is Job's adversary? Wasn't there already a character in the story called that? Yes, Satan. His name, or rather title, can be translated as either "the Accuser" or "the Adversary." Even though the Hebrew word for Satan is not employed, Job is using the same sense with other words to describe the idea that God is his Satan. Recognizing this has profound consequences for how we understand Job's spiritual and emotional health during the story. It's possible that this could make many feel uncomfortable. This is the opposite of the fictional image of "patient Job" that so many espouse without having actually read the book. Yet, perhaps after reading about Abraham, Jacob, Moses and their heated encounters with God, Job's words seem normal. Then again, perhaps they're still hard for any of us to swallow.

All of this leads to some interesting ideas. Job believes that "if one wished to contend with [God]," the endeavor would be a failure. He asks who, if any, has resisted God and succeeded, apparently unaware of the stories of Abraham and Moses (9:3–4). He wonders who would be bold enough to ask God "What are you doing?" (9:12) or attempt to teach him knowledge (21:22). And more importantly, he believes that even if he did succeed in finally summoning God to speak with him, "I do not believe that he would listen to my voice" (9:16). Ultimately, he declares that he has no hope, concluding that God "will kill me" (13:15).

After all, Job concludes, if it's a question about justice, who can summon him? Who, Job asks, can question the judge of everything? (9:19). Yet, instead of this discouraging him, as one might naturally assume, this seemingly cynical and stark dose of reality only provokes Job further. He sarcastically remarks that if God were a mortal like him, that he would take God to court and sue him (9:32–33). Sue God? Yes, Job said he wanted to sue God and not only that, but by wishing for a judge to handle the case between them, also wishes that there was a god higher than God who could judge God for his "crimes." Eventually Job declares that "I desire to argue my case with God!" (13:3) and speaks of his wish to "lay my case before him and fill my mouth with arguments" (23:3–4).

But then the big day came and God showed up. What is fascinating about the encounter between Job and God is also what frustrates so many readers about it: there is *no resolution*. Nothing is ever explained. Job, quite ironically, postulates half way through the book that if he was able to eventually speak with the Almighty, God would not argue back with Job "in the greatness of his power... but would give heed to me." Job concludes that if he could find God's dwelling and meet him, he could "reason with him" (23:6–7). It's ironic because contrary to Job's assertion about the character of God, that is exactly what God ends up doing. And it is the reason why countless readers have found the ending of Job both mystifying and dissatisfying.

Unlike previous occasions, God responds to Job with forceful words, asking "Shall a faultfinder contend with the Almighty? Anyone who argues with God must respond" (40:1–2). Job, previously filled with indignation, backs down. "See," he says, "I am of small account; what shall I answer you? I lay my hand on my mouth" (40:3–4). To which God no less forcefully orders Job to act like a man, saying: "I will question you, and you declare to me." God provocatively calls Job out on his claims that God was not only callous toward the issue of morality, but the reason evil succeeds, saying: "Will you even put me in the wrong? Will you condemn me so that you may be justified?" (40:7–9).

At this monumental moment in the story, after countless speeches by Job about the cruelty of God and innocence of his life, Job replies meekly with these words: "I had heard of you by the hearing of the ear, but now my eye sees you; therefore I despise myself, and repent in dust and ashes" (42:5–9). What is Job repenting of? His words? His actions? It's unclear. The safest interpretation that both honors the integrity of Job's speeches and his words to God is to understand that Job is merely repenting of his presumption to judge not only God's actions, but his very character.

Yet the shocks continue. Speaking to Job's friends, God does not, as one expects, congratulate them for defending him but rather curses them with a threat of death, saying that "you have not spoken of me what is right, as my servant Job has" (42:7). It's a shocking idea: Job spoke what was right? Not the friends? The man who potentially described God as similar to Satan and described God as the reason for why evil persisted was… the right one? For many, this takes a bit of mental adjustment.

The book of Job is unique because it gives us the perspective of a man of faith, blameless and upright, who questions God's sense of justice, and however difficult it is for us to struggle with God's answer, is told that he is right. How he was right, in what way he was, we may never know exactly (precisely because the author is so purposefully cryptic). If nothing else, we can understand this: God affirms that Job was right to speak his grievances aloud.

He was *right* to question God.

He was *right* to argue.

AARON'S SUCCESSFUL REBELLION

There is one story in the Bible that almost no one knows about, let alone realizes that it has to do with this book's theme. Buried in the intimidating and sleep-inducing work of Leviticus, there is a fascinating and odd tale from the consecration of the Tabernacle. While in the desert, Aaron (the high priest of Israel) and his four sons celebrate an eight-day ritual to initiate the altar, a ritual that would prove to be the inspiration for Hanukkah.

After seven days, everything appears to be going well, that is until Aaron's two oldest sons are brutally murdered by God himself.

> Now Aaron's sons, Nadab and Abihu, each took his censer, put fire in it, and laid incense on it; and they offered unholy fire before the

LORD, such as he had not commanded them. And fire came out from
the presence of the LORD and consumed them, and they died before
the LORD. Then Moses said to Aaron, "This is what the LORD meant
when he said,

'Through those who are near me
I will show myself holy,
and before all the people
I will be glorified.'"
And Aaron was silent.

(LEVITICUS 10:1–3)

This is a hard story for anyone to get their head around, and even if it hadn't been included in the least-read book of the Bible, it still probably would have been largely ignored by most readers. The shock of the tale stems from how inhumane God appears. Nadab and Abihu were, after Moses and Aaron, the third and fourth most important people in Israel. God had singled them out as some of the most holy and devout, inviting them to see him in their own theophany (Ex. 24:1; 9–11).

Yet these two young men, sons of God's second most important leader, are brutally murdered for having used the wrong coals to light their fire (yes, that's literally what the text is saying they did wrong). Their fire was unholy due to having used the wrong sort of coal and as such, a pure fire from God came to consume them. Moses remarks in the story that God is showing how he will be glorified, by demonstrating that he will even kill those closest to him (Lev. 10:3). Does that sound like a merciful God? No, it doesn't. Thankfully, we're not alone in thinking that. The events of that day clearly did not sit well with Aaron either. The text notes that though the crowd shouted and fell on their faces at the previous display of fire (9:24), Aaron remained uncharacteristically silent at the death of his sons (10:3).

As if to add insult to injury, because Aaron and his two younger sons were already anointed that day to do their work for the initiation of the altar, Moses warns them that they cannot cry, they cannot show grief, and they cannot go to their dead son/brothers. They must ignore their deaths, Moses tells them, or else God will also kill them for acting inappropriately (Lev. 10:6–7).

At this point, it is important to clarify something: Nadab and Abihu did in fact break God's command. They had violated God's instructions to distinguish between what God called the common and the profane. They had been warned to do this and they failed, apparently for their first time. This is important to note because it underscores the gravity of what happens next to Aaron and his two youngest sons. God personally speaks to Aaron, but instead of consoling him, he threatens him and warns that in order for him and his sons not to die, they must "teach the people of Israel all the statutes that the LORD has spoken to them through Moses" (10:11). In other words, after killing Aaron's sons for disobeying his commands, God commands Aaron to ensure that all the people avoid the same mistake and the death that accompanies disobedience.

What happens next though is where things get interesting. Moses orders Aaron to fulfill God's instructions, as had been previously given in Lev. 8:31–35, and eat the goat of the sin offering in the sacred area. To Moses' shock, he later discovers that Aaron and his two young sons have purposefully broken God's instructions and burned the meat instead! In other words, Aaron has slapped God in the face and Moses reacts with visible anger.

> Then Moses made inquiry about the goat of the sin offering, and—it had already been burned! He was angry with Eleazer and Ithamar, Aaron's remaining sons, and said, "Why did you not eat the sin offering in the sacred area? For it is most holy, and God has given it to you that you may remove the guilt of the congregation, to make atonement on their behalf before the LORD. Its blood was not brought into the inner part of the sanctuary. You should certainly have eaten it in the sanctuary, as I commanded." And Aaron spoke to Moses, "See, today they have offered their sin offering and their burnt offering

before the LORD; and yet such things as these have befallen me! If I had eaten the sin offering today, would it have been agreeable to the LORD?" And when Moses heard that, he agreed.

(LEVITICUS 10:16–20)

Aaron's response to Moses and Moses' agreement are confounding, as is the silence of God, who up until now has been ever vocal. Aaron essentially argues that the sin offerings that his sons have offered have been of no use. God, he argues, has not honored them. As such, he decided in his judgment that he would, like his dead sons, not honor God's statute. Instead of making *a mistake* like his sons, he *purposefully defies* God's ordinance.

However, it is Aaron's second given reason for doing this that is astounding: he suggests to Moses that God would not have been pleased had he and his two remaining sons followed his law. Instead, he argues, it was more agreeable to God for him to defy it in response to that day's events. And as if that wasn't surprising enough, Moses agrees with this. Moreover, God's silence and lack of punishment appear to confirm that Aaron is right.

This is a shocking story: God wants you to be honest, even if it means that you fight him and even disobey him out of frustration. Yet that simple reading of the story is not necessarily the end of the tale. The Jews around the time of Jesus also wrestled with some of the things that affect the meaning of this story and their ideas imply an even more jaw-dropping (if not humorous) conclusion.

The Jewish sages believed that the festival of the initiation of the altar (the first Hanukkah) was linked to the New Moon festival. One of the requirements for the festival was that a goat was to be offered as a sacrifice. Now what was the reason for the New Moon festival?

Well, according to the Talmud*, a collection of the discussions that the Jewish sages had, the answer lay in a rather symbolic and parabolic reading of Genesis 1.

> R. Simeon b. Pazzi pointed out a contradiction [between verses]. One verse says: And God made the two great lights, and immediately the verse continues: The greater light... and the lesser light. The moon said unto the Holy One, blessed be He, "Sovereign of the Universe! Is it possible for two kings to wear one crown?" He answered: "Go then and make thyself smaller." "Sovereign of the Universe!" cried the moon, "Because I have suggested that which is proper must I then make myself smaller?" He replied: "Go and thou wilt rule by day and by night." "But what is the value of this?" cried the moon; "Of what use is a lamp in broad daylight?" He replied: "Go. Israel shall reckon by thee the days and the years." "But it is impossible," said the moon, "to do without the sun for the reckoning of the seasons, as it is written: And let them be for signs, and for seasons, and for days and years." "Go. The righteous shall be named after thee as we find, Jacob the Small, Samuel the Small, David the Small." On seeing that it would not be consoled the Holy One, blessed be He, said: "Bring an atonement for Me for making the moon smaller." This is what was meant by R. Simeon b. Lakish when he declared: Why is it that the he-goat offered on the new moon is distinguished in that there is written concerning it unto the Lord? Because the Holy One, blessed be He, said: Let this he-goat be an atonement for me making the moon smaller.
> (BT Chullin 60b)²

If you're confused, I don't blame you. The Talmud is even more cryptic than the Bible usually is. In this particular case, the Talmudic writers are using a parable or metaphorical story to represent a deeper reality. According to one interpretation of this text, the moon is representative of the world, where God is responsible for having reduced

---

* The *Babylonian Talmud* (BT) is a sacred collection of interpretations, opinions and legal verdicts, having been written down in Babylon during the period following Jesus' death. It is sometimes called the *Oral* Torah and is second only to the Bible for Judaism.

and ultimately created an imbalance. The waning moon, thus, comes to represent the fragility of life and the darkness of death which eventually covers the moon entirely, blocking almost all of its light, and, metaphorically, all hope for the future.

This diagnosis of our world's broken reality is then combined with an interesting oddity in the regulations governing the New Moon festival. Unlike any other festival, this one specifically requests that an offering be brought "unto the LORD." This led the rabbis to presume that since the other sacrifices were offered to God implicitly, this offering "unto the LORD" must have been not an offering *to* God, but on *behalf* of God.

In short, the rabbis argue that God needed the offering. The waning moon is symbolic of death and impurity. Thus, God requests of Israel that they symbolically forgive him for the corruption that exists in the world, which then is followed in the New Moon festival with a *bright* new hope in the sky, renewed each month.

Rabbi Hefter proposes, based on this same interpretation of the Talmudic tradition, that perhaps the unidentified sin offering in Lev. 10:16 is in fact the goat required for the New Moon festival.[3] This adds a new dimension to Aaron's refusal to eat the meat: he's actually refusing to make atonement on God's behalf. Aaron and his two younger sons will not forgive God's perceived imperfections, but will rather hold him responsible.

As Rabbi Hefter concludes in his article:

> The way Aharon handled his grief is a lesson to all on how to build and maintain a living relationship with God. In an honest relationship we dare not repress our feelings lest resentment and alienation grow. Aharon by refusing to eat the sin offering, is insisting on an authentic relationship with God. Not one based upon servile submission and sycophantic platitudes. The intensity and—yes—the recrimination of God implicit in Aharon's behavior is actually the foundation upon which he builds his authentic relationship with God. The preacher

who obsessively apologizes for God and believes he is protecting Him is in fact erecting barriers to Him.[4]

It's a bold reading of an already heretical story (wasn't breaking God's law purposefully already bad enough?) that surprisingly *agrees* with the book of Job's message: even God must be held to account, like any judge. Whether or not it's correct as either an intepretation of the original biblical tale or even as an interpretation of the Talmud, and it may not be, the simple and straightforward message of Leviticus and its story of Aaron's defense of his disobedience still stands as an important milestone for us to heed. According to Aaron, God would rather have faithful and honest disobedience than simple blind obedience from his followers.

DON'T DEFEND GOD

One of the interesting things about the book of Job that many people miss is that there's actually a bigger issue at stake in the book than simply whether God is just. There are issues of scriptural authority present as well. Unbeknownst to many, the book of Job is actually written in direct *opposition* to the books of Deuteronomy and Proverbs. Yes, you heard me right. The book of Job was written in order to contradict the views of two other books in the Bible. Don't believe me? Sounds too radical? Let's take a look.

Deuteronomy 28 warns that anyone who breaks God's covenant will receive a number of curses, among them the following: they will have disaster befall them (v. 20), they will be afflicted with boils all over their bodies which cannot be healed (v. 35), their livestock will be killed or taken away (v. 31), their sons and daughters will be taken away by force, and they will see the food they grow stolen from them either by strangers who steal it (v. 33) or God himself who will prevent the crops from growing (vv. 21, 24).

Does any of that sound familiar? It should. *It's the story of Job's first two chapters.* Only... that's the point. Job didn't do anything Deuteronomy said he needed to do in order to have these curses fall upon him. And this is what most of us miss when we read Job's story: when his friends insist that he did something wrong, it's not because they are uncaring, *it's because they are trusting Scripture.* Deuteronomy had promised its readers that none of these curses would ever fall on those who were righteous. Job's friends trusted that promise, yet, Job insists that God's word in Deuteronomy is wrong. He's arguing that the world does not operate in the way in which *that* Scripture described it. His friends, on the other hand, are insisting that God's Word never lies and that of course, given that fact, it means Job could not have been innocent.

See the conflict? It's not all that far-fetched. It sounds like the debates that Liberal and Conservative Christians still have over the issue of biblical authority. Progressive Christians argue that our experiences in life should help us to interpret the Bible while Conservatives argue that the Bible is the highest authority and overrules our experiences. The book of Job pits these two viewpoints against each other. Job's experience in life contradicts Scripture, yet his friends cannot accept Job's words because of that very fact.

To give you the sense of how radical this claim was, I'll give you a modern analogy. Imagine that Job is a young man named Steve who is living not in Edom, but in today's San Francisco. Instead of struggling with great losses like Job (something that sadly indicated to people back then that he sinned), Steve is gay (something many people today sadly identify as evidence of sin). He comes out to his friends and says that even though he is a staunch believer in God and loves Scripture, he did not choose to become gay and claims that this is the way God made him. His friends argue that because of certain verses in Scripture, it's not possible that he was truly God-fearing and certainly, they insist, it's not possible that God made him this way. Yet, Steve knows that he didn't choose to be gay. But his friends won't hear anything of his defense since Scripture, they believe, says Steve is wrong.

Get it? In this second story, if you're conservative, you find yourself aligned with Steve's friends. Imagine reading a book of Scripture in which the author reveals to you that even though Scripture says something, and even though these friends will uphold it, in reality, they and even *that very* Scripture are wrong, and the main character Steve is actually the one who is right. You would struggle throughout the whole book, precisely because you agree with the friends and yet you've been told that the main character is right.

That's how radical Job's book was when it was first written. It was undercutting the prevailing theology of its time, and did so without a hint of subtlety. It was changing everything. It was valuing personal experience over a scriptural foundation. Radical, no? Even for our time it seems profound.

As briefly mentioned earlier, Job's friends seem to also very closely echo the views of not only Deuteronomy, but Proverbs as well. In Prov. 10:30, for example, it promises that "the righteous will never be removed, but the wicked will disappear from the land." It also promises that "the wages of the righteous is life, the income of the wicked, punishment" (Prov. 10:16). Another verse says that "The righteous is delivered from trouble, but the wicked takes his place" (Prov. 11:8). Yet another states that "No harm happens to the righteous, but the wicked are filled with trouble" (12:21). And Prov. 13:25 says that the righteous never go hungry, but those who are wicked will starve.

See the similarity? Job's friends are simply following what Scripture says. The wise sages of the book of Proverbs, whether Solomon or otherwise, are giving absolute judgments on fate. Righteous people do not suffer. Wicked people do! Yet, here's Job. And here are Job's friends who are clinging to their sacred texts to contradict his testimony.

This opens up a big issue: should we defend Scripture when it conflicts with our real experiences in life? Or, to return to our earlier topics, should Christians ultimately feel the need to defend God at all? Should they uphold the evaluation of scriptures which affirm God's violent actions even if they contradict what we believe to be moral? Is it right to say that if God does it, it's okay, but if we do it, it's evil?

Is this not showing a form of partiality towards God?

Actually, yes.

As shocking as it may sound, Job had actually warned his friends that God would "surely rebuke" them if they showed partiality toward God. "Will you," he provokes them, "speak falsely for God and speak deceitfully for him? Will you show partiality toward him, will you plead the case for God?" (13:7–8; 10). It's an interesting idea. Job takes God's words in Deut. 1:16–18 about judges being required to judge justly and applies it not only to all humans, but even to God himself. In Lev. 19:15, it says that "you shall do no injustice in court" and "you shall not be partial to the poor or defer to the great." Job, quite radically, argues that even God (in this case, "the great") should not be shown favoritism by those who follow or defend him. Such an idea, though, should not strike us as odd for someone like Job. After all, three chapters earlier he had spoken of his desire to sue God in a court of law. So his attitude does make sense.

When God does eventually confront Job's three friends, he tells them that "my wrath is kindled against you" (42:7). He warns them that despite their defense of him and Scripture, "you have not spoken of me what is right." And who has? Job. God describes not only their words but their entire approach as "folly" or "foolishness." The Hebrew word used here, *nebalah*, is defined not only as stupidity, but can also mean "willful sin," "wickedness," and even "grave sin," depending on the dictionary you look at. Defending God with Scripture, according to God himself, is a potential "grave sin."

Although some Christians feel the need to deny the experiences of others that contradict Scripture, the message of Job is that God will judge them. Even though some Christians feel the need to apologize for their faith, to explain away the disturbing passages of the Bible, the message of Job is that God will actually judge you. In Isa. 5:20, it warns that judgment is reserved for "those who call evil good and good evil, who put darkness for light and light for darkness." Christians who defend genocide, even if, according to the Bible, it was done by God, are fulfilling this prophet's very words. Sometimes, Scripture shows us, the best answer is "no," even if it appears to be directed at God.

6

DID GOD SAY IT OR MOSES?

"Jesus was not content to derive his ethics from the scriptures of his upbringing. He explicitly departed from them... Since a principal thesis [of mine]... is that we do not, and should not, derive our morals from scripture, Jesus has to be honoured as a model for that very thesis."

RICHARD DAWKINS[1]

We've spent a long time in this book so far looking primarily at stories from the Bible. For some, these stories may seem to hold limited value. Someone might sigh and remark, "Aren't you stretching or reading into the meaning of these stories too much?" Where, this same person might wonder, can we unambiguously discover God's will? Ignoring the fact that the earliest Christians and Israelites primarily relied on stories and not dogmatic rules, it is true that we as Christians have something that those before the first century didn't: *Jesus of Nazareth*.

To use an appropriate metaphor, he is the pair of glasses we wear in order to see the world and Scripture in a new light. Moreover, he is a pair of glasses that we choose never to take off and which we expect, because of his promise, to someday transform and become our very eyes. So, it is very interesting to realize that Jesus, according to the Gospels, touched on some of the very issues in our discussion.

It turns out that Jesus exhibited a similar disposition for reinterpreting and challenging established scriptural truths about God. This observation is of course not novel, as it is apparent to many readers of the Gospels that the teacher from Galilee was constantly pushing the boundaries of Scripture in his day. When the Sabbath laws became oppressive, he argued not from Scripture, but theologically and philosophically that if the Sabbath was made *for* all mankind, it was not and should not be a burden to any man (Mark 2:27).

When the disciples were accused of picking grain on the Sabbath, which was forbidden by God (Ex. 34:21), Jesus simply argued that David did much worse but was still blessed by God for it anyway (Mark 2:25–26). In other words, Jesus argued in favor of breaking this specific law of God because of a previous instance in which God appeared to not enforce the law and furthermore, blessed the person anyway! When was the last time you heard a minister preach a sermon with that message?

One of the most famous cases of reinterpretation was the story in John of the woman caught in adultery (John 8). In that tale, we are told of how a woman was brought before Jesus on the charge of adultery. She had just been caught in the act, but apparently, the man had conveniently escaped. The crowd proposes to him a dilemma: should they stone her to a bloody death or not? God had explicitly said in Scripture that the answer must be yes (Lev. 20:10). If Jesus answers that ethically they should not, he appears to value his own ethics above the Scripture. So, what does Jesus do when he believes that the Bible is wrong? It shouldn't surprise us: he draws on principles *from* Scripture, rather than specific verses. Quite ingeniously, he dabbles in philosophy once more and argues that the only one who can act as an impartial and right judge of sin is the one who is not guilty of sin himself. Since they are all sinners, he argues, none of them can judge her.

The Scripture that the crowd drew from, though, was very clear: she must die. In fact, one text in the Torah actually says explicitly that the crowd must, by vigilante justice, kill the adulteress *together* (Deut. 22:21). More so, according to John 8:4, some in the crowd had actually witnessed the woman's act, and according to other texts in Scripture, they were demanded by God to begin stoning her first, even before the crowd did (Deut. 13:9; 17:7).

Yet Jesus *invalidates* these scriptures by making an appeal to logic, utilizing principles drawn from other scriptures. He nullifies one set of God's words with the principles of another. All of this should demonstrate well the fact that the idea of arguing with God and as such, arguing with Scripture, was not only a phenomena of the Old Testament, but a well-established practice continued by Jesus. An obvious question, though, begins to emerge: how can something God explicitly said be simply ignored? What does that imply about its authoritative status?

In John 7:22, Jesus strangely says that "Moses gave you circumcision."* The book of Genesis, of course, is very clear that the idea of circumcision was a "covenant agreement" handed down not by Moses, but *by God* to Abraham and all of his lineage (Gen. 17:10–14). Even when Moses is told of circumcision, it is not a custom of his but God's (Ex. 12:48; Lev. 12:3). Interestingly, one ancient writer noticed this contradiction and eventually felt forced to comment on it.

Jesus' statement is, funnily enough, followed by an editorial remark by the author of John (or a later scribe) who adds that "it is, of course, not from Moses, but from the patriarchs." It's fascinating to realize

---

* A similar incident can be seen in a passage in the book of Acts where *circumcision* is referred to as "the custom of Moses" (15:1).

that at least one Bible writer or editor saw the strangeness of Jesus' wording. In fact, this is one of the few times in the Bible where an editor (instead of a character) argues with God! The scribe is correcting a statement from Jesus, God incarnate, arguing that the Son of God misspoke. The funny thing is: even his editorial correction is *still wrong*. Contrary to this anonymous writer's statement, circumcision was not from the Patriarchs, for they had in fact received it from God according to Genesis. Again, the issue at stake here is one of authority. Does the practice stem from a human or from God? If the Bible clearly states it was from God, why do New Testament writers speak of it as from man?*

Let's dig deeper into this issue by taking a look at another example in Mark 10:3–5, where Jesus is asked whether it is lawful for a man to divorce his wife. Jesus famously answers that Moses allowed divorce because "of your hardness of heart." But, there's just one problem with what Jesus seems to have said: *Moses did no such thing*. The law on divorce, found in Deut. 24:1–4, was said to have been given *by God*, not Moses. The passage is given in a lengthy list of laws in Deuteronomy that begins in 10:11–13, which states that God requires that Israel "keep the commandments of the LORD your God and his decrees that I am commanding you today." Yet Jesus said that Moses "wrote this commandment for you," as if its authority came from Moses himself, not God. Why is that important? Because in the story in Mark, Jesus refutes this "commandment" by Moses, arguing that it is merely human, not divine. Jesus' entire rationale for dismissing divorce in the Gospel of Mark is predicated on the idea that

---

* In Mark 1:44, Jesus tells someone he has just healed to "say nothing to anyone," and instructs him to "offer for your cleansing what Moses commanded." The passage in question is a reference to Lev. 13:49; 14:2–4. Once again, the law in question is not a command of Moses but according to Lev. 13:1, the voice of God.

divorce came from Moses, not God. Yet what Jesus says describes as a human command is actually said to be in the Bible from God!

This raises an obvious question: how in the world was anyone supposed to know, prior to Jesus, that the command was from a human and not God, when the book the command is written within says otherwise? In other words, how can someone tell the difference between what Moses wrote and what God *truly* wrote if both are attributed to God in the text? How can we trust what the Bible says if Jesus reveals that sometimes it's not accurate about who is saying what?

A similar incident occurs in Mark 7:9–13, when some Pharisees rebuke Jesus and his disciples for not washing their hands. Jesus' witty response: you are hypocrites.

> For Moses said, "Honor your father and your mother"; and, "Whoever speaks evil of father or mother must surely die." But you say that if anyone tells father or mother, "Whatever support you might have had from me is Corban" (that is, an offering to God)— then you no longer permit doing anything for a father or mother, thus making void the word of God through your tradition that you have handed on. And you do many things like this.
>
> (MARK 7:10–13)

Great argument. Most people cheer. Another point for Jesus. Only there's a problem: Moses didn't actually say that. *God did.* Both of those are statements made by God himself *to Moses* according to the passages Jesus is quoting, yet instead, Jesus is saying that it's from Moses. The problem grows even larger when one examines which texts from the Bible Jesus claims derive their authority from Moses. The two passages are found in Ex. 20:12 and 21:17. The first passage is from the fifth commandment (part of the famous Ten Commandments, the two stone tablets that God was said to have engraved with his very own finger) and the second passage is also a law which was introduced as "The LORD said" (Ex. 20:22). Can you see the problem with this example?

Jesus has described one of the Ten Commandments as the words of Moses, human words (and human authority)! And at least according to one New Testament writer, what you do to one commandment applies to them all (James 2:10). Was Jesus demoting the authority of what Christians have traditionally called "God's Eternal Moral Law"? This is, admittedly, a hard pill to swallow, especially as a Seventh-day Adventist. If there's one thing that many Adventists value in terms of theology (aside from Jesus), it's the Ten Commandments.

Interestingly, even though in Mark 7 Jesus equates the two different sets of laws from God as the words of Moses (a human), he still refers to it as "the commandment of God" and "the word of God." How can this be true? How can Jesus both affirm the Ten Commandments as the words of Moses and of God? For most, it seems to be a hopeless dichotomy: either it's one or the other. Certainly, many fundamentalists would see such a distinction between the two as absolutely necessary. Yet is such a distinction neccesary at all? It seems so confusing, yet, it also may be the most important factor in all this.

THE WORD OF GOD

A great Evangelical scholar of the Bible and bestselling author, Peter Enns, wrote a work on this subject called *Inspiration & Incarnation*.* In this fantastic book, Enns points out that, biblically speaking, the only way to understand inspiration is to accept the existence of contradictions and the human element of error. He argues

---

* Regardless of how one feels about Enns' work now and whether some would still describe it as Evangelical, it cannot be denied that the work cited here was written by him when he was an Evangelical, writing for Evangelicals, from an Evangelical perspective.

that if we accept that Jesus, the incarnate Word made flesh, was both fully human and fully divine, why then do we have trouble imagining that the Word made *written* can also be affirmed as both fully human and fully divine?*

Fundamentalists and more conservative Christians would argue back: either the Bible is the Word of God or it isn't! They would argue that this talk of a mixture of human and divine confuses that fact. Yet, such objections may not prove helpful. Daniel Migiliore, a famous theologian, wisely cautions us that: "If we are embarrassed by the humanity of the biblical writers, we are also probably embarrassed by the humanity of Jesus the Jew from Nazareth and by our own humanity." And he adds that: "If we affirm the full humanity of Jesus, we will also respect the humanity of the Biblical witnesses."[2]

To be believers in the divinity and humanity of Jesus, in essence, requires not only that we understand the Word in flesh as both God and man, but the witnesses to this advent as both a mixture of God and text. Migiliore continues: "Our interpretation of Scripture must therefore include both a 'hermeneutics of trust' (the human words of Scripture convey *God's* Word) and a 'hermeneutics of suspicion' (God's Word in Scripture is conveyed in *human* words)."[3]

This is still likely to remain disconcerting for some. God's word is not, strictly speaking, merely God's word. Migiliore notes perceptively that:

> Recognizing that there are flaws and distortions in all witnesses to revelation is disturbing to many Christians. But if we remember that God's grace and power are made perfect in human weakness (2 Cor.

---

* Ellen White, writing in 1888, appears to have had similar thoughts to Enns when she wrote that "the Bible, with its God-given truths expressed in the language of men, presents a union of the divine and the human. Such a union existed in the nature of Christ, who was the Son of God and the Son of man. Thus it is true of the Bible, as it was of Christ" (*The Great Controversy*, p. v).

12:9), we will have little difficulty in seeing the grace of God at work in the fact that fallible human beings are taken into the service of God's revelation.[4]

Although many writers have discussed these issues, both past and present, one woman in particular shared some wise observations on this subject, especially for her time. A prolific author of the nineteenth century and one of the founders of my particular denomination, Ellen White wrote in 1886 (fourteen years or so before the rise of Fundamentalism), that:

> Everything that is human is imperfect... The Bible is written by inspired men, but it is not God's mode of thought and expression. It is that of humanity. God, as a writer, is not represented. Men will often say such an expression is not like God. But God has not put Himself in words, in logic, in rhetoric, on trial in the Bible. The writers of the Bible were God's penmen, not His pen... It is not the words of the Bible that are inspired, but the men that were inspired.[5]

But this raises the important question: if the words of the Bible are merely a witness to God's inspiration and are subject to human error, what then do we look to, to understand God and his will? To what, or rather, whom, do we direct our vision? The answer is as simple as remembering that the Christian faith, unlike that of Judaism and Islam, is not centered on a book, but *a person.*

"Strictly speaking," Mark Vernon writes in an article for *The Guardian*, "the Judeo-Christian 'people of the book' are not people of the book at all: they are people who look beyond the words of the book to a deeper truth and reality." Or as John Dominic Crossan so aptly puts it, "The person, not the book, and the life, not the text, are decisive and constitutive for us."[6]

Which person? Jesus. Which life? Christ's.

There's more truth to that idea than many Christians consciously realize. When Jesus' ethics run counter to the human directives of

Deuteronomy (even when Deuteronomy says they come straight from God), it is Jesus who wins the argument over the woman caught in adultery. When Jesus' understanding of divorce runs contrary to the instructions of Deuteronomy (even when, again, Deuteronomy says that it came straight from God's mouth), it is Jesus, the *Word made flesh*, who sets Christian ethics, not Scripture.

As Marcus Borg so aptly puts it, "Because Christians find the ultimate disclosure of God in a person and not in a book, Jesus is more central than the Bible. Jesus trumps the Bible; when they disagree, Jesus wins."[7] In these conflicts between the Word of God and the Word made Flesh, "Jesus is the norm, the standard, by which the rest of the Bible is to be understood." Why? Because "as the Word become flesh... Jesus is for Christians the decisive Word of God—decisive in the sense of 'ultimate.' Thus, what we see in him transcends the Word of God in a book, the Bible."[8] In essence, "the Word become flesh—what Christians call 'the incarnation'—triumphs over words in a book."[9] Of course, as Borg points out, there's a paradox in this reality as well since "we know about him primarily through the Bible, and in particular through the New Testament." And it is this paradox, "the interweaving of God, Jesus and the Bible" that "is at the heart of the Christian vision of life."[10]

In truth then, that which we as Christians call the *Word of God* refers not to the *words* of biblical writers, but to the victorious rider of the white horse of Revelation whose "name is called the *Word of God*" (Rev. 19:13), which we affirm is the eternal *Word* who "was God" and "became flesh and lived among us" (John 1:1, 14). I am, of course, being as simple as possible: speaking of Jesus, whose life and teachings is our first and only Scripture since he was, is and remains the only decisive revelation of who God is.

Bromleigh McCleneghan puts it just right when she writes that: "I profess Jesus *as* the Word of God, and the Bible *as* a witness to His life, ministry, death and resurrection."[11] Jesus is, ultimately speaking, the center of our faith. Yet we talk at times as if the Bible, a mere witness to his revelation, was the foundation of our beliefs. The *Word of God* has become the *words about God* and the transition has made us poorer in our theology as a result.

Brian McLaren points out astutely the danger in this, that "just as the bronze serpent that had been an agent of healing in Moses's day could later become something of an idol (2 Kgs. 18:4), so Christian individuals and communities can unwittingly become false Trinitarians, worshiping Father, Son, and Holy Scriptures."[12] Bibliolatry then, and all forms of idolatry which seek to take our eyes away from the center and focus of our faith, must be fought and pushed against by Christians.

THE IDOLATRY OF SCRIPTURE

Bibliolatry. For many, the term is likely new and as such, requires definition. In short, it means "the idolatry of the Bible." It specifically refers to Christians who have come to worship the book *instead* of the God who is the inspiration behind it. In short, they are the sorts of Believers who ask if you have faith in the Bible, rather than asking if you have faith in the Christ that the Bible points to.

I encountered an extreme example of this when I traveled to Israel. I was attending a local Adventist congregation in Jerusalem during their Sabbath School study, which was just prior to the main service. My friend was leading the discussion on the lesson when one of the women stood up and proclaimed that the Bible… *was Jesus*. That's not a typo, that's what she actually said. And yes, she meant that quite literally. She went on to clarify that it *was* Jesus because it contained *his words* and as such, could rightfully be seen as his *replacement and equivalent*.

When I speak about Bibliolatry, that is what I am referring to at its strongest and most radical element. And although this was a visiting member from another country, there are sadly far too many who hold similar if variant extreme views in the United States. Finding its strongest roots in the rise of Fundamentalism in America at the turn of the twentieth century, this extreme view of Scripture was elevated out of a reaction to advancing scholarship in the Bible (much of which we have and will continue to explore) and increasing discoveries in science, particularly further arguments regarding the principle of natural selection.

At the risk of repeating a point too many times, I'll echo Matthew Distefano's quip that the Bible "is not a part of the Holy Trinity—if it were, we would have to call it the Quadrinity."[13] This is what makes bibliolatry so dangerous. Or as Brennan Manning puts it,

> I am deeply distressed by what I only can call in our Christian culture the idolatry of the Scriptures. For many Christians, the Bible is not a pointer to God but God himself. In a word–bibliolatry. God cannot be confined within the covers of a leather-bound book. I develop a nasty rash around people who speak as if mere scrutiny of its pages will reveal precisely how God thinks and precisely what God wants.[14]

Obviously, the majority of the readers of this book will not fall into the category of Bibliolatry. Most Christians would gawk at the woman who said the Bible was Jesus, but nonetheless, the road to Bibliolatry is a slow one and each step matters. No one means to end up at a destination such as Fundamentalism, but many arrive there regardless. As such, even the slightest misunderstandings about the Bible can grow into something worse. As N. T. Wright has noted: "the church clearly can't live without the Bible, but it doesn't seem to have much idea of how to live with it."[15]

A quick survey of some nearby Evangelical churches in Southern California reveal a common thread. On many of their "What We

Believe" pages on their websites, the Bible is listed first, above their beliefs of who God is, making the Bible and not God himself their ultimate top affirmation of faith. One touts that "Because it is inspired by God, it is truth without any mixture of error."[16] A Lutheran church affirms that "the Bible is… free from any error whatsoever."[17] Another states that "As the verbally inspired Word of God, the Bible is without error in the *original* writings… Therefore, it is to be believed in all that it teaches, (and) obeyed in all that it requires."[18] Another states that "We believe the Scriptures… inerrant in the original writings, and that they are of supreme and final authority in all matters of faith and life."[19] Another simply says "We believe the Bible is God's Word. It is inspired and accurate."[20] Another says cryptically that "We believe that the Bible is God's Word, and not only contains truth but is truth (itself)."[21] Another even more cryptically says that "it is the source of God's divine revelation."[22]

Perhaps it shouldn't surprise us then that King James Onlyists tend to kick bibliolatry to a new level altogether by affirming not only everything that those Evangelical churches stated above, but also by affirming that the only Bible God blesses (at least in English) is the KJV translation. If the Bible is so perfect, a translation among many won't do. The need to create certainty drives these ultra-conservative Christians to latch onto a myth: that the King James Version is the perfect English translation. As one San Diego church puts it, "We believe that the King James Version of the Holy Scriptures, is the best English translation of the Word of God as it was given in the original infallible autographs."[23] Another Fundamental Baptist church in the area touts that "God… used holy men through the process of inspiration to move them to write not just thoughts, but every word." It goes on to state that "the King James Bible is the Word of God preserved by God for the English-speaking people."[24]

However, perhaps the King James Onlyists are more sane theologically than another recent bestselling author. Kevin DeYoung is a conservative evangelical pastor and professor who has written many bestselling books. In one of his recent volumes on the Bible, a thin work that can be read in about an hour, he writes that "Scripture is enough because the work of Christ is enough. They stand or fall together. The Son's redemption and the Son's revelation must both be sufficient."[25]

Yes, you read that right. DeYoung equated Jesus's death on the cross with the written pages of the Bible. No, not even King James Onlyists go that far.

Yes, he made the Bible the equivalent of God. No, you're not crazy if that disturbs you.

He writes that "We need Scripture to live forever" and that "Submission to the Scriptures is submission to God," and that "Rebellion against the Scriptures is rebellion against God." He concludes that thought by noting that "The Bible can no more fail, falter, or err, than God himself can fail, falter, or err."[26] He goes on to affirm that "Every word in the Bible is in there because God wanted it there," or as he writes elsewhere, "What Scripture says, God says."[27]

He writes that "The Bible is never wrong in what it affirms and must never be marginalized as anything less than the last word on everything it teaches."[28] Perhaps most shocking amongst all of his seemingly strange beliefs is that he rejects the historic Christian belief that Jesus (the Living Word) or the Gospel has *priority* in the Christian faith. He writes that "We are sometimes told that the final authority for us as Christians should be Christ," but rebuts this claimed "liberal" idea, saying "an evangelical understanding of inspiration does not allow us to prize instructions in the Gospel more than instructions elsewhere in scripture."[29]

DeYoung admits in one part of the book that some have accused his view of the Bible as being idolatrous (probably because *it is*), but defends his beliefs as "a high view of Scripture," and instead argues that those who give priority to Christ are the real idolaters who have created a false messiah, worshiping an idol of their own imagination.[30] If that sounds crazy, it means that you aren't a Fundamentalist. Congratulations!

Near the middle of his book, he warns his readers that "There is a lot at stake with this doctrine," and honestly, I couldn't agree more. DeYoung, one voice among many with similarly outrageous views about God's word, encapsulates why *this* book is so needed. It's not because I'm somehow a more talented writer (I'm likely not), nor is it because I might say something never heard before (also unlikely), but rather it is needed because the truth of Christ and the power of the Gospel are at stake.

The eccentric woman at that church in Israel simply took DeYoung's beliefs to the next level. If Jesus and Scripture are the same authority and Jesus cannot be more authoritative than the Bible, why not simply have an even "higher view of Scripture" and say that Jesus *is* the Bible and make the idolatry go all the way?

In fact, Darwin Fish, founder of "A True Church" (with a congregation of around *fifty*), like the woman in Israel, does just that and affirms: "Believing in Jesus is identical to believing in and obeying the Bible."[31] Or as he says, "The Bible… and God are one and the same."[32] He adds that "God does not separate himself from his word," and then reflecting on a friend who told him that he worshipped the Bible, recalls that he responded: "Indeed!… what it says, we worship."[33] "Jesus Christ," Fish explains, "is all of the Bible."[34] He goes on to argue elsewhere that this view is so important that if you don't believe this radical theology, God will destine you to Hell for all eternity because as Fish seems to say, knowledge equals salvation. Gnostic much?

Of course, it's more than sad that we need to be reminded that Jesus had once said, "If I be lifted up, I will draw all men to me," and not: "If the Bible be lifted up, I will convince all people that it is the equivalent of God." Bibliolatry is a problem. In fact, it's a big one. As J.P. Moreland noted at a speech at the Evangelical Theological Society in 2007, within the North American Evangelical churches "there is an over-commitment to Scripture in a way that is false, irrational, and harmful to the cause of Christ… And it has produced a mean-spiritedness among the over-committed that is a grotesque and often ignorant distortion of discipleship unto the Lord Jesus."[35]

Valerie Tarico, in an article for the *Huffington Post*, makes a correlation between the issue of idolatry in biblical times and the cousin sin of Bibliolatry, noting that,

> Today many Christians assert that the Bible is the literally perfect Word of God, timeless and complete—exempt from addition, deletion, or revision. Many Muslims make the same claim for the Quran, according it such high status that either defacing a copy of the book or denying its divine provenance is a crime worthy of death. In other words, they attribute to the Bible and Quran the qualities of divinity, and they treat offenses against the book as if they were offenses against a god. They behave toward the Bible and Quran precisely like their ancestors did toward the wood and stone carvings that represented the divine for pre-literate people. In an age of widespread literacy, what better golden calf than a "golden" book?[36]

Bruxy Cavey strikes at the core issue of what's at stake, noting in an online essay the example of Paul Hill, a "dedicated and passionate evangelical pastor" who was "committed to the authority of Scripture." As Cavey makes careful note to remind his readers, "he was passionate for God and he professed to love Jesus—but he *followed* the Bible." That was, it seems, his undoing. On July 29, 1994, pastor Paul Hill read in his Bible, prayed, and then went to an abortion clinic where he took out a shotgun and murdered the doctor and his bodyguard as they sat in their car. Hill later commented that he believed it was required of him to do so because of his commitment to *follow* the Bible.

In reflection on this tragedy, Cavey remarks that,

> ...it seems to me that the Bible, detached from the enfleshed word of Jesus, can be a very dangerous book used to justify many destructive and deadly practices... The Bible records Jesus teaching that all of Scripture functions as a pointer to him. If Christians do not move through and beyond the pages of Scripture to follow the person of Jesus, then we are left following a book that can be manipulated to espouse many deadly and destructive teachings.[37]

The issue at stake is one of authority. Is all Scripture equal to Jesus, so that one is not above the other? Is God merely the equivalent of the words in the printed book, or is Jesus the supreme judge of not only humanity but Scripture, operating as our key to interpretation? Kevin DeYoung would reject this idea. Other prominent conservative voices might reject it as well. And I believe that our very souls and livelihoods as Christians are at risk if we *don't* accept that. Bibliolatry and all forms of Christian idolatry must be fought against, for nothing less than our Christian identity depends on our resistance to it.

As John Dominic Crossan writes in a recent book, provocatively titled *How to Read the Bible and Still Be a Christian*,

> We are called Christ-ians not Bible-ians... our very name asserts the ascendancy of Christ over the Bible... And that, of course, is why certain Christians ask "WWJD," that is, "What would Jesus do?" rather than "WWBS," or "What would the Bible say?"... with all due respect to Islamic tradition, we are not "the People of the Book." We are "the People WITH the Book," but even more importantly, we are "the People OF the Person." This is why a favorite Christian quotation from John's Gospel does not say "that God so loved the world that he gave his only Book," but "God so loved the world that he gave his only Son" (3:16). Christianity's godsend is not a book but a person, and that person is the historical Jesus.[38]

Christ once rebuked some very Bible-based believers, warning them that "You search the scriptures because you think that in them you have eternal life... Yet you refuse to come to me to have life" (John 5:39–40). He warned them that in choosing the Bible over him, they revealed that they did "not have the love of God" in them (vs. 42). And in a Christlike manner, he cautioned them: "Do not think that I will accuse you before the Father" (vs. 45), for Jesus had come to the earth to save, not to condemn (3:17). But, the condemnation would come by another means. They would be condemned by someone other than Christ; other than God.

"Your accuser," Jesus revealed, "is Moses, on whom you have set your hope" (5:45). How shocked those Jewish leaders must have been upon hearing that accusation. According to Jesus, when one sets their eyes on Scripture rather than the one which Scripture points to, instead of finding salvation, the Bible itself becomes the very thing that condemns you. And in the end, it all comes down to love. What sort of love? A love motivated and strong enough to say no to God or the Bible when it is for the sake of God's heart.

7

BECOMING LIKE GOD

"Sacred scripture is meant to create a relationship between God and humanity, a relationship in which the human partner is inherently challenged simultaneously to learn from, and critique, the divine."

RABBI DONNIEL HARTMAN[1]

What does it mean to become like God? This is a question that few of us ask. Though we often encourage each other in church to become more like God, we all too often fail to recognize what that actually entails. And for many, our advice on how to do it makes little sense. "Follow the Bible," some will say. Yet, if the goal is to become like God, how is this helpful advice? Does God follow the Bible like we do? "Obey God," some will say. But does God obey God? No, none of this gets to the reality that this book is pointing to: that God wants us to copy him by copying his character of love, and in so doing, it requires us to reject the same sorts of things that God himself rejects, even when they come from God.

In the previous chapters, we have examined various stories throughout the Bible in which men of faith rejected God's expressed will for the sake of what they believed was a more important truth about God's inner character. These stories outlined incredible depictions of the relationship between God and humanity, depictions that revolved around dialogue and fighting, rather than traditional ideas of obedience and submission. There is one other story that we haven't looked at yet which centers around quite possibly the earliest written prophet in Israel: a man named Amos.

In Amos' prophetic work, God comes to him with two visions of how he intends to destroy his people:

> This is what the Lord God showed me: he was forming locusts at the time the latter growth began to sprout... When they had finished eating the grass of the land, I said,
>
> "O Lord God, forgive, I beg you!
> How can Jacob stand?
> He is so small!"
> The Lord changed his mind concerning this;
> "It shall not be," said the Lord.
> This is what the Lord God showed me: the Lord God was calling for a shower of fire, and it devoured the great deep and was eating up the land. Then I said,
> "O Lord God, cease, I beg you!
> How can Jacob stand?
> He is so small!"
> The Lord changed his mind concerning this;
> "This also shall not be," said the Lord God.
>
> (Amos 7:1–6)*

Of course, by now, the shock value of these texts has likely started to wear off. Yet, it is in our best interest to keep reminding ourselves of how radical Amos really is. As a prophet, he is expected to be the mouthpiece of God. This was, after all, a vision he was given. He is, above all else, expected to reveal not his own beliefs, but God's. As

---

* Translation is taken from NRSV, where it says God "relented." The word in Hebrew is the same one that is translated elsewhere in the NRSV as "changed his mind." Thus, for the sake of continued clarity, I have edited the translation to reflect this.

a vision, it's not intended to be a dialogue, but a revelation. And yet here we have a prophet arguing with God, rejecting his ordained will. And guess what? God likes it.

Although God delivers a punishment in the end (7:7–9), it is a *just* judgment against specific wrongs, and not against the entire nation including those who are innocent (cf. Abraham in Gen. 18). Because of Amos *caring* about innocent people more than God's supposed divine superiority, he and countless others gain a blessing. And it's all because Amos, the mouthpiece of God's words, fights God to change those words.

Why does he do so? It isn't because he is somehow morally superior to God, but because this is exactly how God taught him how to act. He is *embodying* God in his choice to resist God. Amos has proven that he has God's character deep within his soul, for just as God's love aches for us to the uttermost, so did Amos' heart ache for his people when he saw them threatened.

THE TEST OF FAITH

God, in a very memorable and poignant verse, urges us, no, compels us: "Come now, let us argue it out" (Isa. 1:18). Like Jacob, we are invited to wrestle with God. We want a blessing, but we seemingly fight against God's will at times to get it. The angel is unwilling to give it. God seems unwilling to give it. Yet we struggle, and we receive it in faith. Abraham, Moses and Job all pushed back against what God seemed to be doing and surprisingly, perhaps heretically, they all succeeded. Instead of obedience to God's words, they were obedient to God's character.

In my third year of college, one of my friends, Daniel Peverini, who went on to pursue his Master of Divinity at Princeton Theological Seminary, was writing an exegetical paper on Moses' encounter with

God. This was part of the same story, which we briefly mentioned earlier in chapter 4, the one where Moses *implied* that God would be evil if he did a certain murderous act and as a result God "changed his mind". My friend's thesis at the time, based on the larger context of that passage in Exodus, was edgy and possibly for those with more conservative values, bordering on blasphemous: he believed that the author of Exodus was presenting God as a deity who was learning and growing from his interactions with Moses. God, in his view, changed for the same reason that we change, because he was learning.

This view of God is not new. It's been around for a long time with both Jews and Christians. A great book which argues for this interpretation (one of many) is Alan Dershowitz' *The Genesis of Justice*. The reason that this sort of interpretation isn't popular is pretty easy to understand: who wants to believe in an indecisive God? Of course, there's another reason too: it contradicts other parts of the Bible. When pastors aren't ignoring such stories about God, they're usually discrediting them, reminding their audiences that "God doesn't change!"* But as biblical scholar David Lamb rightly notes:

> If the text tells us that God changed his mind, but we conclude that that couldn't have happened because we know (from Aquinas?) that God can't change, then we have a problem... When our systematic theology comes into conflict with the Bible, the former needs to be modified, not the latter... we can work to understand how these two apparently contradictory yet biblical descriptions of God can be faithfully reconciled without downplaying the tensions.[2]

I agree with Lamb, but I do think there is a way to reconcile the tension that has not been sought out before. And although my friend's

---

* Some might mistakenly believe that Numbers 23:19 states that God doesn't change, and then use this as a proof-text. However, as Lamb explains well in his own study: "It's not simply that God doesn't ever change, but specifically that he doesn't change regarding his promises to his covenant people" (*God Behaving Badly*, p. 146).

thesis for his paper was definitely justified by the text of Exodus (where it does actually say that God changed!), because I was writing drafts of this book at the time, I had a different view of the story. For some, my view might seem either more radical or more conservative than my friend's. I'll leave that judgment up to each reader to decide.

Allow me to propose the following possibility:

What if God wasn't learning at all from these experiences?

What if it only *appeared* that he was changing?

What if, instead, God was *lying*?

My inspiration for this shocking idea was the interaction between Abraham and Yahweh in Genesis 18, a story we have already covered in detail. In the earlier part of this chapter, I mentioned how Yahweh chose to lie to Abraham. He informed his human servant that he would *investigate* the city of Sodom, and even suggested that perhaps they might be found innocent. This was a bold-faced lie on God's part. As I mentioned earlier in this book, God had already made his judgment and even given his orders to his two angels (Gen. 18:17; 19:13). Investigation, we learned, was not one of those orders. Of course, as the story reveals, Abraham recognized almost immediately that God was lying to him, and called God out for it, condemning God for a crime that God hadn't even verbally mentioned yet (18:23–25).

Yet why would God lie? What reason would God have to say something untrue to Abraham? As I suggested before, God was testing Abraham. More specifically, he was testing Abraham's faith. He was testing to see if it was strong enough, secure enough, and motivated enough to fight back, to fight against God. In other words, he wasn't lying in the way that we typically think of the word, which is with the intent to genuinely deceive. No, rather, God was *provoking* Abraham. God's lie was merely a ruse to provoke a response from his servant. God lied, but only did so precisely because he knew that Abraham would immediately recognize his lie for what it was and reject it. In other words, the ruse is a teaching tool, intended to test whether the student has fully embodied the lesson, or is merely echoing words without fully understanding them.

God, in essence, is testing Abraham as to whether he cares about justice enough that when God, who first taught him justice, appears to betray it, that he will speak out in favor of it. The same thing, I believe, can be seen in the encounter between Moses and God on Sinai. God lies when he says that he plans to destroy the Israelites. The goal of the ruse was to test whether Moses knew God well enough, and cared about the Israelites enough, to stand up and object. God was testing whether Moses could tell the difference between good and evil, even when both came from God. The fact that this is a ruse appears confirmed at the end of the story in Exodus 34, when God reveals that he is an ever merciful God who is always forgiving, the opposite of his previous depiction. Moreover, this revelation matches the initial conviction of Moses, who had demanded that God show him his true ways. The truth, it turned out, was that God was primarily merciful as Moses had believed, not vengeful as God initially pretended.

When the Canaanite woman pushes back against Jesus, he praises her for doing so precisely because that was the requirement of the test. The reason that Jesus ignores her cries but oddly never tells his disciples to dismiss her is so as to test her. Jesus purposefully misrepresents himself to the woman as a prejudiced individual in order to test whether she has enough faith to believe that Jesus is different from this bigoted portrait. This is why, when she resists him, she is praised for her faith. She passed the same test that Moses and Abraham once did.

Likewise, when Jesus in John's Gospel rejects his mother Mary's request, it is again another test. Will Mary accept the devil's mask that depicts Jesus as uncaring and disinterested, or will she push against it and affirm that Jesus (God) truly does care about even small things like happiness at a wedding. She approaches the servants because she knows her son well enough to know that he will not do as he has spoken, and it is because of her faith in her son's goodness that Jesus responds and fulfills the request. Like the Canaanite woman, like Moses, and like Abraham, Mary too passes the test of faith.

When Jacob is attacked at night, this again appears to be a test. As the daylight breaks and Jacob can see that he is wrestling with God (or God's emissary), we might imagine that he must confront the fact that God's will is against him and that he is supposed to submit to God's will. But instead, Jacob resists God's will by fighting back and demands a blessing from God. What sort of test is this? The test is whether Jacob, when faced with a God wearing the devil's mask, will affirm the mask or uplift the character of the one hidden behind it. Will he recognize that God is wearing a mask at all? When he demands a blessing from his divine opponent, he affirms that he believes that God seeks his blessing, not his curse. As such, he demonstrates that he knows the true divine heart, which is why God names him Israel. The Israelites are those who fight God and win. They win, because they reject the devil's mask and affirm the goodness of God.

I believe that this is exactly what was happening with every such story that we have covered in which God appears to want or decide to do something evil or bad, is called out for it by his leading servant, and then "changes." Yahweh, I argue, is attempting to provoke his servants in each case. He's trying to provoke them to give him a response. He's trying to get them to stop being merely servants. He's trying to get rid of their blind obedience. He's trying to transform them into *representatives* of him.

Unlike the other religions that surrounded Israel, all of which believed that their religions were unchanging and that their God's will was impossible to grasp, Israel was the nation that fought God. They were the ones who believed that not only were they tasked with *knowing* God, but with *becoming like him*. To do that, they would need his mind. To accomplish that, Yahweh would need to test them, provoke them, and ultimately fight with them to move them from the apathy of blind belief and into the light of conscious action. If they were truly to be his servants, they would need to *know* him so well, that even if he wore the devil's mask, they would reject it, knowing all too well that the devil and God have nothing in common.

God, in the end, wasn't changing. Instead, we were, and so was our view of what God was. We were becoming more like him. We were beginning to *think* like him. And with that growth, it meant that God was writing a new covenant with humanity, one not written on stone which needed to be read and observed, but one which was written on the heart and lived out as if natural (Jer. 31:33). And such a covenant would require testing, a testing which revealed whether one knew the heart of God, or only followed the mere words of God. If one only did the latter, then God could betray Godself and the individual would never be the wiser. But the mark of true faith, these biblical stories reveal, is that someone with faith recognizes the mask, spots the betrayal, and affirms that God is the opposite, that God is ultimately good. In doing this, the biblical heroes prove that they are *friends* of God, precisely because they prove that they truly know him.

FROM LUTHER TO BONHOEFFER

Perhaps that sounds too outrageous? Maybe you assume that this is the strange idea of a modern mind? In that case, you might be surprised to learn that Martin Luther and John Calvin both came to the same conclusion. For example, it was Luther who once radically said that although "it seems absurd that we are called lords and conquerors of God… in theology it is right and godly to say that God is conquered by us," because God "exhorts us to fight and shows us that it is to Him a most pleasing sacrifice to be conquered by us."[3] How was this possible? Because as Luther elsewhere argued, "In reality... it is [all] a game" and "God plays with [us] to discipline and strengthen [our] faith."[4] He gives the example of a father who suddenly takes away an apple from his child in order to motivate the child to implore him for the apple. Luther describes this game as a "test" of faith, a divine ruse.

According to Luther, the test is determined by our ability to affirm the goodness of God. We must recognize that even if God wears the devil's mask, it is only a mask and we are to push back against God in full faith of that fact. Thus, Luther argues forcefully in one sermon: "if God himself appeared to me in His majesty and said: 'You are not worthy of My grace; I will change My plan and not keep My promise to you,' I would not have to yield to Him, but it would be necessary to fight most vehemently against God himself." The ability to conquer God in such a fight he says is only due to the fact that we are fighting God with God's own Word, with his very character. Thus he can say that "There is sufficiently abundant protection in the promise of God... against this lofty temptation [from God]."[5]

Regarding this, Calvin was in perfect agreement. He writes eloquently in his commentary on Genesis:

> For we do not fight against him [God], except by his own power, and with his own weapons; for he, having challenged us to this contest, at the same time furnishes us with means of resistance, so that he both fights against us and for us. In short, such is his apportioning of it is conflict, that, while he assails us with one hand, he defends us with the other; yea, inasmuch as he supplies us with more strength to resist than he employs in opposing us, we may truly and properly say, that he fights against us with his left hand, and for us with his right hand.[6]

Likewise, Karl Barth and Dietrich Bonhoeffer, to name two more recent theologians, also affirmed this view. Barth argued that a place "where there is knowledge of the truth and of the Christian religion" can only be such a place "where a man stands wholly and utterly against God, and in this resistance against God he is marked by God... he is heard and blessed, and in this very blessing he sees the face of God and in it he knows the truth."[7] Likewise Bonhoeffer argued that Jacob's battle with God demonstrated what it meant to "become holy" as a Christian, affirming that it was because Jacob "dares to talk back to God, to refuse to do what he says," that God was able to transform his life.[8] In other words, rather than submission or obedience, the path to "be holy like God is holy" was paradoxically disobedience. Though in truth, this disobedience was actually obedience to the original divine call.

This same premise can be found in philosophical form in the works of Søren Kierkegaard and Paul Tillich. Kierkegaard argued in his book *Fear and Trembling* that Abraham "strove with God" and ultimately "conquered God," and because he defeated God was "greater than all."[9] How did he conquer God? Because he doubted God's command to kill Isaac and trusted that there was something higher or more true about God than the divine command which he knew and was confronted by. Thus, whereas before "direct opposition to the universal" (i.e. God) would have been a sin, now it becomes faith precisely because it is by means of the divine that one confronts the divine.

In my own denomination, Ellen White herself also stumbled across this idea. Commenting on Exodus 32, White argued that God had planned to "test the perseverance, faithfulness and love of Moses" by proving whether Moses recognized that it would be evil for him to accept God's proposal to kill all the Israelites. The question was whether Moses "valued more highly the prosperity of God's chosen people than a great name [for himself]."[10] In other words, White argued that the test given to Moses was similar to the one given to Christ in the wilderness when Satan provoked Jesus to give up God's mission for the sake of receiving the world. She remarked that "Many men would have said: 'It is the purpose of God. If he wishes to destroy Israel, I can not help it. They will be destroyed.'" And yet, as she notes emphatically, "Not so Moses."[11] Instead, "Moses discerned ground for hope where there appeared only discouragement and wrath."[12] Why? Because Moses knew God's character and knew that what God had said was contrary to it. Thus, Moses passed the test before him, by placing the wellbeing of others ahead of any concern for God's literal words.

So, although none of these great writers attempted to emphasize this conception of God to the extent that I am doing here, developing and applying it to a large and encompassing range of issues, they all recognized its central validity and logic. I believe it's time that we all began to do the same. Much of our struggle with the Bible is due to our inability and failure to take these biblical insights into account. After all, what good is inerrancy if the Bible reveals that God himself can test us with error for the express purpose of proving whether we will reject it? The goal of Scripture has never been to make us trust that we have the unerring words of God, but whether we can recognize and trust the true heart of God, even if the words of God attempt to use error to test us.

SAYING NO TO THE BIBLE

If we accept this understanding of God, we are recognizing something monumental: that God wants his people to imitate Moses, knowing God's true character so well that if God decided to test us by acting different, we would reject the change (even though it was God) and affirm who God truly is. To quote Tillich, we would be seeking "the God beyond God." Or put another way, we would be going beyond the words *from* God and seeking something deeper, the heart *of* God. When God's words don't match his heart, it is because God is testing whether we know the latter well enough to recognize the difference.

Like Luther, we are asked to reject anything from God's lips that does not match his revealed character. We are, like Abraham, to call God back to his senses, exclaiming: "Far be it from you!" This is not done because we are arrogant or because we believe God needs to hear it, but because God wants to know that *you* know that God isn't that way. To use a different example: if your mother had been wonderful to you for your whole life, but then suddenly shifted one day and acted distant for no reason, you would recognize something was different, wouldn't you? If you didn't see anything different, it would mean that you never knew your mother well enough to notice the change. Similarly, if your view of God can't recognize when he begins to look more like the devil than Jesus, it means your view of Jesus isn't that far from the devil. God doesn't want that, and that's why this test is so important.

This is why although God calls us to fight and defeat him, paradoxically it is our defeat of God that is his true victory. For what we are actually defeating is the mask God is wearing which tests us, and who wins is the heart of God. For as Calvin himself said, God is the one giving us the means by which to win the fight. We fight from the heart of God against the mask of God. And so, when we radically say no to God's ruse, when we win the "game" as Luther calls it, it turns out that we're actually faithfully saying yes to the heart of the divine.

What I mentioned before deserves repeating: this dismantles most of our current debates about the inspiration of Scripture. Whereas Conservatives and Progressives have been fighting over the doctrine of inerrancy, it turns out that debate is entirely worthless. Even if Conservatives were right in believing that the Bible contains the very words of God, it turns out that according to that same Bible, God's words aren't always trustworthy because sometimes God is testing us with them. If that is true for God's speeches with his servants recorded in the Bible, it is likely just as true a possibility for us, his servants reading the Bible.

In fact, it's even more of a reality for us than it was for Moses. For in his case, and Abraham's, and Jacob's, and even the women of the Gospels, they all had stood in the presence of God, and were able to interact with him directly. On the other hand, we have only testimonies *about* God, which *supposedly* reveal what he said or did in the past. This complicates things, for if we are not supposed to necessarily accept whatever God directly says, how much more should we be wary when reading reports by humans about such divine speech?

When we read texts from the Bible in which God is depicted as bloodthirsty and vindictive, this similarly should force us to question whether the portraits are accurate to begin with, let alone a potential test. For in the case of Moses, God reveals what he plans to do, allowing his servant the opportunity to object and for God to reveal that he wasn't going to do it to begin with. However, we are confronted in the Bible by depictions of things God already did that match or exceed the evil faced by Moses, and statements supposedly made by God which no human is depicted fighting against. In these cases, what are we to do? Should we view these as ruses? Or something else?

Some of the ancient Jews did, in fact, view these issues similarly to what I've described. For example, the sages in the Talmud describe certain rules as never having been intended to be enforced. When Deut. 21:18–21 states that parents should kill their sons, along with the rest of the city, if they are disobedient and rebellious, the Talmudic writers argue that the law was impossible to be followed and as such, was given not for the purpose of actually following it, but rather to challenge its readers to question and analyze why it was impossible (Sanhedrin 71a). In other words, the law's purpose was to test humans as to whether they knew the law well enough to realize that the law was impossible to follow.

Intriguingly, in the Zohar, a thirteenth century document from medieval Spain which records various mystical Jewish traditions, the same text is mentioned (Zohar Balak 197b). It tells a story of how when Moses was transcribing the Torah, he stopped when God gave this specific law. "Write!" God commanded, but Moses refused. Instead, he implored God to change his mind about a law such as this, for he believed no good parent would ever think of such a thing. God promises, like in Exodus 32, that Moses will be rewarded if he writes it, but like before, Moses stands his ground and refuses. Finally, God reveals to Moses that the law is not intended literally. Only with the realization that the law is not actually to be followed, does he finally write it down.

Whether or not the Zohar is simply relating an edifying fictional story, or whether the Talmudic sages are merely attempting to explain away a horrific text from their past, both works point in the direction that this book is aiming for. Sometimes God says things with the expectation that we will object to and reject them, and that applies to the Scriptures we hold just as much as the God who inspired them. And this is in fact what we saw was at work in the way that Jesus handled Scripture. He recognized that the laws Moses wrote down were a mix of human and divine initiative, even if the Bible itself only ascribed them to God. When God supposedly said that divorce was good, Jesus dismissed it, saying that it was actually Moses who had been the driving force behind such stipulations.

In other words, Jesus confirms for us as Christians that when we read the Bible, we aren't always saying no to something God said, such as Moses did, but we are sometimes simply saying no to the human writing about God. The Bible, as we explored, is a mix of human and divine, and while the divine element ensures that we treat Scripture with humility, the human element demands that we take seriously the fact that we are reading words that can and do indeed contain error, whether intentional or simply as a byproduct of human nature. Remember, Jesus didn't say that Moses was right but that times had changed; rather, he rejected Moses as wrong and said it was a deviation from God's order and something not approved by God.

DOING GREATER THINGS

Jesus was remembered by the early Christians for saying many things in the course of his ministry. Some of his words are remembered fondly, like the Golden Rule. Others, on the other hand, have proven less palatable. Among these ignored sayings of Jesus was one verse that perhaps ranked as one of the most controversial statements he ever gave.

> Very truly, I tell you, the one who believes in me will also do the works that I do and, in fact, will do greater works than these, because I am going to the Father.
> (JOHN 14:12)

In what way does Jesus intend for us to do "greater things" than he did while on the earth? I believe that this verse serves an important purpose in reminding us of something that the Syrophoenician/Canaanite woman and his mother had learned: Jesus has not come to replace Moses or the Bible. He has not suddenly brought the challenges to an end. No, rather, he's continued them. Just as God wanted Moses to challenge him, and just as Jesus challenged Moses, we are also to challenge Jesus as the revelation of God, just like those two bold women did.

Sometimes Christ-centered Christians become trapped when they assume that Jesus' words are the new inerrancy doctrine. They reject a *Divine Command Theory* in the Old Testament, only to apply it to a select few texts in the Gospels. These red-letter readers (referring to Bibles that print Jesus' words in red color) have adopted the same mentality that many fundamentalists do, only they've shrunk their authoritative canon. Instead of the entire Bible, only certain parts are considered to be authoritative.

The problem with this view is that it is not only unbiblical, it's un-Christlike. Jesus demonstrated in his ministry that he was *continuing* the confrontations. God didn't stop pushing us to resist him when Jesus came, rather, he taught us how to resist him even better. Jesus, after all, came to this earth as part of an ancient culture, at a distant and removed time from the past, and he had to act and speak in a way that made sense to *that* time and culture. That means there are things that Jesus said and did that were only done because of the people he was trying to communicate to.

What does that mean for us? It means that part of our job as Christians, followers of the slain Lamb, is staying true and faithful to Jesus' message in every age and culture. It is our commission as disciples to ensure that Jesus' words are not only preserved, but that they are growing and adapting, remaining the true revelation of God's love for every age. And that means that sometimes, things that Jesus said *then*, may not be perfectly suited for *now*. It means that at times, as his disciples, we are to embody his message deep within ourselves for the purpose of understanding how to change it when needed and best apply it to those around us today.

Does that sound too radical? Is it hard to believe that Jesus himself invites you to wrestle with his words as well? Well, Paul didn't think so. Early on in his ministry, that famous apostle made clear that part of his ministry to the Gentiles involved changing Jesus' commands. Why? Because the Gentiles were not the Jews, and a new culture demanded better contextual teachings. Among the many challenges that Paul faced in setting up new Christian communities in the

Greek regions and Metropolises was the issue of newly formed mixed marriages. The typical convert to Christianity was a woman and her child, or slave. As such, these newly converted Christian women (and occasionally men) found themselves unequally yoked to unconverted Pagan spouses.

After restating Jesus' command that nobody should be divorced under any circumstances (1 Cor. 7:10–11; cf. Mark 10:2–12 and Luke 16:18), Paul proceeds to alter Jesus' message for a new audience:

> To the rest I say—I and not the LORD—that if any believer has a wife who is an unbeliever, and she consents to live with him, he should not divorce her. And if any woman has a husband who is an unbeliever, and he consents to live with her, she should not divorce him… But if the unbelieving partner separates, let it be so; in such a case the brother or sister is not bound. It is to peace that God has called you… However that may be, let each of you lead the life that the LORD has assigned, to which God called you. This is my rule in all the churches.
> (1 COR. 7:12–13, 15, 17)

Paul argues that Jesus' instructions forbidding divorce are not applicable to Christians in such cases. He emphasizes that this is what he says from his own opinion and "not the LORD" (vs. 12). Notice what Paul is most interested in: the "peace that God has called you" to. Maintaining peace between relationships is the "rule" that Paul seeks while contextualizing Jesus' earlier messages. He knew that Jesus' overall trajectory was toward peace and that his life was lived toward that goal for all humanity. And so, with that in mind, Paul used the trajectory of Jesus to alter some of Jesus' actual teachings, in the same way that Jesus altered some of the Bible's teachings in order to emphasize the trajectory that the Bible pointed to.

So, what does that mean? It means that, indeed, Jesus *is* our standard. He is, as Marcus Borg pointed out in the previous chapter, what trumps the Bible every time. Yet, this is not the full story. For what we have learned is that there is one thing that trumps the past incarnation of Jesus, the Resurrected Christ who lives, reigns and triumphs as God above presently. *That* God works in all cultures, places and times, and not only just in first century Judea. And how does the Resurrected Christ speak to us today? *Through the Holy Spirit.*

> I still have many things to say to you, but you cannot bear them now. When the Spirit of truth comes, he will guide you into all the truth... He will glorify me, because he will take what is mine and declare it to you.
>
> (JOHN 16:12–14)

The Holy Spirit's purpose post-Resurrection is the same as its purpose was pre-Christ. Its purpose has always been to grow us closer in our relationship to God, to inch us closer to the image of love. Jesus was trapped in his context, but the promise of the Spirit was one that surpassed those limitations. Unlike the historical Jesus who had to minister only to those of the first century, the Holy Spirit would continue to grow the church in the years to come, so long as they listened, followed, and *struggled* with it.

Jesus' promise that the Holy Spirit would "guide you into all the truth" that Jesus couldn't give was not merely a reference to Paul and the other New Testament writers, but to you, myself, and all believers. It is a promise that just as Job, Abraham, Jacob, Moses, Amos, and the women of the Gospels struggled and fought with God, so too are we invited to lock hands with the God of all creation and in fighting him, come to better understand the character of his divine love.

BECOMING GOD'S FRIEND

As you may recall, I began this book with a story from my time at college. I described a philosophical challenge put forward by the Greek philosopher Socrates, who asked, "Is the good loved by the gods because it is good, or is it good because it is loved by the gods?"

This has come to be known as the *Euthyphros Dilemma* and it has generated much consternation and conversation over the centuries since it was first put forward.

When C.S. Lewis was challenged by someone regarding it, he gave the answer this book has been seeking. In a private letter, he wrote of how absurd it was to assume that whatever God did was good. He said that the "ultimate question" was whether "the doctrine of the goodness of God or that of the inerrancy of the Scripture is to prevail when they conflict." His answer? The goodness of God. For, he wrote, it is "only that doctrine [which] renders this worship of Him obligatory or even permissible." And then he went on to write the following profound point:

> To this some will reply "Ah, but we are fallen and don't recognise good when we see it." But God Himself does not say we are as fallen as all that. He constantly, in scripture, appeals to our conscience: "Why do ye not of *yourselves* judge what is right?" [Lk. 12:57]—"What fault hath my people found in Me?" [Jer. 2:5] And so on. Socrates' answer to Euthyphro is used in Christian form by Hooker. Things are not good because God commands them; God commands certain things because He sees them to be good. (In other words, the Divine will is the obedient servant of the Divine reason). The opposite view (Ockham's & Paley's) leads to the absurdity, if "good" means simply "what God wills" then to say "God is good" can mean only "God wills what He wills." Which is equally true of you or me or Judas or Satan. But of course, having said all this, we must apply it with fear and trembling. Some things which seem to us bad may be good. But we must not corrupt our consciences by trying to feel a thing as good when it seems to us totally evil.[13]

This is indeed our calling from God. Winning a fight with the Creator means becoming like Job, who although he at one point in his suffering came to believe that Yahweh was evil, had so carefully followed Yahweh's ways that when he lost faith in Yahweh, he himself still continued to act as a representative of Yahweh. In essence, he had come to mirror God, becoming a mini-Yahweh, a reflection of God. He no longer had to believe that God was the reason for morality in order to know that morality was right. In other words, he could reject God and yet still be possessed by the Holy Spirit because he continued to live out the heart of God and perhaps without realizing it, mirror the God in whom he didn't believe.

Faith, in conclusion then, is knowing who God is and having the guts to stand up to God or even the Bible and say, like Abraham: No, far be it from you! Faith is knowing God so well that even when his Word tells us something that disagrees with his character we know that it cannot be true. Instead, we take it as a test and push back against it just like the heroes of old. Yet faith is also knowing God so well that even when we disagree with God, we continue to wrestle with it, recognizing that at times, our own sense of justice may not be as high and pure as we assume.

We must remember that to be in the image of God is to have his character dwell in us. That is morality. That is righteousness. That is faith. Abraham, the pillar of faith for millions of believers today, was called a friend of God (James 2:23). This then is the call of *our faith*: to grow and mature to the point that we can know God well enough to know his character. And that means being able to say like a friend, when the occasion calls for it, "no." This is, in the end, what a faithful reading of Scripture looks like, to say nothing about our relationship with God.

INTERMISSION

REALIZATION

8

PYROTHEOLOGY

Some of you are likely reading this with what I call "faithful horror." You may feel disoriented and dizzy, unsure of which rug was pulled out from under your feet and whether you can still stand back up. Theologically, this first section of the book has rewritten or at the very least, challenged your understanding of biblical authority to a degree that you never suspected would be possible using the Bible alone to do so.

And perhaps that is the most frightening part of this book so far: *all of this has come from the Bible.*

In the first section of this book, we explored the topic for which this book is named: the radical concept that sometimes we should say no to God, and not simply because we feel some urge to, but because God himself urges us to fight him. In it, I laid out a number of biblical stories most Christians systematically ignore or simplify, ranging from the Old Testament to the New, which together outlined the fact that from Israel's very foundation, God intended for his people to fight him. It's in the very name! In some sense, the earlier section was my personal attempt to illustrate that the Bible, by principle, does not support the authoritarian inspirational view which Fundamentalist and deeply Conservative Christians adhere to. By that I mean, the

Bible itself does not systematically support the belief summarized by the popular idiom: "The Bible says it! I believe it! That settles it!"

As one of the professors from my denomination's main seminary, Darius Jankiewicz, puts it:

> "While such a declaration may initially convey the impression of deep piety, it ultimately proves to be a hollow and selfish premise, which promises much but does not deliver." Embracing the sorts of difficult questions that we are exploring in this book and will continue to look at, he argues, makes that sort of slogan "too simplistic to embrace."[1]

One of the issues I dealt with in some of the previous chapters was the conflict between the lives we live and the text we read, or put another way: experience versus Scripture. I did not simply wish to, as other writers have, force readers to confront the dilemma which Job did and then make a decision as to whether to follow the personal experience they felt or Scripture. Rather, I wanted to show that *on principle* it was acceptable (and good) to not only argue with God, but it was possible (and sometimes required) to reject his words and very will. I attempted to present the foundation for the case that if Abraham, Jacob, and Moses could all do it to God's face, then we who have only the written words on a printed page can feel much more secure in our rightful struggles with Scripture.

I doubt that every Evangelical or Conservative leaning Christian who reads this far will suddenly take everything I've written and change their long-held views. I would hope that at the very least, these past chapters will encourage you and others to open your Bibles once again and read through the biblical text with new eyes. Some of you will think that I've opened Pandora's box, while others will believe that I've cracked open Heaven's gates. Whichever way you view this material, as welcomed or uneasy, it is without a doubt controversial in our polarized religious context.

Unfortunately, it's going to get worse. The rabbit hole is far deeper and to use a biblical analogy, the wrestling match with God goes deep into the night. Peter Rollins, the Irish theologian we have looked at before, calls this experience "Pyro-Theology." Literally it means fiery (Pyro) talk about God (Theology). It's a fancy way of saying that he believes *you need to burn the church down to discover if it was worth anything to begin with.*

To explore that idea further, Rollins reflects on the first debate Christianity ever had regarding the requirements of men to undergo the Jewish rite of circumcision. The early church initially debated whether or not a requirement by God, enshrined in the Bible, was truly needed. It was a fundamental question that divided Christians. In truth, he argues, it was incendiary. It was a question that transformed and lit on fire the church and as such, Rollins identifies similar revolutionary inquiries by the church simply as "Circumcision Questions." They are called this, not only because of the first question that spawned the rest, but also because of their very nature. They are, as he writes, "never concerned with addition (working out what needs to be added to the message as it currently stands) but with subtraction (debating what needs to be cut away)." He points out that "a circumcision question asks us to remove something previously thought of as vital in order to help unveil, in an apocalyptic way, the central scandal of Christianity."[2]

As such, these questions he argues are never the result of "constructive theology," but are always a work of "Pyro-Theology." The former seeks to build up, but the latter seeks to burn down. The question that this book seeks to ask is no more incendiary for the church today than circumcision was for the early church. Especially for many Evangelicals of deep conviction (and those like them), the status and understanding of the Bible is almost as central to them as circumcision was to the Jews back then. Touch it and you touch everything else.

If that sounds radical, to burn the church down to discover what's left, it may just be because you don't read your Bible enough. Think about it: the Jewish people only came to understand better the role God intended for them when their temple burned down not once, but twice. It was only because of the First Temple burning that the Hebrew Bible or Old Testament began to take the shape we now know. In truth, we only got certain books like Lamentations because of it. Likewise, it was only because of the Second Temple's burning that the Christian New Testament began to take its own shape. In fact, we likely owe our first Gospel account (Mark), and perhaps those that it inspired after it, to those impending fires. In each of these cases, burning the very image of God's presence was required before the vision of the people of God could be focused on where his presence really was.

Rollins actually goes a step further, suggesting that perhaps the flames themselves which burn our sacred temples, and not what survives, is of true value. In other words, the fact that the flame can burn away the chaff is more true than simply what wasn't devoured and left under the ashes. It means that the fire that burns away what is false is what is actually true. He writes that if this is true, then it means that in the words of Buenaventura Durruti, "the only church that illuminates is a burning one."[3] Those were mocking words for the original anarchist who spoke them, but they seem almost prophetic in this light. After all, was it not Jesus himself who said in Luke 12:49: "I have come to set the world on fire, and I wish it were already burning!"

Ellen White, a bit less radical compared to Rollins, but perhaps no less for the nineteenth century, echoed similar sentiments when she wrote that "If the pillars of our faith will not stand the test of investigation, it is time we knew it."[4]

Some have feared that if in even a single point they acknowledge themselves in error, other minds would be led to doubt the whole theory of truth. Therefore they have felt that investigation should not be permitted; that it would tend to dissension and disunion. But if such is to be the result of investigation, the sooner it comes the better. If there are those whose faith in God's word will not stand the test of an investigation of the Scriptures, the sooner they are revealed the better...[5]

For some of you, and especially some of my fellow Adventists, that might be a bit shocking to read. It's not a quote, let alone a sentiment, that is often repeated these days in churches. Did she really say that if a belief cannot be proven true and people lose their faith because of that... it's a good thing? Yes, she did. In fact, she wanted it to happen as soon as possible. Like a cancer, she wanted it cut out immediately. She went on to state elsewhere that: "Age will not make error into truth, and truth can afford to be fair."[6] But what happens when the truth *is* fair and it doesn't go the way we thought it would? What happens when the truth, that great pillar, fails to withstand the shaking of an investigation?

Using the analogy of an earthquake, she said, "If so, *let it fall.*"

Or to use Rollins' different analogy, "let it burn."

That's quite radical, even by today's standards. In fact, so ready was she for this, that she adds once again: "the sooner (it happens) the better." Moreover, she goes even further, implying in the next sentence that anyone who is closed to this possibility actually has the spirit of Satan in them.[7] For it is only Satan who wishes to protect falsehoods behind the idolatry of misplaced certainty.

Again, even though this book is an act of Pyro-Theology, it is not written simply for the purpose of *watching* the temple burn. "This work of pyro-theology," Rollins describes, "will involve outlining the present understanding of God, exploring the way Crucifixion and Resurrection open up a different reality, and charting what might arise should we be courageous enough to step into this reality."[8] In other words, like all theology, it is aimed at redirecting us toward the Gospel. That is precisely what this book is attempting to do. As such, this material, it is hoped, though possibly destabilizing in the present, will prove a rock for you in the future upon further reflection.

Given all of this, after we've agreed that the Bible encourages us to say no, and after we've better understood the portrait that the Bible paints of the God who invites us to fight him, when do we ourselves decide how or if to say no? There is seemingly no single right answer for this and that can often create a large spiritual anxiety for many. There is no end of conservative pastors who would warn you about (or condemn me for) the "dangerous" ideas in this book. If we decide to both affirm the Bible's accorded freedom to disagree with God and the Bible's flawed human fingerprints, then the process of choosing what to say no to definitely appears to become challenging.

How then does it look to apply this in the church today? If this is the relationship we have been called by God to have with him, if this is the hermeneutic through which we are called to read Scripture, then how do we go about doing it ourselves? At what point do we cross from stories about biblical characters fighting God to fighting God ourselves? Luckily for us, we don't have to start from scratch.

In the forthcoming chapters, we will look at various issues that are (or *were*) controversial and divisive in the church. For some, issues such as these may seem obvious targets for the biblical message this book is exploring. However, before tackling them, I wish to draw our attention to a different but equally important topic, one that undergirds those others and yet is insidious because you may not even think of it as something to worry about. I am, of course, speaking of *orthodoxy*.

PART TWO
INCARNATION

9

SAYING NO TO ORTHODOXY

> *"There is no excuse for anyone in taking the position that there is no more truth to be revealed, and that all our expositions of Scripture are without error. The fact that certain doctrines have been held as truth for many years by our people is not a proof that our ideas are infallible."*
>
> ELLEN WHITE[1]

Having been raised in a conservative church, within a denomination where many of the more fundamentalist stripe believed that they were superior in their understanding of Scripture as compared with other Protestant churches, I grew up with a sense of always "being right." Although this feeling was focused on Scriptural issues, like a cancer, the disease had effects in lots of other areas. As my height rose, so did the time I spent watching various televangelists who all seemed to prove that this sense was indeed accurate. By the time I was a young teenager, I had memorized the arguments, proof texts, and intricate dates of obscure prophecies in order to defend my beliefs from anyone who should dare question them.

As a homeschooled teen with too much time on my hands, I became active on online chat rooms, regularly debating on topics of religion, which often led to private messages that grew more intense.

I should feel proud to say that I often won the debates, but I'm not. Because even if I technically "won," I actually only frustrated them to give up, or generally pissed them off, and in truth, neither of us left the experiences with a blessing. Christ wasn't there. I was merely flexing my muscles and rhetorical skills. I was proving to myself, not them, that I knew more. Two experiences that illustrate this stick out in my memory most vividly.

I was around sixteen and while browsing at a thrift store for some interesting books, a middle-aged woman approached suddenly and pointed to a copy of the novel *Left Behind*. "You should read that," she said enthusiastically, probably assuming that she was saving a wayward young soul. I smiled and nodded, "It's a good piece of fiction." Adventists firmly reject the doctrine of a secret rapture, and so the book series was the subject of many vigorous sermons that picked apart its logic. She looked at me with a wink, perhaps indicating some age-old arrogance, and replied: "It's much more than that. It's the truth." Perhaps I should have smiled and walked away. Instead, I debated. I gave her a five-minute condensed version of one of the hour-long sermons I'd heard. When I finished explaining why the prophecy in Daniel had been misconstrued by the authors, her eyes looked withdrawn. She just stared at me, dumbfounded. She finally spoke only seven words: "Ah. I can see that you've studied." With that, she turned away from me and walked off, probably dazed and regretful.

I felt proud and victorious at the time. I had defeated the woman at her own game. And that, it turns out, was the problem. Did she actually remember any of the many facts I cited? Had she found a change of heart? No. All I had done was confuse her enough to realize that she wasn't going to be able to carry a conversation with me. I still think back to that moment and wonder, what if I had approached it differently? What if I had redirected the conversation away from prophecy to the Gospel and asked her how she came to know Christ? What if instead of meeting her on the battlefield of disagreement, I had asked her to join me in fellowship?

The other memory that sticks out to me happened at a Walmart when I was around thirteen. My mother was shopping and I, like always, was browsing the electronics section. Somehow, I came to have a conversation with another shopper about the Bible, and particularly the doctrine of the Sabbath. As you can guess, for Seventh-day Adventists, the issue of the Sabbath is pretty important. I was quoting scriptures to her left and right to support my position, but she would disagree and simply tell me that I was misquoting them. This was frustrating to my young brain, hyped up on televangelists who assured me again and again that I was indeed "right" and that people who disagreed with me were "wrong." So I did what kids do; I acted immature. I started asking random people, including a nearby employee, if anyone had a Bible. I was, frankly, obnoxious. And I still recall what she told me in response: "What do you think you're trying to prove? You've lost me."

As she walked off, I felt victorious. The disapproving glance of the nearby employee didn't bother me, because I knew I was right. That's all that mattered, I thought. But now, looking back, why in the world would I think that it did matter? Rather than seeking harmony and finding common ground, I was obstinate and full of myself. Where was Christ? The Spirit had long since fled. I may have been *right* in some technical sense of knowledge, but I couldn't have been more *wrong* in my practice. Like a cancer, the orthodoxy of my denomination infiltrated me and made me into someone who wanted to be "right" more than loving. I now know without a doubt that this most definitely wasn't what Christ had called his children to follow as an example.

BEING RIGHT

By orthodoxy, I do not mean the Eastern church which carries that name. Orthodox, rather, literally means "right belief" and has been the rallying cry of Christians for centuries as a catch-all phrase that describes those who claim to have the best theological beliefs. Because of the nature of such a word, countless people who profess to believe in Christ have, still do, and probably will continue to argue for the foreseeable future about which believers have the *correct* or orthodox beliefs and which do not. People with differing beliefs are labeled "heretics," which comes from the word Heterodox, indicating those who think "differently." As one might easily guess, for some, orthodoxy as a word brings to mind more negative images than positive.

Christians have, nearly since the time the church began, attempted to prove that their beliefs and interpretations (and theirs alone) are right. However, the reality is that when people actually read the Bible for themselves they often find that they are in disagreement with each other about what it means. As bestselling author and biblical scholar Peter Enns writes, "The Bible does not have a good track record of promoting unity among those who read it."[2]

In conservative churches, divisions over issues always prove to be problematic. "And that's the great irony here," Enns writes. "The long Protestant quest to get the Bible right has not led to greater and greater certainty about what the Bible means."[3] That's why I believe that the often overlooked letters of 1–3 John are particularly helpful in this discussion. Long before our modern debates, our ancient forebears struggled with the same sorts of problems.

There, in those ancient epistles, we read of how *some* early Christians decided that if *other* Christians didn't believe the same as they did, then they were no longer going to be considered Christians. Ironically, the letters that are typically famous for their treatises on love are actually some of the most divisive and sectarian pieces of literature in the entire Bible, and certainly the New Testament. Bad theology sometimes comes wrapped in pretty bows, a fact that shouldn't surprise any Christian.

The writer of 1 John describes how he is writing "these things to *you* concerning *those* who would deceive *you*" (2:26). There is, from the outset, an *in*-group and an *out*-group; an *us* and a *them*. So, who were these? They were fellow Christians from their own congregation (2:19). Apparently, a schism occurred over a doctrinal issue. The other group of Christians came to value Christ's divinity so strongly that they eventually came to believe that Jesus had not actually come in the flesh when he was on Earth, but rather that he was fully a divine being who had only appeared to *look* human (4:2–3). This idea eventually became a major doctrinal controversy that a number of early Christians adopted, but was later deemed a heresy, called Docetism.

The writer of 1 John writes that although they worship Christ, recognize him as divine, understand themselves to be Christians and are separated by only one doctrinal issue, they are not actually Christians and Jesus rejects them and their worship (1 John 1:6). In fact, contrary to how the writer of 1 John calls his readers "children of God," he says that the other Christians are *not* the children of God. Instead, he calls these other Christians the "children of the devil" (3:10). In fact, he goes even further, arguing that these other Christians are "antichrists" (2:18). He says that not only are they *currently not* God's children, but he informs his church community that they *never were*, even when they all believed the same. He writes that: "They went out from us, but they did not belong to us; for if they had belonged to us, they would have remained with us. But by going out they made it plain that none of them belongs to us" (2:19). Even later, he further alludes to them as atheists (5:10).

This is important because it reveals that when 1 John famously speaks of loving your brothers (and sisters), it does *not* include those *other* Christians who left their specific church. Those individuals are not considered part of their family by the author of 1 John. This is somewhat incredible to imagine (and painful to empathize with) when you realize how small these churches were at the time, that they met usually in people's homes, and that most churches were made up of *families*. This means that likely some of those separated by the schism were family members. So, when the writer of 1 John tells his congregation that they are to love their brothers, those who believe the same as them, it also means that if they had a real blood brother who left, they were not to show the same care for them.

He continues this train of thought, alluding to the belief that if those Christians who think differently than they do are not considered part of the fellowship of Christ (to "abide in him"), their doctrinal differences will prevent them from being saved and put them "to shame," no matter how convinced they are or how much they believe that they love Jesus (2:28). He writes that: "Whoever has the Son has life; whoever does not have the Son of God does not have life" (5:12).

Finally, the author of 1 John reaches the application stage of his instructions, imploring his readers not to listen to the *other* Christian believers.

> "They are from the world; therefore what they say is from the world, and the world listens to them. We are from God. Whoever knows God listens to us, and whoever is not from God does not listen to us. From this we know the spirit of truth and the spirit of error."
> (1 JOHN 4:5–6)

The logic is a bit circular. The writer argues that the other Christians are from the world, continuing his theme that they are the devil's children. He warns his congregation not to *listen* to anything they say, telling them that only those from the world would listen to them. The threat is implied: if one of his congregation listens to what these others have to say (or even dares to consider it), it means that they are already lost, since only the lost world would listen to them. Remember, he previously said that the others were never truly Christian because they left. Similarly, he's arguing that if his congregation takes steps to listen to those who left, they would be revealing that they too had left the fold. He goes on to argue as well that anyone who listens (or agrees with him and his congregation) is from God, since they are obviously right and from God. Anyone who doesn't listen (or doesn't agree with how they think) is not from God.

When you turn to the second letter, far shorter and less theologically dense, addressed to an anonymous "Elect Lady," one finds the same theology repeated. He writes that "I was overjoyed to find some of your children walking in the truth, just as we have been commanded by the Father" (vs. 4). The author is happy to find "some" of the Elect Lady's children walking in the truth. But then he warns her of the command to "love one another." By this, he does not mean for her to love all people (like the Gospel of John teaches), but of the command in 1 John to love only those who think the same as you. He warns her, as he did the others, of the dangers of those who are different from them:

> Do not receive into the house or welcome anyone who comes to you and does not bring this teaching; for to welcome is to participate in the evil deeds of such a person.
>
> (2 John 10–11)

Think about those instructions. "Do not, even if they are your own blood family, welcome anyone who comes to you." The command is absolute, the same as what you'd expect from the rules of a malicious cult. If you know someone who holds theological beliefs opposite of your own, the author basically teaches, don't help them, even if they're in need. Don't give them an ear. They don't deserve it. Moreover, if you show them kindness, it will be counted as evil against you.

In 3 John, the author* writes to a Christian named Gaius, who he describes as someone who believes the same as him and like him, refuses to talk with others that disagree with him (vs. 3). But afterward, we learn that an individual is causing the author issues.

> I have written something to the church; but Diotrephes, who likes to put himself first, does not acknowledge our authority. So if I come, I will call attention to what he is doing in spreading false charges against us. And not content with those charges, he refuses to welcome the friends, and even prevents those who want to do so and expels them from the church.
>
> (3 John 9–10)

We learn that this man, Diotrephes, is a leader of a church. In fact, it appears that he is one of the "brothers" who believes the same as the author of 3 John. Yet, this pastor has closed the doors of his church to our author, refusing to accept the letter from him or welcome and greet any of the members of his church who visit. He even expels them from the church. This Diotrephes has accused them of what the author calls: "false charges." What were these charges?

This is the key to understanding what hasn't been said explicitly: all of the actions that Diotrephes makes are exactly the same things that 1 John and 2 John instructed his church members to do to anyone who held different theological convictions. What do we learn from this? We discover that Diotrephes' "false charges" are likely accusations. He is claiming that our author (of 3 John) holds *false* theological beliefs and Diotrephes, in response, will act toward them just as our author instructed him to act toward those who are different.

---

* Many scholars are unsure of who wrote these letters, and even whether they all share one author or several. There is no conclusive evidence that the two smaller letters didn't come from the same hand as the first, and since tradition tells that they were all by one person, I have felt most comfortable with assuming the same. But 2 and 3 John could equally have come from others in the same community who shared the same ideology.

In short: the letter of 3 John provides an ironic and unexpected twist to the message of these three letters. The author, the Elder John or otherwise, has taught again and again how to act toward those who believe differently and has ironically found himself being the recipient of that same teaching by one of his own church members who now no longer views his teacher as orthodox. The greatest irony? The author does not recognize the comedy of the situation and instead becomes angered that the church leader has treated him with such disrespect. He, it turns out, does not like his own teaching when it is used against him.

And then, finally, he wrote his concluding message:

> Beloved, do not imitate what is evil but imitate what is good. Whoever does good is from God; whoever does evil has not seen God.
> (3 JOHN 11)

Without realizing it and missing the irony of it all, our author of this very small epistle warns his readers to not imitate evil, not thinking about the fact that the very evil that he is upset about is the same evil he promotes. While we can see the folly in this sort of thinking and the ironic results of such divisive practices, we must take the time to reflect on how we today also share many of these same misconceptions about unity. In spite of the fact that we might all agree with the theology of the teacher (as opposed to the Docetic believers he was fighting), we can agree that the way he went about promoting his beliefs was entirely wrong.

Instead of creating a safe place within the church to have dialogue and to reason with one another (as God himself invites us to do with him), this early Christian leader chose to segregate and cast out those who would not readily admit to his own views. And this is the danger we face today: even when we are technically right, we may be terribly, horribly, and ultimately wrong. We may cause damage and heartache where there need be none. After all, can we imagine Jesus acting in this fashion with his disciples? No, because in spite of their seeming stupidity and consistent inability to understand Jesus (and their predisposition to believe the wrong things), Jesus never cut anyone off. In fact, even when the disciples wanted to cut others off, Jesus said they were never to do so (Mark 9:38–41; Luke 9:49–50).

Today, we do not usually face the large-scale theological controversies that the author of 1–3 John dealt with. Typically, we fight over minor theological quibbles. But regardless of the content, our disposition is usually the same as that ancient author and our ability to calmly handle theological variety is just as lame. At the risk of citing one of my denomination's own thought leaders too many times, Ellen White wisely cautioned the fledgling Adventist church at the time that: "We cannot then take a position that the unity of the church consists in viewing every text of the Scripture in the very same shade of light."[4] She explained what should be common sense: that *different* people see *different* passages in Scripture *differently* and that, most importantly: "this is all in the order of God."[5]

We only need to look at a few examples to realize that this is true. Perhaps the most instructive for us today is the account in Acts 15 of the first church-wide decision that was ever made in Christianity's early history. The early church announced three or four doctrinal pillars for Christian gentiles (that's most of us), requiring: "that you *abstain from what has been sacrificed to idols*, and from blood, and from what has been strangled, and from sexual immorality" (Acts 15:29).

This council, the first of church history, announced that "the Holy Spirit" thought their idea was good (Acts 15:28). Yet, Paul, who was there at the council, went around telling his new congregations that the church was assuming too much about the Spirit's direction. According to Paul's own testimony, he not only did not enforce the first requirement about food offered to idols, he actively dismissed it in his teachings (1 Corinthians 8). For Paul, the requirement, supposedly given with help by the Spirit, was something that only people weak in their faith would believe in (see Romans 14). And surprisingly, the church has agreed with Paul ever since.

This should give us pause. Wouldn't the Spirit have led the wider church in its fledgling moments in the right direction? Many would assume yes. Looking at the example of Paul, we discover the answer is a resounding no. A single apostle, versus the wider church leadership (and apparently, even the Holy Spirit), understood what was to be orthodox belief in the future... in spite of the fact that many at the time would have seen his resistance as *heresy*.

To quote Peter Enns again, as I will do many more times in this chapter (because his book, *The Sin of Certainty*, is simply brilliant): "Many factors influence how we 'follow' the Bible. None of us rises above our place in the human drama and grasps God with pure clarity, without our own baggage coming along for the ride." He goes on to wisely note that "We all bring our broken and limited selves into how we think of God. We're human, in other words. We can't help but think of God in broken and limited ways, as creatures limited by time and space."[6]

As the example of 1–3 John proves in conjunction with the many divided churches that exist today, people like to hold on to their beliefs and rarely allow themselves to be challenged about them. When you reflect back on the many bloody battles of church history, what is the typical common thread that ties them all together? The preoccupation with correct thinking. And all too often, this preoccupation is about issues we can no longer understand the need to fight about. This problem, Enns argues, can itself become a sin.

> It is a sin because this pattern of thinking sells God short by keeping the Creator captive to what we are able to comprehend—which is the very same problem the Israelites had when they were tempted to make images of God (aka idols) out of stone, metal, or wood.[7]

Idolatry, it turns out, can involve not only the Bible, but even our commitments to beliefs about it. It also speaks or hints at a certain arrogance. After all, most debates regarding orthodoxy are about the fear of heresy. They revolve around specific issues and typically involve one group, having an established view, being challenged by a newer or more novel idea from another group or person. There typically is an unspoken understanding on the side of those who are being challenged that their views are both "the truth" and "unchanging." Thus, the very existence of an alternative view becomes disconcerting to them.

In my own church, we have typically suffered from this dilemma more than some others in recent history. It has become like an insidious disease to have church members not only believing, but actively speaking about how "we have the truth," to the extent that the most conservative of my church do not even think they have anything to learn from any other denomination.

A professor from Andrews University put it this way:

> Under such circumstances, dogmatism trumps other values; the aphorism "my way or the highway" becomes a reality; personal and communal growth is stifled; theological development suffers; and the concept of diversity becomes anathema. Ultimately, such communities tear themselves apart, all for the sake of an ideology. A lonely driver with a sticker on his hatch door proclaiming "The Bible says it! I believe it! That settles it!" becomes just that—a lonely driver on the highway of his or her own presuppositions.[8]

Peter Enns, channeling the same sorts of thoughts, notes that this sort of mentality "reduces the life of faith to sentry duty, a 24/7 task of pacing the ramparts and scanning the horizon to fend off incorrect thinking, in ourselves and others, too engrossed to come inside the halls and enjoy the banquet."[9] He warns that "when holding to correct thinking becomes the center, we have shrunk faith in God to an intellectual exercise, a human enterprise, where differences need to be settled through debate *first* before faith can get off the ground."[10] Furthermore, he writes that:

> My beliefs or thoughts about a person are unavoidable, and often helpful in deepening the relationship—but they may not always be right, and the relationship shouldn't rest on getting them right. After all (and I know this may be hard to believe), I occasionally (by which I mean often) have mistaken beliefs regarding my wife, which she is only too kind to point out to me. But this skewed knowledge does not nullify our marriage.[11]

A great example of this can be seen in the case of Job. As we explored at length in the first part of this book, Job is quite unorthodox in his views. Whether we watch him proclaiming that God is evil, that there is no true morality, or that the world should be destroyed before God can save it, Job hits one heretical home run after another in his baseball game from the ashes. His friends, on the other hand, so often criticized by careless readers, are quite orthodox in their own views. In fact, they're so orthodox that they are somewhat boring. Their words mirror Deuteronomy and Proverbs with little room for their own theological imagination.

And so, it is quite surprising when we discover that God announces that Job has "spoken right of me." To speak right about God is the very definition of orthodox! If you were the friends in that story, this would have made no sense. The story of Job is a story in which God calls the heretic orthodox and the orthodox heretics! Exactly what Job said that was right, however, is never clarified.

But maybe that's actually the point. The fact that God doesn't clarify is our indication that what is important to God is not whether we get things right, but whether we speak from our hearts honestly about God. God doesn't tell us what is orthodox about Job because he wants us to understand that orthodoxy isn't as simple as merely quoting from books of the Bible as his friends had been doing. As Enns aptly notes:

> When we learn that it is okay to let go of the need to be right—that God is not going to pounce on us from behind the corner and give us a whipping but actually welcomes this step of faith—only then will the debilitating stress of holding on to correct thinking begin to fade.[12]

To mention another example of the many problems that orthodoxy presents, look no further than the letter of Jude in the New Testament. It's a letter that is written specifically against false teachers and which defends orthodox thinking staunchly. Its whole purpose for being written was to defend what had been correct thinking in times past. Yet, I'd like to point out a curious thing about this early proponent of orthodox thought: look at what book he quoted from in order to defend his correct views.

> It was also about these that Enoch, in the seventh generation from Adam, prophesied, saying, "See, the LORD is coming with ten thousands of his holy ones, to execute judgment on all, and to convict everyone of all the deeds of ungodliness that they have committed in such an ungodly way, and of all the harsh things that ungodly sinners have spoken against him"
>
> (JUDE 14–15)

Now here's the million-dollar question: from what book in the Old Testament is he quoting? Normally I'd suggest you go and Google it, but it's a trick question. So, I'll just tell you the answer. It's *not* from the Old Testament at all. Well, it's not from yours anyway.* It's from the Book of Enoch (or *1 Enoch* as it's called by scholars). If this strikes you as strange, it should. Jude defended his

---

* For Ethiopian Orthodox Christians (and even Ethiopian Jews), the book of *1 Enoch* is considered Scripture and included as part of the Old Testament/Tanakh in their printed Bibles.

orthodox thinking using a book that *used* to be orthodox at one point for his community and then was *later* viewed as heretical by others in different communities.

In fact, it wasn't the only time. In vss. 11–12, he similarly quotes from another apocryphal book (the *Assumption of Moses*), mentioning a story that in his community and time was apparently accepted as orthodox but which like *1 Enoch*, became seen as heretical by *later* orthodox thinkers. That's pure irony, and it illustrates the problem with orthodox thinking: it's only orthodox today, with absolutely no guarantees for tomorrow.

Perhaps that's precisely the reason why Jesus never instructed his disciples on what books made up the Bible. In spite of the fact that the Jews were bitterly divided between themselves on which of the different formulations of the canon was correct and which books should be considered Scripture, the incarnate Word of God chose to remain silent on the entire issue. Though he quoted often from books such as Deuteronomy, Psalms, and even Tobit,* he didn't seek to impose a divine command regarding the authority of these books.

---

* Because this is sure to be a controversial claim for some, it deserves a longer explanation. Jesus alludes to and draws from Tobit on numerous occasions, mostly found in the Gospel of Matthew. Compare Matt. 7:12 (and Luke 6:31) with Tobit 4:15; Matt. 25:34–36 with Tobit 4:16; Matt. 6:20–21 (and Luke 12:33) with Tobit 4:9; Matt. 6:3–4 with Tobit 4:7–8; Luke 11:41 with Tobit 4:10–11 (and Tobit 12:9). In fact, one of the only times Jesus comments on the canon appears to be in two places within Matthew's Gospel. The first is in Matt. 7:12 when Jesus rewords Tobit 4:15 and claims that what he has said is found in "the Law and the Prophets" (a shorthand reference to the canonical scriptures). Likewise, in Matt. 22:23–28, he accuses the Sadducees of not understanding the Scriptures in response to them asking a question derived from the book of Tobit. A possible inference from this is that Jesus has indirectly affirmed Tobit as Scripture. Whether this is correct, it is true that early Christians understood Jesus to be affirming books like Tobit. Even outside the canonical New Testament, Jesus is said to have quoted from Tobit. In the *Gospel of Thomas*, the sixth saying or logion of Jesus quotes twice from Tobit 4.

That's a fascinating fact since, for those who defend orthodoxy, the issue of which books make up the Bible is one of the most contentious. What does it mean that Jesus chose not to settle an issue that divisive? It says this: *that God loves to challenge our thinking, not to do it for us.*

Luckily, we have an even better biblical example to look to which illustrates this. When Jesus spoke on the subject of divorce, he had a very simple policy according to two of the Gospels: don't do it... *ever.*

> "Therefore what God has joined together, let no one separate."... He said to them, "Whoever divorces his wife and marries another commits adultery against her; and if she divorces her husband and marries another, she commits adultery."
> (MARK 10:2–12; REPEATED IN LUKE 16:18)

Jesus' guidance in Mark and Luke regarding divorce posed a problem for some, among them the Gospel of Matthew. Matthew, an anonymous Greek speaking Christian convert,* was worried that Jesus was contradicting Scripture. After all, contrary to Jesus' statement, it was not Moses who allowed divorce, but God himself in the Torah. So Matthew, and likely many in his community of faith, understandably felt uncomfortable with this situation.

Now, let's be clear: the orthodox approach to this issue is fairly straightforward. If Jesus said you can never get divorced, then that's that. He said it, I believe it, and that should, in theory, settle it. Divorce, as such, should never be allowed. *End. Of. Story.* The living Word of God said it and what more would you need to hear to believe it?

---

* For those that don't know this already: the three Synoptic Gospels (Matthew, Mark, and Luke) are all anonymous. The names were added much later to the books because of legend and tradition. The Gospels themselves, however, don't claim who wrote them. John's Gospel claims that it is written by the "Beloved Disciple," however, it never reveals who that was and John is never said to be the name of either that disciple or the author of that Gospel.

However, as you might have guessed, Matthew didn't think the way many conservative Christians do. Instead, he sought to "interpret" Jesus. Rationalizing that since Jesus was a Jew and the Hebrew Bible *does* say God approved of it, Matthew harmonized the two and as a result, changed Jesus' message.

> And I say to you, whoever divorces his wife, *except for unchastity*, and marries another commits adultery."
> (MATTHEW 19:9)

Suddenly, Jesus' radical statement, reported by Mark and Luke, that prevented any and all divorce has been transformed into a restricted *approval* of divorce. Matthew changed Jesus' teaching using his knowledge of the Bible and theology, and shocking enough: put that change into Jesus' own mouth!

But if that seems shocking, what the apostle Paul did decades before makes Matthew seem timid in his approach. Needless to say, Paul is seen by quite a few as the bastion of orthodoxy. Almost every conservative position finds its roots or support in some statement by Paul. And this is why it's so interesting that he did something many would unilaterally consider so unorthodox.

As mentioned previously in another chapter, among the many challenges that Paul faced in setting up new Christian communities in the Greek regions and metropolises was the issue of newly formed mixed marriages. Paul offered some interesting advice to these new Christians (1 Cor. 7:12–15). After restating that Jesus had forbidden *any* sort of divorce (affirming the tradition in Mark and Luke's accounts), Paul says that if the non-Christian partner is the one wishing for a divorce, the Christian may indeed grant it so that they keep the "peace" (vs. 15). He argues that Jesus' instructions forbidding divorce are not applicable to Christians in such cases. He emphasizes that this is what he says from his own opinion and "not the LORD" (vs. 12).

All of this, of course, flies in the face of what one should think would be the "correct path." It would seem relatively clear that the orthodox or correct position would be to simply repeat what Jesus had originally said, unaided by man. Yet, what we see in the Bible is something different: God *in conversation* with man. For Matthew and Paul, it was never as simple as: "God said it! That settles it!" And for the rest of us, stuck shifting through God's orders in the Torah, Jesus' rejection of them, Matthew's harmonization of them both, and Paul's addition to them, we are left to wonder: who is right and which should be followed?

Again, this highlights another problem with orthodoxy. It wants things to be tidy and neatly organized by God when in reality, the Bible doesn't offer anything like that for believers. Paul was comfortable adding his own thoughts to Jesus' instructions because he understood that the life of faith was a conversation between friends. Conversations between friends are never rigid or simple and because they are rooted in trust, sometimes can even involve one implying the other is an evil person (remember Moses in Exodus?), if it's done for the sake of calling his friend back to his senses.

Matthew felt free to alter Jesus' very words because, again, like a friend, he didn't simply take his friends words as unchanging. He assumed that he knew him well enough to read between the lines. Or perhaps Matthew simply believed that he knew Jesus well enough to know that what Mark had originally written was not accurate to what he knew of Christ's teachings. The point is: Matthew wasn't forced to simply accept the tradition, but was actively shaping and interacting with it.

Enns reflects on this messiness and sense of trust in his book, writing that:

I believe that the Bible does not model a faith that depends on certainty for the simple fact that the Bible does not provide that kind of certainty. Rather, in all its messy diversity, the Bible models trust in God that does not rest on whether we are able to be clear and certain about what to believe. In fact, the words "belief" and "faith" in the Bible are just different ways of saying "trust." And trust works, regardless of where our knowing happens to be.[13]

Orthodoxy doesn't work because people expect from it something it can never give: certainty. God calls us in the Bible to trust him, but in trusting him, to also disagree and fight *for* him, even when it sometimes appears that we are fighting *against* him. If we are to model a true biblical orthodoxy, we must be willing to realize and readily admit that our orthodoxy may be someone's heresy from the past and someone's heresy in the future. Orthodoxy is typically a goal, not a destination. It's where we want to be, but usually when we think we've arrived, we discover we've only reached our layover on the way there.

Of course, it is clear that Abraham and the other heroes of faith earlier explored had orthodox beliefs. By that I mean, when Moses appeals to God to have God act better, his affirmation of God within his rebuke is the definition of orthodoxy. And what is that orthodoxy? Simply this: that God is love, that God is faithful, and that God is good. That is the underlying orthodoxy of every character who fights God. Even Paul, in changing the rules for divorce, stakes his idea on the belief that God wants *peace* more than rule obeying robots. And ultimately, by having an orthodoxy like that (an orthodox belief in the orthopraxy* of God), they reveal that they trust God's character. And that, by all means, is a view of orthodoxy we should all embrace, just as they did.

---

* Orthopraxy refers to correct *praxis*, a word that refers to a person's way of living or acting.

10

SAYING NO TO PREJUDICE

> *"The text [of Scripture] is structured in such a way that it challenges us to go deeper, for it does not merely offer us examples of people who wrestled with God but also presents us with situations in which we are invited to do the same."*
>
> PETER ROLLINS[1]

For many Christians, the authority of Scripture is intricately tied up in the issue of the Bible's inspiration. To claim that something is inspired is tantamount to claiming its authority, and in claiming authority, the implication is that the authority is incontestable. This is partly why theories such as *inerrancy* can seem so convincing to some at a logical level. If biblical authority is assumed to mean something that is not questionable, then the claim that the Bible is without error makes sense. However, a good question for any believer should always be this: can something be authoritative and yet still allow you the freedom to disagree with it?

For many conservative Christians, the answer is a cautious no. For them, the Bible is either one or the other, but it can never navigate both. It is either always right, or never trustworthy. Jonathan Brown sums up this sentiment well, writing in his own work on religion that,

It is in this sense that saying "no" to scripture is fatal to its authority and signifies a turnover in epistemological eras. The move from assuming that scripture contains the truth but need only be understood properly to saying "no" to scripture because it says something unacceptable or impossible is a blow that shatters the vessel of scriptural reverence. It means that some extra-scriptural source of truth has been openly acknowledged as more powerful and compelling than the words of God in scripture. If scripture is read with a hermeneutics of suspicion... then dire problems can appear on every page.[2]

Arguments like those outlined by Brown make sense to many readers. So, what is a Christian to do? To explore this question, we need to first recognize something that should be, but clearly isn't always obvious: *we have already said no to many things in the Bible, and by extension, God.* Most conservative voices speak about this issue with the worry of a slippery slope of diminishing biblical authority, and yet they ignore that we have been sliding down that slope for quite a long time already (and moreover, most would affirm it as a good thing).

THE BIBLICAL CASE FOR SLAVERY

As a case example, let's look at the circumstances of slavery in the United States during the 1800s. I want to specifically explore the question of why slavery was so heavily supported by Christian Americans both at the level of the pew warmers as well as the ministers. Though a strange and almost abhorrent thought today, Christians once heavily and sincerely debated the issue of slavery in the Bible, and most, not just many, argued persuasively that God was in favor of it.

Biblical stories feature slavery time and time again in many of their narratives, but this goes without saying. The world in which the biblical writers lived was inundated with slavery. It was a reality that needed no explanation. However, the Bible doesn't merely refer to the existing reality of slavery, it also supports it. It outlines how to sustain and support an institution of slavery and human trafficking.

Yet, God didn't just wink at the idea of slavery. If supporting the structure of an already existing institution of slavery wasn't bad enough, God actually endorsed it in one verse, commanding that his people *should* take others *into* slavery (Deut. 20:10–15).

In Ex. 21:1, God informs the Israelites that if they take a slave when he is single, he is to go out as a single man when freed. If he comes into slavery married, he must be freed along with his wife. However, what happens if the master forces his slave to marry another, or he falls in love with another slave during his indentured servitude? Well, tough luck. If he becomes married and is freed later, he is not allowed to have his wife freed. Instead, he can only choose to declare his love and lose his freedom forever, being branded and serving as a slave for the rest of his life, in order to avoid losing his wife. Oh yeah, and if he has children, they are slaves too and he'll have to abandon them in order to become free. Specifically, vs. 4 acknowledges that children born to slaves are automatically considered slaves as well.

This horrendous situation is not only described, but prescribed by God. God not only endorses slavery, but gives a law in the Bible that commends that it is his will for families of slaves to be separated.

At this point, the divine rules get even more disturbing. Exodus states that if a slave master beats his slave to death, he should have some sort of punishment, but if the slave survives and can walk after a day or two (even though he nearly died), the slave master should not be punished, because, as God is recorded as saying, "the slave is (merely) property" (21:20). Similarly, in Ex. 21:32, God declares that a slave is worth only thirty-two shekels, the amount someone must pay to the slave master should their bull gore their slave. And Ex. 21:7

states that God allows fathers to forcibly sell their young daughters to be slaves if the circumstances require it.

Leviticus states that people should take their slaves from the nations around them (25:44). In Josh. 9:23–27, it states that God sometimes curses a group of people to become slaves forever (in that particular case, the Gibeonites). And Lev. 25:44–46 states that foreign slaves will remain the slaves of their respective Israelite owners forever, their children becoming slaves perpetually for the benefit of their master's family. In fact, the verse goes on to regulate that Israelites were not to be ruthless toward fellow servant Israelites (but leaves the legal impression that God permitted or at least winked at the Israelites who might be ruthless to non-Israelite slaves). And Lev. 19:20–21 states that sins done against slaves, especially sexual sins, are treated as a lesser offense in God's eyes, since the slave is only property.

If you think things changed in the era of the New Testament, well, they didn't. "Paul" writes in Col. 3:22, some instructions for slaves.

> Slaves, obey in everything those who are your earthly masters, not with eyeservice, as men-pleasers, but in singleness of heart, fearing the LORD. Whatever your task, work heartily...

Continuing that train of thought, the letter of Titus instructs other Christians regarding their slaves.

> Bid slaves to be submissive to their masters and to give satisfaction in every respect; they are not to be refractory, nor to pilfer, but to show entire and true fidelity.
>
> (TITUS 2:9)

As if that wasn't bad enough, 1 Peter goes even further.

> Servants, be subject to your masters with all respect, not only to the good and gentle but also to the unjust.
>
> (1 PETER 2:18)

However, in 1 Tim. 6:1–2, we read further that slavery is something that is in perfect harmony with Christian practice. Moreover, the letter claims that Christian slaves need to work even harder to please their Christian masters, more than even their worldly ones.

> Let all who are under a yoke as slaves regard their own masters as worthy of all honor, so that the name of God and the teaching may not be reviled. Those who have *believing masters* must not be disrespectful on the ground that they are brothers; rather they must serve all the better since those who benefit by their good service are believers and beloved. Teach and urge these things.

THE BIBLICAL CASE AGAINST SLAVERY

For centuries, Christians fought with each other over the issue of slavery. The dilemma? Those Christians who wanted to be rid of the institution had to struggle with the reality that their sacred texts promoted, presumably from God's own lips, the practice. As such, Christians who were against slavery had to turn to a few texts in the Bible that appeared to contradict the others.

These Christians recognized that although the Bible largely supported slavery at all levels, some writers of the biblical material appeared to go against this trajectory. Isaiah wrote that it was better to God for his people to set slaves free and seek their liberation than to practice a religious fast (Isa. 58:6). In Lev. 25:17, it states that God's people are not to oppress one another and in vs. 10, it states that *liberty* is to be proclaimed to all people in the land. And in Lev. 19:33–34, it likewise states that you are not to do any wrong to the stranger in the land and to treat him as you would yourself, which would seemingly exclude then the possibility of slavery (cf. 19:18).

In the New Testament, Jesus stated that his followers were not to act like the Gentiles and exercise lordship and authority over one another (Mark 10:42–43). That would seemingly outlaw slavery since the institution was built on the concept of exercising dominion over another human. And 1 Tim. 1:10 actually condemns people who partake in the selling of slaves.

Quite ambiguously, Paul states in 1 Corinthians that:

> Each one should remain in the condition in which he was called. Were you a bondservant when called? Do not be concerned about it. But if you can gain your freedom, avail yourself of the opportunity.
> (1 CORINTHIANS 7:20–21)

Statements like that, while bolstering abolitionist Christian views, also seemed to serve the purposes of slave owners who could argue that Paul had clearly stated that slaves should be content to be slaves. As such, in many ways, the battle over scriptural authority usually favored the pro-slavery side more than it did the anti-slavery side, even when the text was possibly anti-slavery.

RUNAWAY SLAVES

The Bible is littered with human fingerprints. We've explored a number of them already and slavery is just another example. What these demonstrate is that without our ability to stand in judgment of Scripture, issues like slavery would quickly grow out of control. The ability to say no to things in the Bible is paramount for our freedom to correctly intuit the will of God.

One of the more interesting verses in the Old Testament with regard to slavery, specifically dealt with the issue of runaway slaves. This sort of law should have been equally important and drawn by Southern Americans, since the South was dealing with an issue exactly like that with the Underground Railroad.

> Slaves who have escaped to you from their owners shall not be given back to them. They shall reside with you, in your midst, in any place

they choose in any one of your towns, wherever they please; you shall not oppress them.

(DEUTERONOMY 23:15–16)

Like today, Christians in the South cherry-picked which laws and verses they believed still applied. Although Deut. 23:15–16 strictly forbids people to return a runaway slave to its master, Christians in the Southern and some in the Northern United States did not believe that *that* law still applied to their situation anymore. So, while Deuteronomy, Exodus, and Leviticus could continue to be cited for their eternal laws favoring slavery as an institution, the laws supporting a slave's rights were dismissed as temporary or culturally conditioned.

Some tried to make sophisticated arguments, such as Bernard Whitman, who argued in his pamphlet from 1831 that the slaves mentioned in Deuteronomy were not possibly the equivalent of the black slaves in America. He argued at length that the runaway slave of Deuteronomy must be from a foreign nation and as such, was a different case than if a Hebrew slave ran away from an Israelite master. In that case, he argues, "the whole face of the thing would be changed." He explains that the property laws outlined elsewhere in the Bible would have then applied.

> But if we now put the other case, viz., that of escape from a Hebrew master, who claimed and enjoyed Hebrew rights, is not the case greatly changed? Who could take from him the property which the Mosaic law gave him a right to hold?… With this view of the matter before us, how can we appeal to the passage in question, to justify, yea even to urge, the retention of fugitive bond-men in our own country?… It may be, that the fugitive has left a severe and cruel master… (but) we cannot sit in judgment on cruel masters belonging to tribes different from our own… We pity the restored fugitive, and have reason enough to pity him, when he is sent back to be delivered into the hands of enraged cruelty… The responsibility, however, for bad treatment of the slave, rests not in the least degree on us of the North. The Mosaic law does not authorize us to reject the claims of our fellow

countrymen and citizens, for strayed or stolen property—property authorized and guarantied as such by Southern States to their respective citizens.[3]

Some might be confused as to how the issue could be ignored. How could Christians even be slave owners in the first place? How could they talk about a slave owner's property rights, while ignoring the rights of the human being used as a slave? These questions, so apparent to us, only a few hundred years ago would have fallen on mostly deaf ears. And that fact alone should probably frighten us.

Whitman continues in his tract to outline a defense of Christian slave owners, a defense that is as sincere as it is horrifying.

> It is not too much to say, that no man, in his sober senses, can believe or say, that there are no Christians in the South, who are owners of slaves. There are thousands of masters and mistresses, of exemplary Christian lives and conversation. There are many thousands, moreover, who have never been taught to doubt, and never have doubted, the lawfulness of slavery. They have felt that they violated no sacred obligation in holding slaves, provided they should treat them in a Christian manner. Whether they have neglected their duty in putting by all discussion of the subject, and all serious examination into it, is another and a different question. I suppose there are Christians elsewhere, besides in the South, who neglect some of their duties, and who are not absolutely perfect. If perfection is the only proper test of a Christian state, I fear that we of the North might have our title to such a name called in question… When will the time come, in which men shall cease to pronounce sweeping judgments of condemnation on their fellow men, without examining into their case, and giving them a fair and impartial hearing? I earnestly hope the day-break is approaching, although at present it seems to be receding. But—it is sometimes darkest just before day.[4]

Luckily for the millions of black slaves in the South, the daybreak hoped for by Whitman was actually the darkness that he feared. Then again, the analogy he used was probably quite apt. His values were twisted upside down so that Christ's ethics appeared to him as the devil's. The Bible does, after all, condemn such individuals, noting that "they loved darkness rather than light" (John 3:19, KJV). How apropos, then, those words were. They loved darkness because to all who are spiritually blind, darkness seems indistinguishable from light.

Illustrating this is the fact that Whitman argues later that it is the Christians urging slaves to run away and gain their freedom that are truly *un-Christian*. Why? Because he argues, "they treat with scorn" the instructions of Paul and Peter to have slaves obey their masters. Northern Christians were un-Christlike, Whitman argued, because they didn't subjugate Christ's ethics to the apostles' words. They were, in short, not respecting the authority of Scripture.

FIGHTING A FAMILIAR HERESY

So how could Christians be so sophisticated in this abhorrent and ancient practice? There are many reasons and no single cause. However, Whitman does give us some insight into the logic of the slave owners and the theologians supporting them. We shouldn't be surprised if we recognize the thought process.

> There then stands the Mosaic statute, which was the perpetual law of the Jews. There it stands, not to be erased by the hand of the most zealous Abolitionist. He will probably think very ill of Moses, and not be very courteous toward me for venturing to quote him... In the name of all that is called reasoning now, in morals or religion, how is the ownership of slaves which heaven has given express leave to purchase, to be deemed a crime of the deepest dye—a malum in se—an offense to be classed with murder and treason? Let those answer his question, who decide a priori what the Bible ought to speak, and then turn it over in order to see how they can make it speak what they wish. But there is no bending or twisting of Moses' words... If Abolitionists are right in their position, then Moses is greatly in the wrong. More than this; then has the God of the Hebrews sanctioned, with his

express leave, the commission of a crime as great as that which he has forbidden in the sixth or seventh commandment... What shall we say then? Shall we consign Moses over to reprobation? Or are we to regard him as an ignoramus? One or the other, or both, follow from the reasoning and the premises of heated Abolitionists.[5]

If that long exposition didn't explain his position well enough, Whitman finally concludes with a line of logic that seems very familiar to far too many of us: "I have said that Moses needs no aid of mine in the way of apology. When he speaks the words of the God of the Hebrews, it is for us to listen, not to call in question."[6]

With that statement, Whitman helps us get to the core of the problem in the theological debate between Christian slave holders and abolitionists. The slave owners took the position that the words of the Bible were non-negotiable, that to argue with anything would mean to find error with God himself. In short, they supported the familiar *heresy* of *inerrancy*. As Charles Hodge exclaimed, "If the present course of the abolitionists is right, then the course of Christ and the apostles were wrong."[7]

On the other hand, the famous and eventually victorious abolitionists refused to accept a view of Scripture like that. Instead, they dared to do something radical: they said no to what God said in Scripture.

They said no to some verses and picked others that supported their cause to fight the other verses. They pitted Scripture against Scripture in order to reclaim it. "Christian opponents of slavery," wrote Henry Brinton, "elevated biblical principles of justice and equality above individual passages that approved exclusion."[8] *Principle above and even against the very words of Scripture.* It sounds so radical. The ironic thing is that few if any Christians remember, let alone are aware of this. They forget that the debate over slavery was in many respects a theological fight over scriptural authority.

As Darius Jankiewicz, of Andrews University explains it, "because the Bible never condemned slavery, the Southerners considered the abolitionist cause *unbiblical*, and the fact that slavery was not practiced in the North a result of *shifting cultural trends* rather than a position founded on the Scriptures."[9]

One can get no better sense of this than reading the words of Henly Thornwell, a southern Presbyterian minister and proponent of slavery, who wrote:

> The parties in this conflict are not merely Abolitionists and Slaveholders; they are Atheists, Socialists, Communists, Red republicans, Jacobins on the one side, and the friends of order and regulated freedom on the other. In one word, the world is the battleground. Christianity and Atheism the combatants, and the progress of humanity is at stake.[10]

Likewise, the Episcopal bishop Henry Hopkins charged that those who opposed slavery were engaged in "a willful or conscious opposition to the truth." He rhetorically asked,

> ...who are we, that in our modern wisdom presume to set aside the Word of God, and... invent for ourselves a "higher law" that those holy Scriptures which are given to us as "a light to our feet and a lamp to our paths," in the darkness of a sinful and a polluted world?[11]

SACRED AND IMPORTANT TRUTHS

On the other hand, the early Seventh-day Adventist movement in the 1800s took a strong stand against slavery. Ellen White, one of our founders that I've quoted before, argued that slavery itself was a sin, and that "in the sight of heaven it is a sin of the darkest dye." Furthermore, she stated bluntly that "God is not with the South, and He will punish them dreadfully in the end." She described those Christians holding a pro-slavery view as "a degraded company, a Godforsaken company," arguing that the "angels of God fled from (them) in disgust."

In this same letter, dated from the beginning of the Civil War in 1862, she rebuked a fellow Adventist who publicly expressed pro-slavery views.

> You have never looked upon slavery in the right light, and your views of this matter have thrown you on the side of the Rebellion, which was stirred up by Satan and his host. Your views of slavery cannot harmonize with the sacred, important truths for this time. You must yield your views or the truth. Both cannot be cherished in the same heart, for they are at war with each other... But notwithstanding all the light given, you have given publicity to your sentiments. Unless you undo what you have done, it will be the duty of God's people to publicly withdraw their sympathy and fellowship from you, in order to save the impression which must go out in regard to us as a people. We must let it be known that we have no such ones in our fellowship that we will not walk with them in church capacity.[12]

Slavery was such a sin that it was upheld by Mrs. White as a deal breaker for Adventist membership. And yet, we might imagine that the individual Mrs. White wrote to was similar to Bernard Whitman in his views. After all, Whitman and the Adventist she wrote to might have protested: how can you call something a sin that is promoted by God in the Bible!

Note though that she did not argue that the Bible didn't promote it, nor did she argue that it was due to a Bible verse that they should oppose it. Look closely at her language she used. She said that his views could not harmonize with *"the sacred, important truths for this time."* This was a reference to something that became known in the early Adventist movement as "present truth," the idea that God revealed his will to his church over time with greater and greater clarity. In this case, she argued that morally it had become clear how horrible slavery was. In other words, no matter what biblical arguments someone might have to support slavery, it was simply wrong (even if parts of the Bible supported it).

Abraham Lincoln (to paraphrase a statement and rephrase it as a question) asked with regard to the issue of slavery, "Are we on God's side?" As Brinton notes ironically, "An answer based only on biblical quotations may put us on the side of Southern theologians who supported slavery and lost their way."

"This tree of Abolition is evil," declared Reverend Henry Van Dyke in 1860, "and only evil—root and branch, flower and leaf, and fruit; that it springs from, and is nourished by an utter rejection of the Scriptures." So sure of this was he, that he went on to argue that:

> When the Abolitionist tells me that slaveholding is sin, in the simplicity of my faith in the Holy Scriptures, I point him to this sacred record, and tell him, in all candor, as my text does, that his teaching blasphemes the name of God and His doctrine.[13]

Ellen White, although not self-identified as an abolitionist, provides insight into the mentality of those who fought against the institution of slavery. In order to be right with God, they argued, you had to either "yield your views" of the Bible's support for slavery or yield "the truth" that God had made it clear in the present that it was a sin. They had to choose between Scripture and experience. They had to reject a picture of God that their own scriptures supported.

THE THORNY ISSUE OF PREJUDICE

One of the most toxic and oft-cited arguments in favor of slavery within America was a peculiar interpretation of the story of Noah known as "the Curse of Ham." The story is recorded in Genesis 9 and tells a very odd tale in which Noah builds a vineyard and becomes drunk. His son Ham sees his father naked and goes to tell his brothers, and finally when Noah awakes he curses Ham's son

Canaan to become a slave to Ham's other two brothers for the rest of eternity. If that story sounds *ridiculous*, that's because, frankly, it is. To this day, scholars can't quite figure out what the offense is, nor are Christians sure that a drunk Noah has the moral high ground.

Regardless, southern Christians took the position that the drunkard Noah was righteous and argued that when he cursed Ham's son, it was the curse of black skin. There were many arguments for this, none of which were in the least bit correct. These countless Christians argued that since God had cursed Canaan for all eternity to be a slave to his brothers (who were believed to be the ancestors of white people), then Americans could enslave black people simply because "the Bible tells me so." Just as Adam lost humanity their intimacy with the divine, Ham had lost his descendants their freedom. *Instead of Original Sin, it was Original Slavery.* Black people were literally believed to suffer a double curse, one binding them to sin and another to slavery.

Even though this interpretation has no exegetical merit and was a perfect example of people interpreting the Bible to make it say whatever they wanted it to (although, as seen earlier, they accused abolitionists of doing that same thing), the truth is that they were right about one thing only: the curse of Ham was indeed intended by its biblical author as a prejudicial command of perpetual slavery based on ethnic prejudice. The prejudice of this curse in Genesis may not have been aimed at black people, but it was indeed aimed at the inhabitants of the land of Canaan with the exact same intent that the southern Christians used.

The curse of Ham explicitly gives biblical authority to the Israelites to enslave the Canaanites *forever*. For what reason? As mentioned before, no one is quite sure what Ham did. The story doesn't even explain why Canaan is the one cursed when it was his father who supposedly did something wrong. The truth may be that there doesn't need to be a reason: the story's purpose is simply to validate the prejudice and superiority of the Israelites over the Canaanites. Everything we hate about the Christian interpretation of Ham's curse toward black people should also be everything we hate about the Israelites' use of Ham's curse toward the Canaanite people. The principle of racial prejudice and ethnic enslavement remains the same.

But was Ham's curse the only time this occurred? No. The Bible is filled with ancient examples of ethnic prejudice. For example, in Gen. 27:46, Rebecca exclaims that she is "disgusted" with Hittite women and says that if her husband Jacob takes a wife from among them, she will consider it better to die than live with one. What was so terrible? No one knows anymore. But the biblical author of that passage in Genesis assumed that any Israelite would know and agree. Like all shared stereotypes and prejudices, the name of the "other" is enough to unite mutual hatred.

In Genesis 19, the famous story of Sodom's destruction is narrated. Less discussed in church but just as infamous is the tale of Lot's two young adolescent daughters getting their father drunk in a cave and giving birth. Although the original story was likely intended to praise the women for shaming an unrighteous man who had offered them up to a mob in Sodom,* the story was surely twisted by other Israelites to designate their descendants as "bastards" and "inbreds." In Deut. 23:3, God demands that the Moabites and Ammonites, the descendants of Lot's daughters, never be allowed to worship him or join Israel. Whether or not a Moabite wishes to worship the God of Abraham, that God declares he doesn't want the worship of the descendants of Abraham's nephew.

---

* I have published this new interpretation of the story recently in an academic journal. For the full argument, see Matthew J. Korpman, "Can Anything Good Come From Sodom? A Feminist and Narrative Criticism of Lot's Daughters in Gen. 19:30–38," *Journal for the Study of the Old Testament* 43.3 (2019): 334–342.

Even when it came to the earlier issue of slavery, God's supposedly righteous laws displayed abhorrent racist discrimination. In contradistinction to slaves who were Israelite, who had to be freed eventually, God commands in Lev. 25:44–46 that the Israelites may take non-Israelite slaves as their property forever, considering their children to be born into perpetual slavery without hope of escaping it. The great Jubilee year of God's favor was never to fall on the non-Israelite.

As such, we can say that the Bible supports the principle of prejudice and discrimination toward people outside of one's own group. Racists, in principle, can find support for their hatred of the "other" within the Scriptures. But the reverse is certainly true. In contradiction to such texts, the Bible contains commands that move in the opposite direction. Take Lev. 19:34, where God said: "You shall treat the stranger who sojourns with you as the native among you, and you shall love him as yourself, for you were strangers in the land of Egypt." Likewise, by describing all human beings as descending from one human couple, the Bible effectively eliminates any claim of superior ancestry and promotes a vision of a united human family (Gen. 1:27).

When the book of Ruth celebrates the origins of Israel's king David, it emphasizes the fact that Ruth, his grandmother, was a Moabite (someone the Bible forbid from joining God's family). Her celebrated faith is a testament to the fact that the Bible's prejudice can be overcome. Look at Joseph and his celebrated marriage to the daughter of a pagan Egyptian priest (Gen. 41:45,50). Or, take the example of Job, whose book opens with the statement that a non-Israelite foreigner, an Edomite, is the most righteous man that ever lived (outshining even Abraham, the father of God's people).

In the New Testament, Paul was clear that "there is neither Jew nor Greek, there is neither slave nor free, there is no male and female, for you are all one in Christ Jesus" (Gal. 3:28). Again, the idea is repeated in Colossians: "There is not Greek and Jew, circumcised and uncircumcised, barbarian, Scythian, slave, free; but Christ is all, and in all" (3:11). Or, as Peter put it: "God shows no partiality" (Acts 10:34). Jesus is said to be the one who breaks down our walls of division (Eph. 2:14). We see that illustrated in John's vision recorded in the book of Revelation, where he saw "a great multitude that no one could number, from every nation, from all tribes and peoples and languages, standing before the throne and before the lamb" in the future New Jerusalem (7:9). James 2:9 warns that "if you show partiality, you are committing sin and are convicted by the law as transgressors."

Like slavery, the Bible has a mixed record in which different writers promote different and contradictory proposals as they battled it out for what they believed was the heart of the God they worshiped. My point is that we today are no different. Just as many writers in Scripture rejected God's commands when they appeared to be unjust (like those who embraced the book of Ruth in contradiction to Deuteronomy), so too are we similar when we say no to such texts and condemn all types of segregation and prejudice.

GOING BEYOND ABRAHAM

It is that last point that cannot be emphasized enough. The practice of saying "no" cannot be overlooked any longer. As Rabbi Hartman writes in his recent work, reflecting on Abraham's feisty exchange with God in Genesis 18:

> Abraham, upon encountering a revelation of God's intent that he deems to be morally flawed, turns and challenges God to live up to his (Abraham's) conception of the good. This challenge, however, occurs within the context of immediate and ongoing revelation, which ensures not only direct communication but also an immediate response and resolution... We, however, who communicate with God only through sacred scripture, are left with a text that remains the same even after our moral challenge. We may choose to reinterpret

it, or to ignore it, but its explicit meaning and its moral inadequacies remain forever within our tradition, low-hanging fruit for either the devil or his minions to use to give religious justification and sanction to that which we now know to be morally inadequate.[14]

Whereas Abraham could have an answer immediately, and we can still read that resolution within the text, there remain texts in our Scripture which have no such resolution and will never be resolved, despite our objections to them. Because of this, our struggle with the divine and with Scripture must not only go on, but must be emphasized and carefully practiced so as to never allow, as Hartman points out, the potential for the devil and his minions to use them.

So, in conclusion, whereas many reading this book might imagine that the concepts outlined within it are new or novel, the reality couldn't be further from the truth. Christians, as can be seen from the preceding pages, have practiced the concepts in this book even when they haven't been consciously aware that they were doing it. The reality is that almost every Christian in America today now agrees unanimously (without even thinking much about it) that the God they serve does not approve of slavery, even though the Bible is very clear that God did and by virtue of silence, should still. Even if they are not consciously aware of what they are doing, these Christians have made a decision to reject certain verses and accept others, all on the basis of the incarnate Jesus and the Spirit's movement upon their conscience.

If we can realize that we've done it before and see in retrospect how important it was that we did, how might that better help us in regard to what still needs to be done in the church's future?

11

SAYING NO TO PATRIARCHY

> *"As an ordained woman, it pains me to wrestle with texts that seem to command my silence. My spirit limps from the struggle... But this struggle is not one of simple obedience and acquiescence... we cannot ask our congregations to consider them Holy Scripture unless we are willing to wrestle with them ourselves. We begin our pastoral witness by refusing to let go until we are blessed."*
>
> SARAH JOBE[1]

In the summer of 2015, my denomination met as a worldwide body in San Antonio, Texas. We were voting on the question of whether the Adventist church would, as a worldwide body, be in favor of or against the freedom for church divisions to independently recognize the ordination of women to Gospel ministry. The vote was needed because of the fact that the Seventh-day Adventist church does not, as a whole, recognize women as ordained, but some conferences and divisions in North America, Europe, and China have independently taken the step to do so. This vote was to allow the freedom for the church to approach this issue both independently and in a large-scale manner. The vote was almost a tie, but unfortunately ended with a small majority winning against the issue. Inevitably, the result caused much heartbreak among the female and allied ministers present and around the world who had hoped that the church would finally recognize their equality.

The issue touched me personally. My mother has been a devoted follower of Christ since she was young. She had wanted to pursue theology in undergrad (at the same school I would later attend), but given the attitudes about women's ministry in the 1970s, nobody encouraged her. Churches were preaching Paul's words about women and authority. As a young woman, who was she to challenge someone like Paul? In fact, even when she tried to push about the issue, one of the male administrators advised her to get a "Bible Worker" associate degree alongside her Bachelor of Social Work. What she didn't realize—and I only discovered decades later by searching up the old bulletins—was that the associate degree's classes were identical and cross-listed with the Bachelor of Theology, with the exception that the classes for the Associate had a small warning: they could never be used as credit for the Bachelor. In other words, you could take all the same classes, do all the same work, but should you feel called to pursue ministry later, you'd have to start over and take the classes all over again, effectively deterring anyone from doing so.

It's hard not to perceive that this program was essentially created for women in order to prevent them from ever achieving a degree that would allow them to later pursue ministry. It's hard not to see the degree as a disgusting attempt to discriminate and patronize those women who were passionate for Christ but who were considered inferior to male evangelists. But when God wants someone, degrees don't matter.

When my mother graduated and moved to Florida, she was unexpectedly thrust into a church whose pastor was largely absent.

Suddenly, many of the pastoral duties were given to her and before long, she was regularly preaching. Of course, she was never paid, even though she carried the church on her shoulders. After several years and before leaving for Texas, that church voted to ordain her as an elder, a fairly rare and radical move at the time for a conservative church. It was a token effort and my mother, humble as ever, wasn't sure she wanted it. After all, would Paul have approved? Did the Bible allow it?

When she moved to Texas, she found that the nearby church, also conservative, was in the same situation. Much to her surprise they asked whether she was ordained and having learned that she was, the church made the radical decision to recognize her ordination. And like before, she was again preaching and leading the congregation in the wake of a mostly absent male minister. Was she paid? Nope. More and more she wondered, was this fair? And moreover, was it right to quote Paul in order to allow this?

That's when I entered into the picture. When she was pregnant, she was preaching. When she gave birth, I was at her side as she preached. Growing up, I can still remember as a toddler imitating her, preaching to a closet full of stuffed animals. The Spirit was alive and well in my mother. She was contagious, not only to me but others. But she was a woman and so her gifts were always valued secondarily to her male colleagues.

This reality is maddeningly common across various conservative-leaning denominations. Many have chosen to object to the idea that God has ordained women, quoting scriptures here and there which they believe limit the role a woman can have within the church. Always, their cry repeats: they are simply upholding the Bible and the authority of Scripture. Again, though, does this not sound so similar to much of what we have already studied? Are those against women's ordination listening to one set of scriptures (for instance, parts of

Paul) and ignoring others (such as other parts of Paul and countless alternative texts)? Are they emphasizing one vision at the expense of what other visions Scripture holds? And more importantly, is their choice to choose one vision over another reflecting Christ or their own human prejudices?

PAUL'S CELIBACY

Nearly two-thousand years ago, a Pharisaic convert to the fledgling Christian movement wrote an impassioned letter to the church at Corinth. In this now oft-quoted epistle, a man known to many simply as Paul laid out the theological framework for a new and daring vision of the Christian faith. And what was part of that radical vision? In short, he encouraged those of the Corinthian congregation not to marry (1 Cor. 7:1–13). To be more specific, those who were engaged or betrothed, he urged to remain so and not "tie the knot" (7:26). For those who had yet to find someone they wished to commit to, Paul urged that they not keep looking (7:27). Instead, he called on them all to become like he was, celibate for the cause of Christ.

To marry another, argued Paul, betrayed the early church's conviction in the belief that Jesus' return was imminent. If Jesus was coming in the lifetime of Paul, then members of the body of Christ were not to be distracted from their missionary work. Time was too short. Marriage would, by necessity, require the attention of one believer to love and care for another, someone that without, they might have been freed to spend more time working on behalf of Christ.

Although Paul explains the logic of his thinking, it does not change the fact that he could not know that Christ would not return in his lifetime. Although we can appreciate and relate to the zeal that Paul held for the coming Advent and his commitment to risk everything, we also recognize how dangerous such advice could have potentially proven to be. Paul was like all of us who come after him, constrained to a limited and imperfect view of how soon Christ's return would and will ultimately be.

His daring proposal for reform in the Corinthian church would shock many of us today and still occasionally does for those who stumble across it in the pages of their Bible, but its message serves as an important point of discussion in our current debates on Women's Ordination in various Christian churches. Why? Simply put, had the early Christians followed Paul's words and abstained from marriage, remaining celibate, we would likely not be here today debating the very issue. In other words, to state what should be obvious by the fact that I am writing this *as* a Christian: most of the early church ignored Paul's daring advice. And, we might add, rightly so.

PAUL'S OPINION

However, the biggest shock is not what Paul said that they should do, nor that the early Christians ignored what he said, but rather how Paul described his belief: as his personal opinion, as advice (1 Cor. 7:6–7,12). That's right, in what is one of several occasions in his letters (cf. 1 Cor. 7:12; 2 Cor. 11:17), Paul admits that what he is writing is by no means something that he has received as a revelation from God and cautions the church at Corinth to, in a paraphrased sense, take it or leave it (7:7). He writes explicitly in 7:25 that "I have no command of the Lord, but I give my opinion…" In fact, as some commentators have noted, Paul appears to be emphasizing his opinion precisely because some of the church in Corinth had previously misunderstood Paul's wishes to be a command.

How is this, though, instructive to our debates on Women's Ordination? Precisely because Paul makes a similar appeal in the context of a verse that has remained at the forefront of the debate: 1

Tim. 2:8–13. Although most of the discussion that surrounds this controversial and heated text begins with vs. 11 and its injunction for women to not have authority over men, the overall discussion of the chapter actually starts a few verses earlier in vs. 8 in which Paul says "I *desire*." His desire, to summarize briefly, is three-fold: that men pray with lifted hands without anger, women dress moderately, and that they do not have authority over men.

The word used by Paul, translated as "desire" by the NRSV, is the Greek word βούλομαι *(boulomai)*, which means a personal desire or wish. Yes, read that once more and let it sink in. The passage in 1 Timothy is not a command from God for how to structure the church. It is the author's *opinion*. He is expressing a "desire," not an imperative he believed was sent from God or even official church teaching he was passing on from Jerusalem. He was giving personal commentary.

This detail seems to have been overlooked by those on both sides of this debate and it is quite unfortunate, as I believe that it provides an important insight for our discussions. Without this context, the debate can quickly become muddled and lose focus. As another biblical scholar, J. Paul Sampley explains, "Paul establishes what *he thinks* is the ideal, how *he thinks* things ought to be, and he depicts that as the *goal* or paradigm toward which people ought to aim and with regard to which people should order their lives."[2] On careful reflection, his words in 1 Timothy on women (his desire), "is based solely on Paul's individual authority… rather than on a principle intrinsic to the good news."[3]

The question, then properly, is not "what does Scripture teach" but "what did Paul personally desire that is recorded in Scripture?" That little change of focus shifts how many would approach this passage and also how they might think to apply it in the life of the church. It allows us to contextualize his statements. In fact, scholars have often noted that the beginning of 1 Tim. 3:1a could, in fact, be the intended conclusion to the entire discussion of women in 2:8–13. If so, it is possible according to some scholars to translate and understand the verse as reading "This is a reliable opinion." It proves to be a fitting conclusion to Paul's expressed "desires," even if we today would disagree how reliable an opinion it really was.

CHANGING DESIRES

Let us briefly return to Paul's opinion on marriage from his letter to Corinth. To illustrate the development of Paul's opinions and how they change, we should examine a different issue: widows. In 1 Cor. 7:8, Paul explicitly says that the young women and widows should remain unmarried. He concedes that they should marry only if they are "aflame with passion" (7:9). Yet, this apparently didn't remain his position. In a twist of irony we find the use of βούλομαι in the letter of 1 Timothy once more, this time in 5:14. There we read that: "I would have (βούλομαι) younger widows marry, bear children and manage their households, so as to give the adversary no occasion to revile us."

If the letter is written by Paul as tradition has maintained, it appears that Paul has changed or nuanced his opinion since he wrote to the Corinthians.* Now he actually wishes and desires that young widows would in fact settle down and marry, whether or not they are "aflame with passion." By saying he wishes for these Christian women to marry, he also wishes for Christian men to marry them, take care of them, and by the logic of his earlier words in Corinthians, have their time inevitably taken away from the ministry. In other words, he's also

---

* Most scholars, though, would likely conclude that 1 Timothy is authored by a later writer after Paul had died. In that case, the point still stands: the Bible, in its historical progression, contains changing views on the topic within the scope of what Paul was believed to have taught.

changed his opinion about celibacy. This appears to be quite a change and demonstrates that his views, rather than set in stone, were subject to change (and if not his, those of his community who contributed to Scripture).

Whatever the reality was that lay behind the "desire" written in 1 Timothy regarding women speaking in church, whether it was only meant for a specific church and occasion (cf. 1 Cor. 7:26) or was part of a broader desire for affecting change in the church as a whole, it is and remains an opinion, not simply in the eyes of those of us today who disagree with it but also in the very eyes of the author himself. We should not lose sight of that. It may have been inspired by a specific circumstance, but like the issue of celibacy in the church of Corinth, following its counsel today will have negative consequences for the body of Christ.

If Paul could change or adapt his opinion about whether widows should marry, if he cautioned that his words on marriage were only his opinion, and if we can see that he expressed his concerns about women in authority as a personal wish: why should we assume that Paul could not have likewise changed his opinion on the latter issue? Bringing these texts together leads us to understand the futility of all of these debates and helps us realize that in an ironic twist, for anyone to make a case based on the personal wish recorded in Timothy that women shouldn't be ordained is ultimately as shaky an argument as for anyone to claim that because of Paul's opinion found in 1 Corinthians 7, we should not be marrying. I believe this is all illustrative of my overall point: *an opinion is to be evaluated and weighed, not dogmatically adhered to.** Paul himself felt the need to change and did.

---

* And of course, as this book as a whole has shown, even when it's not an opinion, one should not remain dogmatically adhered to it regardless!

Why should we not do the same as we read his words in the twenty-first century?

REJECTING SEXISM

Aside from these issues though, one must ask what motivates one to hold such views? This is a question supporters of Women's Ordination ask of those who are firmly against it. While those antagonistic to women's ministry often cite certain verses from the Bible as their justification for doing so, that answer doesn't go deep enough to be satisfactory. Even if one agrees that the verses they cite say what they do, the question equally applies to the biblical writers just as much as it does to their contemporary readers. What is the motivation of using Eve as a scapegoat for limiting women (1 Tim. 2:12–14)? In truth, the answer is well known: patriarchy and sexism. While many of those against women's ministry would reject the labels as hyperbole, the truth is that the Scriptures are stepped in sexism.

Patriarchy has been around for a long time. So it should be no surprise that it fills the pages of the Bible. The Ten Commandments, supposedly God's cherished moral law, are addressed exclusively to men, and even assumes in its very structure that women are considered part of their property (Ex. 20:17). The laws in Leviticus are primarily, if not exclusively, addressed to men and when it does decide to address women, it's in the context of sex (such as forbidding it with animals, Lev. 20:16). When one reads of the ancestors of Jesus in Matthew and Luke, one gets genealogies of Joseph, not Mary. When one wishes to know about the children of Adam and Eve, one hears stories of Cain, Abel, and Seth, but only learns of nameless daughters in a short and obscure reference (Gen. 5:4).

And when women aren't ignored in the Bible, they are typically and often sorely mistreated. In Numbers 5, a ritual is prescribed (supposedly from God) in which a husband is given the right to bring his wife to the temple if he feels jealousy. Although he may have no evidence, the ritual gives him the right to force his wife, alongside a priest, to drink water mixed with the dirt of the temple floor. The goal, the ritual promises, is that any child that she is carrying will be killed within her if it stems from another man. No limit is placed on how many times a jealous husband can repeat the ritual. Likewise, women were not allowed to make oaths to man or God without their father or husband approving of it (Num. 30:1–16). That's right, not only could women not object to drinking dirt, but they couldn't make promises to God about their own lives without seeking the approval of their jealous husbands.

If the woman was free, single, and raped, she was required to marry her rapist (Deut. 22:28–29). Although slaves were to be freed after a certain period of time, a daughter sold by her father (something actually allowed by God) was denied that eventual freedom (Ex. 21:7). Moreover, a slave master could beat their female slave to death without punishment so long as she did not die the very day of the beating (Ex. 21:21).

Again and again the Bible shocks us with the antiquated views of women that it promotes. When the invading Abimelech is crushed by a stone thrown by a woman from atop a tower, saving the city's inhabitants, his last request is that his armor bearer kill him so that it may never be said that a woman did it (Jdgs. 9:54). According to some of the stories in the Hebrew Bible, there was nothing worse than a man being made to become like a woman, which is why mobs of men would sometimes seek to gang rape a man in order to symbolically murder him as a woman (See Gen. 18 and Jdgs. 18). Even in the New Testament, one finds egregious statements such as the one by the author of 2 Timothy when it notes that there are "silly women, overwhelmed by their sins and swayed by all kinds of desires, who are always being instructed and can never arrive at a knowledge of the truth" (2 Tim. 3:6–7).

The truth though is that although the Bible is filled predominantly with patriarchal and sexist views, it does shed light on periods of history where that wasn't the case. In the Hebrew Bible, one great example comes from the book of Judges. Within that collection of stories, all of which takes place prior to a male Davidic dynasty or kingdom, a number of stories are told of women who had agency. In particular, the story of Deborah stands out as a prime example (Jdgs. 4–5). Here, the Scripture reveals the portrait of a woman who ruled over part or much of the land of Israel, but unlike her male contemporaries or predecessors, she was also a spiritual leader: a prophet (4:4). She instructed Israelite men in both political and spiritual matters (4:5). But unlike Samuel who also shared the office of judge and prophet, Deborah was also a military leader who was expected to fight (4:8). One cannot imagine a more pro-feminist portrait of a woman in Israel than the image painted of this female Israelite leader.

In the book of Nehemiah, we learn that a powerful spirit-led woman was leading the prophets of Jerusalem (Neh. 6:14). In the book of Ruth, a woman uses her sexual prowess to secure her future husband. In the book of Judith, contained in most Bibles around the world but excluded from recent Protestant editions, a Jewish widowed woman independently saves her city by a combination of prayer, shrewd speech, and sharp objects. Likewise, within a mirror story found in Judg. 4:17–24 and 5:24–27, a non-Israelite woman named Jael disobeys her husband and sleeps with another man so as to murder an enemy of Israel, for which she is praised above all women by God's prophet. Similarly, in Genesis, stories are told of women who disobeyed God's own supposed laws in order to gain what was rightly owed to them by those same laws (i.e. Tamar in Gen. 47, and Lot's daughters in Gen. 18). Again and again, women manage to raise their heads through the layers of patriarchy in the Hebrew Bible, demonstrating that their words and witness cannot be silenced and that the Holy Spirit is empowering their voices even thousands of years after their actual voices have passed away.

Likewise, in the New Testament, female agency is seen time and time again. There were female apostles, some such as Junia who were called such (Rom. 16:7), and others like the legendary Thecla of Iconium whose early stories were never included in the formal New Testament (*Acts of Paul* 3:1–4:18). The Gospels present Mary Magdalene as the first apostle (or as later tradition called her, the apostle to the apostles), though they never use the term. Other gospels outside the canon, such as the *Gospel of Mary* and *Philip*, do appear to know of a tradition that presented Mary as continuing her ministry after the death of Jesus like the other apostles. Back within the canon, female deacons are also mentioned in the New Testament, such as Phoebe (Rom. 16:1), and women are listed as the highest respected office of the church, those called to be prophets, such as Philip's daughters (Acts 21:8–9; cf. Paul who encourages women to prophecy in 1 Cor. 14:39). Moreover, the book of Acts portrays women teaching or evangelizing to men about the Gospel, such as Priscilla (Acts 18:24–26). The letter of 2 John is addressed to an elect lady, which is either a female name for the corporate church or an actual woman who was running a church community. Likewise, according to Paul, women could speak in tongues (1 Cor. 14:39) and the book of Acts records that women were at Pentecost (Acts 1:14–15) and were among those who began to speak in tongues (2:1–4).

In other words, women in the New Testament had the freedom to be called as prophets, apostles, teachers, evangelists, deacons and to speak in tongues. Basically, women could be almost all of the offices of the church that Paul listed (1 Cor. 12:28 and Eph. 4:11–12), precisely because "all of you are one in Christ Jesus" (Gal. 3:28).

Outside the church's structure, women had agency and ran businesses, like Tabitha/Dorcas (Acts 9:36–42) or Priscilla (Acts 18:2). That's not to say that life was perfect for women at that time, nor that patriarchy wasn't pervasive, but rather that the patriarchy didn't get to have the final say. Unfortunately, because of a couple of verses (one of which looks not even to be authentic), Christians have tried to ignore these texts in order to support patriarchal interpretations. Whether they realize it or not, because many of them adhere to an idea of inerrancy, they are already saying no to God by ignoring some texts in favor of others. *The real issue is whether they are saying no to the right things*, as Abraham did.

In Liberation Theology, there is a common anecdote: God is always on the side of those who are oppressed. It's a truism in the Bible that repeats again and again. So, when one group aims to ignore some verses and props up others to oppress one group, and another group aims to ignore verses and prop up others to defend and uplift one group, which scenario does God seem more likely to be in favor of? If the debates over slavery are any example, it's clear that God would be, and if he would be, is currently and always has been, a feminist. It's time we recognized this and consider those Christians who defend patriarchy the same way that we now do those who dare to publicly state that they support slavery: misguided and anti-Christian. In other words, lost souls who need to be evangelized and saved from themselves.

Just as Priscilla heard the disciple of John the Baptist, Apollos, preaching a message that fell short of the truth brought forward by Jesus Christ, and took him aside to evangelize him, so too does the world need more women preaching the good news of Jesus to those Christians who are lost in an older and more obscure vision of the clarity that God has brought through Jesus. And like Aquilla, her husband, men can help this effort by supporting and/or partnering with those women spearheading such efforts.

LADY WISDOM?

Perhaps the single greatest argument in favor of the full equality of women is the simple fact that the Bible makes it clear that men and women are both equally made in the image of God. In Gen. 1:27, it is clear that both genders are created in the divine image, giving no favoritism to one over the other. Likewise, when Jesus spoke of God, he employed a number of feminine metaphors, describing God as a mother hen wishing to gather her chicks (Matt. 23:37), or as a woman seeking a lost coin (Luke 15:8–10). These are not unusual images, for in the Hebrew Bible God is described as a female master (Psalm 123:2–3), as a mother eagle or bear (Deut. 32:11–12; Hos. 13:8), as a human mother (Isa. 66:13; Psalm 131:2; Hos. 11:3–4), as a woman who is breastfeeding her child (Isa. 49:15), and finally, God is said to have given birth to humanity like a woman (Deut. 32:18).

Yet, there is another fact from Scripture that is almost never said: that Jesus himself was affirmed to be a woman. Although that claim may strike you as impossible, it's very much real. In 1 Cor. 1:24, Paul describes Jesus as the incarnation of "the wisdom of God." This is a theologically powerful statement, for it can only be understood in reference to two other texts: the books of Proverbs and the deuterocanonical/apocryphal text of the Wisdom of Solomon. In the book of Proverbs, readers are introduced to Wisdom, personified as a woman called Lady Wisdom. There, she describes her identity, history, and purpose:

> The LORD created me at the beginning of his work, the first of his acts of long ago. Ages ago I was set up, at the first, before the beginning of the earth… When he established the heavens, I was there, when

he drew a circle on the face of the deep, when he made firm the skies above, when he established the fountains of the deep, when he assigned to the sea its limit, so that the waters might not transgress his command, when he marked out the foundations of the earth, then I was beside him, like a master worker; and I was daily his delight, rejoicing before him always, rejoicing in his inhabited world and delighting in the human race. And now, my children, listen to me: happy are those who keep my ways. Hear instruction and be wise, and do not neglect it. Happy is the one who listens to me, watching daily at my gates, waiting beside my doors. For whoever finds me finds life and obtains favor from the LORD; but those who miss me injure themselves; all who hate me love death.

(PROVERBS 8:22–36)

Christians have long argued that the character of Lady Wisdom was a description of Christ pre-Incarnate (see Col. 1:16). During the debates over the divinity of Jesus in the fourth century at the Council of Nicaea, arguments about this text centered on what it meant for Wisdom to be "created." What was never debated was the fact that they were accepting a text about a woman as describing Jesus Christ, a historical male. But this was only truly made possible because of the other text mentioned before, the Wisdom of Solomon. Written perhaps only a few decades to a century before the birth of Jesus, the book's message was almost contemporary with the rise of Christianity.

> For wisdom is more mobile than any motion; because of her pureness she pervades and penetrates all things. For she is a breath of the power of God, and a pure emanation of the glory of the Almighty; therefore nothing defiled gains entrance into her. For she is a reflection of eternal light, a spotless mirror of the working of God, and an image of his goodness. Although she is but one, she can do all things, and while remaining in herself, she renews all things; in every generation she passes into holy souls and makes them friends of God, and prophets; for God loves nothing so much as the person who lives with wisdom… Compared with the light she is found to be superior, for it is succeeded by the night, but against wisdom evil does not

prevail. She reaches mightily from one end of the earth to the other, and she orders all things well... If riches are a desirable possession in life, what is richer than wisdom, the active cause of all things? And if understanding is effective, who more than she is fashioner of what exists?... Because of her I shall have immortality, and leave an everlasting remembrance to those who come after me.
(WISDOM OF SOLOMON 7:24–28, 29–30; 8:1, 5–6, 13)

The anonymous author of the book of Wisdom continues to describe Lady Wisdom, noting that "in kinship with wisdom there is immortality" (Wis. 8:17) and addressing God in prayers, describes how "you made all things by your word" (9:1), how "wisdom... sits by your throne" (9:4), and how "even one who is perfect among human beings will be regarded as nothing without the wisdom that comes from you" (9:6). Echoing Proverbs further, he agrees that "she knows and understands all things" (9:10). According to this author, going further, it was Lady Wisdom who "delivered" Adam from his sin in Eden (10:1). It was Lady Wisdom who "saved" the world during the flood, guiding Noah (10:4). Likewise, it was Lady Wisdom who saved the Israelites from Egypt and guided them across the Red Sea and on their Exodus (10:15–18). If it hasn't seemed clear, the Wisdom of Solomon is describing Lady Wisdom not only as a creation of God (like Proverbs), but as if Lady Wisdom and God are one and the same. This idea is strengthened in 11:1–4 when instead of describing Wisdom, the author begins and continues henceforth to directly address Wisdom and God as if they were the same entity.

It was this book, the Wisdom of Solomon, that influenced the description of Heb. 1:2–3 which noted about God that: "in these last days he has spoken to us by a Son, whom he appointed heir of all things, through whom he also created the worlds." When he concludes that "He is the reflection (απαύγασμα) of God's glory and the exact imprint of God's very being," this draws upon the only other use of that word in Wis. 7:26, demonstrating which of the two texts about Lady Wisdom was on the mind of the author of Hebrews.

One of the greatest contributions of the Wisdom of Solomon for Christian thinking was its simultaneous ability to both describe God and Wisdom as if they were the same person, and yet to still insist that somehow they were distinct. This is most clearly seen in Wis. 9:17 when the author asks, "who has learned your counsel, unless you have given wisdom and sent your holy spirit from on high?" Here, seemingly, there are three entities depicted: God, wisdom, and a holy spirit. Whether the original author intended such a conceptual tripart distinction, it helped make it possible for early Christians to identify Jesus as both Lady Wisdom and God.

JESUS IS A WOMAN (AND A MAN)

However, clear exegesis aside, the idea itself is surely to come as a shock: the early Christians were okay imagining Jesus as a woman? The answer is, surprisingly, yes. Although they recognized that Jesus had come to earth in his incarnation as a man, they recognized that before his incarnation, at the throne of God, Scripture had described a portrait of Jesus, the eternal Logos, as female. Even before, the Jewish author of the Wisdom of Solomon was willing earlier to imagine God as both male and female, by distinguishing and simultaneously mixing together Lady Wisdom and the Divine.

This understanding remained with the early Christians for a time and can most plainly be seen in some of the Gnostic influenced writings. The word for wisdom in Greek is *sophia*, and as such, many Gnostic Christians (given their interest in gnosis, or knowledge) referred to Jesus by the feminine name of Sophia. Although they had very strange and heterodox beliefs, some of them at least recognized that the Christ they worshipped was a dual representation of male and female. That single insight, first understood and given evidence to by Paul and Hebrews, is worthy of our reconsideration now more than ever.

Just as both man and woman were created in the divine image of God, so too did the earliest Christians affirm that God's divine image made human was representative of both woman and man. God's son was not only a son, but his daughter. Sound too radical? Well, we are asked in the Bible to say to Lady Wisdom (to Jesus Christ): "you are my sister" (Prov. 7:4). We are asked to consider her an "intimate friend" (7:4). If we are encouraged to call the image of God our sister, why is it so strange to consider calling God our mother, or referring to her as "she"? He is not a man. She is not woman. But the reality is that while God is indeed genderless, since gender is a gift from God to us through creation, God must be affirmed in all his and her multiple and beautiful ways. When I was a freshman, just beginning my journey into academics, I still remember my surprise when I first heard Wonil Kim, my Old Testament professor, refer in class to God as "she." Many students squirmed, unsure how to react. He told us that day that our reaction was indicative of why it was important to say things like that, to help us enlarge our vision of what God is depicted as in the Bible. Whether I fully understood it then, I now realize how right he was. If Christ, the image of God, is my sister, so too is God. Many years later, Kim is still not only a daring professor, a fantastic mentor, and one of my dearest friends, but he also remains a shining example of the effort we must make to grow our understanding of God beyond the simplistic frameworks we have grown too accustomed to.

This is imperative, for until we see God, Jesus, and the Holy Spirit for what they are, the source of the divine image in both genders, we will continue to make un-Christian and, dare I say, demonic arguments against the equality promised in Christ. God and humanity are reconciled in Christ because Christ and God saved and identified with *all* humanity, not merely or primarily with one half of it. If we are asked to call Christ our sister, it is because all too often we have disregarded and neglected the sisters of our community. As Jesus would say in his ministry, "just as you did it to one of the least of these who are members of my family, you did it to me" (Matt. 25:40). As Christians, we call everyone our brothers and sisters in Christ, and seeing Christ as Lady Wisdom reminds us that all those we call sister are cared for by Christ.

Yet, we cannot avoid one more important contribution that this theology of Wisdom provides us: the recognition that Christ represented and saved not only our static gender norms, but all sexual diversity. A theology of Wisdom opens the way to understanding Christ as intersex, and not only that, but as one who covered the entire sexual spectrum. In Christ, all of humanity's sexual diversity is embraced and redeemed by God's love. Nobody is left out of the kingdom of heaven for the way in which they were born. For all those who were born without a static or specific gender, God embraces you, for he/she/it has no gender, and yet all identities are encompassed by the breadth and love of God. For those born with signifiers of both genders, those born intersex, Christ embraces you, for Christ transcends and embraces both. And for all those who find themselves in some sense different from what is often considered the norm, God invites you to call him "sister" and "friend," for there is no greater ally to the disenfranchised and oppressed than Christ.

12
SAYING NO TO HOMOPHOBIA

> *"Neither Peter in his work to include Gentiles in the church nor the abolitionists in their campaign against slavery argued that their experience should take precedence over Scripture. But they both made the case that their experience should cause Christians to reconsider long-held interpretations of Scripture. Today, we are still responsible for testing our beliefs in light of their outcomes—a duty in line with Jesus' teaching about trees and their fruit."*
>
> MATTHEW VINES[1]

During the Summer of 2015, when I was taking a two-week intensive history class, I first witnessed homophobia in a place I never would have imagined seeing it. The class was being taught by a visiting professor who was far more conservative than anyone actively teaching at the school. Toward the end of the class, the five or so students in the class began discussing various controversial issues. Eventually, as if by clockwork, the topic of homosexuality was raised. I remember that at one point, I mentioned how I believed it was never the right of a pastor to kick out someone from the church merely for who they were, who they were married to, or because of whatever struggle they faced. The church was to be a place for all people to find a space within. I thought that would be a pretty non-controversial opinion, but I was wrong.

The visiting professor became heated and to my surprise, adamantly informed me that he had every right in a church he ran to kick out a gay couple. Some of the students agreed, others silently showed discomfort. We all liked him, and although we would have all said Christ typically shone through his kind demeanor, the light that was shining then was satanic. This wasn't simply an academic or doctrinal disagreement. It took on a different character from other topics we had discussed and it was clear that something dark and ugly resided within his heart, something that the Gospel of Christ had promised to root out.

When I was beginning my work as a student pastor two summers later, the issue reared its head again. When I read my church's handbook for ministers, and I quickly noticed that parts of the text had not been updated for decades. Amongst many arcane and odd rules that made no sense anymore, there were others which were simply rejected by most. To my surprise, on the same page that banned any homosexual men or women from being members, so too did it ban any remarried men and women.

While at one point that rule had indeed been enforced decades back, most ministers I knew today allowed remarried couples in their churches without so much as a word. Why? Because a large number of Adventists in North America have been divorced, a statistic that is shared by just about every Christian denomination. If ministers enforced that rule, the membership would be greatly diminished. Perhaps more importantly, because so many have been affected by divorce (including many pastors), most ministers inherently disagree with the idea of punishing people for simply continuing to pursue love. Empathy, in short, takes precedence.

And yet, there was a deep and painful irony. Whereas the remarriage rule was routinely broken and ignored, the adjacent rule about homosexuality continued to be invoked by people such as my earlier professor. Why? Because unlike remarried divorcees, LGBTQ+ individuals are a small minority and many pastors have no connection to any of them, and as such, are not affected by the issue. Ministers and members feel no need to reevaluate their position as they have regarding divorce. They can afford to be hypocrites toward them because if they do, there are no negative consequences personally or communally as a result.

This realization suggested to me that if, in an alternate reality, the LGBTQ+ community were not a minority, if they made up half the church, then the church would also ignore this old rule. This hypocritical attitude angered me then, and it still does now. Was this the sort of model that Christ had called the church to follow? Was this a model of church leadership that Paul had ever displayed? No. Bigotry and hypocrisy never had a place in the church when it began and it should have no place now.

DEFENDING EQUALITY

One cannot honestly reject sexism and defend the equal rights of women without also recognizing the plight of those who are also routinely and openly still discriminated against throughout the world on the basis of sex: the LGBTQ+ community. Christian communities, like many Western faiths, have traditionally been some of the worst offenders against such sexual minorities. Instead of showing the grace and love of Christ, Christians have more often imitated and incarnated his enemy, the devil, in both word and action.

The world, though, has changed in great and tremendous ways, many of them positive both for humanity and the Gospel as a whole.

Within the United States, the 2020 Democratic Primaries have already demonstrated this with the rise in popularity of Mayor Pete Buttigieg, an Army veteran and gay Christian who was married in a church to his husband. Almost every aspect of that description would have seemed impossible a hundred years ago; much of it would have seemed implausible only twenty years ago. Perhaps the most unbelievable aspect is that Buttigieg has won most of his acclaim and popularity by his public affirmation of faith and his willingness to accuse conservative Christians such as Vice President Mike Pence of hypocrisy. Rather than alienating Christian voters, Buttigieg has won the support of many who see him as a faithful example of Christianity. Clearly, Christian attitudes toward the LGBTQ+ community are changing in profound and important ways.

As each decade passes, more and more churches have changed their views on the role that such individuals have within the plan of God. On the more conservative side of the spectrum, almost a majority of Evangelical churches have switched from believing that gay sexual attraction is a sin to believing that people can be born gay and not be sinful (but must remain celibate). On the more progressive side, a large number of Protestant churches have revised their beliefs to accept LGBTQ+ relationships as entirely blessed by God. The Episcopal Church in America routinely performs LGBTQ+ weddings. In short, regardless of where one falls on the spectrum, Christians attitudes have for the most part come to accept that LGBTQ+ persons are children of God and not inherently sinners.

DAVID AND JONATHAN

With the increased attention that such an issue has garnered socially, an equally growing attention has been given by people to the biblical material and its relevance to these issues. For example, a number of scholars have raised questions about David and Jonathan's relationship. The author of 1 Samuel reports that "Jonathan loved him as his own soul" (18:1), and when David weeps over Jonathan's death, he states that "your love to me was wonderful, passing the love of women" (2 Sam. 1:26). The suggestion by some scholars is that this is not quite a normal proclamation for a man with as much of a sexual libido as David to make about another man.

Others have argued that given Near Eastern cultural attitudes toward men (which are unusually intimate), that this is merely a statement describing a friendship. This could be possible, but some of the evidence suggests that's not an adequate answer. For example, the text reports that Jonathan and David kissed each other (1 Sam. 20:41), reports that Jonathan had stripped naked for David to prove his loyalty (1 Sam. 18:1–4), and Saul accuses Jonathan of shaming his mother's nakedness, a statement which carries a sexual connotation (see 1 Sam. 20:30). When the text states that "Jonathan took great delight in David" (19:1), it uses the same Hebrew word that was used to describe Shechem's sexual desire to marry Jacob's daughter Dinah (Gen. 34:19).

None of that proves that David was bisexual or that Jonathan was gay, but it does present the possibility. Many conservative Christians have violently rejected the idea and accused anyone suggesting this of distorting or maligning the Bible. Here's the real question though: why would it upset anyone *if* David was bisexual? Why should it be a contentious issue to begin with? The possibility is there and can't be entirely explained away, and yet, the visceral reaction many have to the suggestion demonstrates the hatred they harbor in their hearts, knowingly or not. One cannot both claim to love their LGBTQ+ brothers and sisters but also argue that David can't be both bisexual and "a man after God's own heart." If you claim to believe that LGBTQ+ people have good hearts, why should David's be any different?

Perhaps a bigger issue at stake in that discussion is the fact that it shows how backwards our own moral priorities are. David is one of the single most bloodthirsty and unholy individuals ever described in Scripture. He routinely appears to condone murder and has a disregard for innocent lives. He was also a serial polygamist who disobeyed the Deuteronomistic instructions on marriage for kings. And yet, somehow, compared with that, the mere idea that David was possibly not heterosexual is what enflames so many moral passions? Something tells me that a spirit other than God's is at work in such emotional reactions.

SEEING OUR PREJUDICES

Whether or not David was bisexual is ultimately irrelevant. The reality is that there were LGBTQ+ people who existed in Israel, who, like in many countries today, had to hide their attractions and undergo persecution from those who claimed to be God's servants. And just like David, and perhaps more so in some ways, they were children of God. Any discomfort a Christian feels about imagining a biblical character as non-heterosexual says more about the sexism and discriminatory attitudes we carry within ourselves than it does about God or one's view of morality.

This can be illustrated wonderfully by the story of Jonah when God commanded him to go to the capital of Israel's enemy, Nineveh, and warn them about their impending destruction. There, one reads of a prophet of God who ran away from God because he didn't wish to do what God asked of him. What is often forgotten is *why* Jonah ran away. It was not out of fear of the Ninevites, but because according to Jonah, he was worried that God would forgive them if they repented (see Jonah 4:2). Jonah hated the Assyrians just as much as any other Israelite, and like them, he used God as the justification for his hatred. As long as he believed that God was against them, then he could also believe that he should be. The story of the book of Jonah, however, is that when God reveals that he doesn't hate the Assyrians, Jonah admits that he would rather not exist than worship a God who loves those he hates. In other words, Jonah's religious justification for hating others was, in the end, merely selfish hatred, with absolutely nothing godly part of it.

This same message was repeated later by Jesus when he told his famous parable about the Good Samaritan (Luke 10:25–37). Unfortunately, many today misunderstand this story for the same reason we often don't understand Jonah's message: we lack the hatred that the author of the story assumed we would have. It is an understatement to say that Jesus' audience hated the Samaritans. Like Jonah, there was no considering the possibility of a "good" Assyrian or Samaritan, in the same way that we cannot today imagine the words "good" and "Nazi" together. The moment that Jesus describes the Samaritan as righteous, his audience, like Jonah before, would have rejected the message. They cannot even consider whether they should seek to act like the Samaritan did, for they are unwilling to even consider the possibility that a Samaritan could ever be good.

Jesus' parable forces the crowd to reevaluate their own prejudices and to realize that instead of being happy that one of their enemies was living how God wanted, they would rather, like Jonah, reject God's love than embrace the object of their anger. The message of the parable, like Jonah's book, is to remind us that our hatred and prejudice derives from our own wicked hearts and has nothing to do with the God who is affirmed as love itself (1 John 4:8). We use God as an excuse to scapegoat and project our hatred on to others. This, however, is the work of the devil, not God.

All too often Christians say that they are called "to love the sinner, but hate the sin," yet they fail to recognize that this can frequently become an excuse to hate both, consciously or not. If I must always state what I hate before I say what I love, which of the two truly has the power over my feelings? If a loving couple, close friends, or even parents don't act that way toward those they truly love, and both are representative in the Bible of God's relationship with us, why then do so many insist on acting in such a contrary way and defend it as love? It's time we recognized that such actions are not loving. Concerned, perhaps, but not loving.

DOES THE BIBLE TELL ME SO?

But aside from our unacknowledged prejudices, there is the larger issue of interpreting the Scriptures that we do have. While David may have a question mark over his sexuality, that question mark will not resolve for many the exclamation mark that appears to exist over the texts in the Bible that speak on sexual divergence. Surprisingly though, for an issue that riles up so many, the Bible has little to say about it. There are only two explicit references to male homosexuality in the Old Testament and only one in the New Testament. Female homosexuality is mentioned explicitly only once in the entire Bible. That's not as much as you would assume would be needed to create the sort of culture wars that exist across the world currently.

Based on my description, there are several questions that have likely arisen in some readers' minds. The first is why I have limited my list to "explicit" references, rather than "possible" references. The answer is simple: if you can't demonstrate what you need theologically from the texts that are clear, then anything else isn't even worth exploring. Part of the same problem is also the fact that sometimes those things which appear possibly related aren't at all. For example, the story of Sodom and Gomorrah has nothing to do with the question of homosexuality. We know this because, like the children's song goes, "the Bible tells me so." The sin of Sodom is listed by the prophets several times and never is homosexuality one of their listed sins (for example, see Ezek. 16:49–50).

Second, there is a duplicate version of the same story found in Judges 18. There, a tribe of Israelites comes to the door of where a traveling Levite and his concubine are, demands that the house owner throw out the Levite so that they can rape him. Instead, the Levite man throws out his female concubine and the crowd rapes her all night until she dies. The gruesome story ends with the Levite reporting to the other tribes that the mob sought to murder him. In other words, sex was not the goal, but the means by which these Israelites wanted to kill the Levite. By raping him, the crowd was symbolically emasculating him and condemning him to, what they considered to be, a worse death. With that story in mind, the tale of Sodom makes more sense and one can understand why the prophets never condemn those cities for sexual immorality: it was never about sex, only power (which is what rape is almost always truly about). If the entire Israelite tribe of Benjamin could seek to murder someone through same-sex rape, then the Sodomites are not exhibiting sexual attraction, but a common culturally shared method for brutality that was accepted or known by heterosexual communities, even those of the biblical faith.

That is a perfect example of why supposed "possible" references to homosexuality in the Bible are not a good place to start. So, sticking with the few confirmed ones, we can notice something curious about my earlier description: the Bible, in both testaments, *only* outright condemns male homosexuality, not homosexuality as a whole. In Lev. 18:22, it states: "You shall not lie with a male as with a woman; it is an abomination." And later, in 20:13, the warning is enlarged with a consequence: "If a man lies with a man as with a woman, both of them have committed an abomination; they shall be put to death; their blood is upon them."

Together, these are the only two texts that touch on the issue of homosexuality, and neither condemns anything except *male* homosexual *sex*. There is no condemnation of *lesbianism*, male same-sex *attraction*, or male same-sex *sex-less marriages*. While that last idea sounds silly to say, Paul proposed it as an idea to heterosexual couples (see 1 Cor. 7:29, "let even those who have wives be as though they had none"). This simply underscores the fact that the two texts in Leviticus do not actually condemn "homosexuality," and to claim that they do is to go beyond the actual words or ideas of the Bible.

Some will object to this and claim that the instructions of Leviticus, though directed to men, are intended to apply to both sexes. This would be a reasonable suggestion if the instructions were from any other book besides Leviticus. However, Leviticus is uniquely specific about which rules are assumed by its author(s) to apply to both men and women, and those which are applicable only to men or women. In fact, a great example of this immediately follows the instructions about male same-sex acts. In Lev. 20:15, it states that: "If a man has sexual relations with an animal, he shall be put to death," and then states that "if a woman approaches any animal and has sexual relations with it, you shall kill the woman." When the book of Leviticus wants you to know something applies to both men and women, it clarifies that fact.

Why then would it have only condemned male same-sex acts and not female? Thankfully, the book of Leviticus appears to tell us in the next verse following the prohibition. In Lev. 20:14, it states that: "If a man takes a wife and her mother also, it is depravity; they shall be burned to death, both he and they, that there may be no depravity among you." At first glance, the text may be confusing. The sin being punished is incest between the mother and daughter. The law is not forbidding polygamy (rather, it's assuming its acceptance), and *it is not concerned about two women sharing a marriage bed.* It is only concerned with what happens when a mother and daughter both share a marriage bed: i.e. incest. The law, in short, assumes that the mother and daughter will not only share a husband, but will have the *freedom* to sleep together and share sexual activity with their husband.

To get even more explicit and to the point: this law appears to assume that men in polygamous marriages with two wives have marital rights to have threesomes with their lawfully wedded wives (a social possibility alluded to in the Bible on occasion, cf. 2 Sam. 16:20–22).* The reason why the previous verse does not condemn female same-sex acts appears to be due to the fact that to do so would be to interfere with the marital rights of Israelite husbands who were linked to multiple women. If his wives were considered part of his property, and both were lawfully married to him, then any interference with what he *could* do in their shared bed was a line too far for many to consider crossing. The exception to that freedom was when such marital rights appeared to create other known violations, such as incest. Contemporary culture and patriarchy, in the end then, were likely the reasons why female same-sex acts were apparently not condemned in ancient Israel.

As such, to be clear: the two quotes from the book of Leviticus only appears to condemn male same-sex *acts*, not homosexual *attraction* or *romantic relationships*. Female same-sex acts appear to get a pass because of the culture in which these rules were made. But if the culture of marriage at the time was responsible for the different

---

* While I am arguing that the law assumes the possibility (for it never forbids such an idea anywhere), it does not mean that I'm claiming such a possibility was a common marital practice in Israel. Contrarily, the Bible gives some hints that it may have been more common to sleep with each wife individually. Yet, my point here is not what was commonly practiced, but what is theoretically allowed and how that affects the way the law was given. For example, while it is true that there is no evidence that anybody observed the year of Jubilee (Lev. 25:1–10), that doesn't change what the law about it assumes.

treatment of female same-sex acts, what makes us sure that male same-sex acts weren't also being treated that way as a result of contemporary opinions? One rotten fruit usually spoils the bunch. In the New Testament, Paul references same-sex acts twice. The most important of these, Rom. 1:26–27, states that pagan "women exchanged natural intercourse for unnatural" and that "men committed shameless acts with men and received in their own persons the due penalty for their error."* But there are some problems here, the most obvious of which is this: female same-sex acts aren't dismissed in the same way as the male is (unlike the men, they aren't condemned and never said to suffer from consequences), and furthermore, though described as "unnatural," it is never called a sin. Paul never forbids female same-sex acts, just like (and probably because) Leviticus didn't, even if he apparently disapproved of it.

If homosexuality is the great sin that conservative Christians fear and preach incessantly about in our generation, why is it that God never outright condemned female-same sex acts anywhere in the Bible, never forbid homosexual attraction or love anywhere in those same scriptures, and only forbid male homosexual *penetration*? Even if Paul was loosely interpreted as forbidding lesbianism, why did God allow (by virtue of silence) such things for over a thousand years prior in Israel? Does that sound like the most pressing spiritual issue humans face? Of course not.

Moreover, as any Christian instinctively knows, no truly divine instruction from God is going to be so arbitrary as to forbid one gender from an act and wink at the other (and especially not because

---

* Most biblical scholars debate whether this description and Paul's other have more to do with pagan festivals where drunken orgies would take place, rather than what we currently debate about, which are committed and monogamous relationships between same-sex couples. Remember, in ancient times our scientific and medical ideas of sexual orientation did not exist.

it benefits polygamous husbands). The very fact that this is what we possibly find in Leviticus points us to the reality that like many other things in the Bible, the laws on homosexuality were more influenced by ancient culture than God's eternal blueprint. They are more like the laws in Leviticus against sowing multiple crops in the same field or weaving clothing made from more than one fabric, in other words: they are not part of God's moral design, but culturally specific rules. The fact that this might be the case does not of course inform Christians how they *should* act and believe today, but it does remove the impetus for why they believe they're supposed to act the way that they have been, and that's a great first step.

SLIPPERY SLOPES ARE GOOD

Putting all these discussions aside, there's something vitally important we should recognize. Though many who argue against the acceptance of the LGBTQ+ community make the case that certain Christians are on a slippery slope, falling away from biblical authority, the truth is that they themselves have already fallen away, whether they have realized it yet or not. Leviticus was clear that the penalty for two men sleeping together is death (20:13), and yet current conservative objections no longer interpret this text as applicable within our current culture. Instead, the conservative argument is that same-sex *marriages* shouldn't be allowed (something that the Bible never discusses)* and that LGBTQ+ people should be allowed to have civil unions, or simply live their lifestyles in private. While there is much there in

---

* To illustrate how illogical this is, consider the following: if Paul can imagine heterosexual marriages where two people love each other but don't have sex, why is it not possible that he would approve of male homosexual marriages that involved male same-sex attraction but not sex, as outlawed in Leviticus? The issue in Leviticus is not attraction, but the specific act, and only limited to one gender. Given this, the entire argument against same-sex "marriages" is a literal biblical farce.

those attitudes that can offend many regarding ideals of equality, the reality of these arguments is simply this: most conservative Christians reject specific scriptural instructions about homosexuality.

What many of them have done is reinterpreted the demand for a *present* death penalty in Leviticus as a *future* promise of a judgment given by God. And yet, many of them will not even allow for that harsh of an interpretation, arguing that since God judges the heart, even those who are LGBTQ+, while they believe them to be sinning, may not be held in judgment for it depending on their hearts. Again, neither of these ideas are what Leviticus states and it is not the interpretation that most Christians historically held. It is rather a move away from biblical authority. These conservative Christians who yell what sounds like hatred at sexual minorities would often be the first to raise their objection should a *true* fundamentalist raise their voice and call for the death of a gay man. And it is this fact that alerts us to the reality that most conservatives are no longer resting their authority on a simple interpretation of the Bible, but have moved it.

For most of these Christians, their reasons for rejecting the death penalty and even assured judgment is Jesus. The realization that Jesus' messages conflict with a literal understanding and application of Leviticus has caused many modern conservative Christians to ignore the book's specific calls for death. Given this, something should readily become apparent: the claim of Bible "literalists" is that any divergence from the Bible unmoors someone from it. According to their own logic, they have already become unmoored. So why then, if there is no anchor in Leviticus anymore, do such Christians object to what more progressive Christians argue regarding the full acceptance and loving embrace of LGBTQ+ individuals? If conservatives have already adjusted their interpretation of Leviticus because of Jesus to a certain point, why is it any different than those who have adjusted it further?

The truth is that there isn't a good justification for this behavior. Like the parable of the Good Samaritan and like the story of Jonah, our prejudices are often defended with the claim that God is behind them, and almost always we discover that God is not the reason we have our prejudices, but merely the shield we artificially use to avoid facing our own distorted hearts. Surprisingly, Jesus actually did potentially discuss the issue of sexual divergence in the New Testament. In Matt. 19:12, Jesus warns his first century disciples that "Not everyone can accept this teaching, but only those to whom it is given." Continuing, he explained that "there are eunuchs who have been so from birth, and there are eunuchs who have been made eunuchs by others, and there are eunuchs who have made themselves eunuchs for the sake of the kingdom of heaven." Again, and ending his teaching, he warns: "Let anyone accept this who can."

For many Christians, this warning has been interpreted to refer to celibacy. This conclusion is drawn by people assuming the definition of a "eunuch" as someone who served in the court and had his genitals removed (castrated) so as to avoid defiling the women there. Yet, this was not the only meaning of the term at the time of Jesus. The research of Jeff Miner and John Connoley, along with others, have noted that a number of ancient sources, including the Talmud, the Apocrypha, and Sumerian documents, refer to men who are eunuchs not by castration, but who are naturally sexually effeminate and uninterested in women.[2] These are not eunuchs who are simply celibate or asexual, for some records indicate that such eunuchs acted as prostitutes, presumably with other men (since the term eunuch was synonymous with a distaste for women). Or as Fritz Guy, one of my professors, once noted, eunuchs "were sometimes described in terms remarkably similar to modern stereotypes of homosexual men."[3] As such, the word eunuch is being used at the time to refer to a range of sexual divergences from the normal heterosexual societal expectation.

If this aspect of the word is what Jesus has in mind when he speaks of those who are born in such a state, his use of the word *eunuch* refers then to sexual divergence and those who cannot embrace their variation within society, which would have included not only those who were celibate, or asexual, but those with same-sex attraction. Jesus here, it appears, is affirming that such sexual divergences can come naturally and serve a purpose in the Kingdom of God. How much better would it be if, despite our disagreements on a host of issues, we could simply agree to love and accept our diverse neighbors as Jesus taught?

Whether we are discussing the oppression of women on the basis of their sex or those who are oppressed because of what sex they are attracted to, Christ calls us not only to take seriously the parts of the Bible that reflect our prejudices, but even more so those texts that God gave specifically to combat those same prejudices. If the devil can quote Scripture for his own purposes, and if the religious leaders of Jesus' day could know their scriptures so well and still not recognize Jesus, it should become abundantly clear that any approach to the Bible that does not start and end with the love of Christ will lead one to a different path than the one that those on the road to Emmaus experienced (Luke 24:13–35).

For those who worry about the consequences of rejecting certain scriptures in favor of love, grace, and/or equality, I would put forth the following question: do you really believe that assuming a more accepting and more loving God is a greater danger than assuming a more reserved and more demanding God? If the answer is yes, how would you have acted with Jesus had you grown up in the first century? His disciples didn't understand him, sometimes thought they knew better than him, and the religious leaders of his day rejected him as being from the devil. They believed that Jesus was working contrary to God's established scriptures and breaking social taboos.

Nobody recognized him for what he was, despite knowing the Bible as well as they did.

Why then would anyone assume that they would have done any better? The religious leaders then, like many evangelicals today, were afraid of the negative consequences of believing that God was more loving and inclusive than what Scripture had already stated. How did it turn out for them? They ended up killing God because they were afraid that God would judge them if they didn't protect the status quo that, unbeknownst to them, God was announcing the end of. How painfully and sadly ironic. Woe on anyone if they should continue to make that same mistake, killing Jesus again and again in the hearts and souls of those who already reflect the love of Christ they themselves lack.

13

SAYING NO TO DIVINE VIOLENCE

> "What Jesus makes clear is that everything a Christian does and thinks and believes—including what we believe about the Bible—is through the lens of Christ crucified... [So] here's the fact of the matter: the violence found in the Hebrew Scriptures will somehow have to be reconciled with the nonviolent rabbi from Nazareth. There really are no two ways about it... [because] anything contradictory to the nature of Jesus is contradictory to the nature of God."
>
> MATTHEW J. DISTEFANO[1]

One day, in between classes during my undergraduate studies, I ran into a graduate student I knew in the hallway. He was busy discussing class readings with another student. He saw me, said hello, and we began speaking about some project of mine. Somehow, and I'm at a loss to remember why, the topic of the Canaanite genocide came up. I was the one who mentioned them as an illustration of disturbing texts in Scripture, and I expected that he would agree about how troubling they were. Instead, he gave a puzzled look as if he had never considered the topic before, and then proceeded to say something that gave me chills: "Well, God must have had a good reason for it. He'd never kill an entire people without a good reason. Why is that a problem then?"

To say that I was disturbed was an understatement. This guy, while certainly more conservative than most, had seemingly gone through enough classes on ethics and other topics to have by now developed a sense for the moral problems such a topic posed. Hell, the very fact that he was a human being should have been enough to cause problems. And it was that second point, rather than the first, that eventually came to haunt me. My colleague in the hallway was responding intellectually to an issue involving human lives, rather than empathetically. He had turned off his emotions and in so doing, had begun to speak from a callous and emotionless place which most psychologists would call sociopathic. He saw numbers and evil where I saw people and messy reality.

Almost unconsciously, he demonized the individuals in order to justify inhuman actions against them. In truth, this is always the way in which we avoid empathy for the "other." If one can be made less than human, to become demonized, then it becomes easier to disregard their human rights and allow inhuman consequences to befall them. It happened in Nazi Germany to the Jews, and it happens to some of us today when we seek to defend the ancient Israelites' depictions of their ancestral wars. As long as we don't recall that there were innocent women and children murdered, so long as we conceptualize those women and children as irredeemably evil (despite the fact that this conflicts with all of Jesus' own claims about how God, grace, and sin works), then it seems acceptable to defend the worst action against them: annihilation.

By caring more about God than the people, strangely, God quickly appears more like his famous adversary, Satan. Surely, that must be a problem. How can God be the origin of goodness and somehow require a lack of empathy, a major characteristic of goodness, in order to avoid looking like Satan? If we have to betray our faith in order to embrace something in it, then it seems reasonable to suspect that there is a cancer in our faith and it's best we recognize it now rather than wait until we learn that the cancer has already spread to our very souls.

GOD'S PEOPLE: ISRAEL OR ISIS?

I touched upon the question of biblical violence at the beginning of this book. The Bible, as many realize (some reluctantly so), is filled with violent and downright bloodthirsty passages. A number of these texts were reviewed earlier. With psalms that fantasize about crushing infants' heads and laws decreeing the extermination of all pregnant women in cities, the biblical texts at times border on the obscene and grotesque. As many atheists have rightly pointed out, the Bible is no children's book and if it carried a rating, it might be well above the standard R.

In our current politically and militarily charged climate, it is more likely that a new reader of these passages will find similarities between the people of Yahweh in the Hebrew Bible and the terrorist group ISIS, than with Jesus or the disciples. At this point, given how much this book has covered, this is not all that radical to say.

Not too long ago in Syria, some ISIS militants shot a 7-year-old boy in front of his parents. Why? Because while he played with his friends, he said a curse alongside God's name. That sort of act might repulse our moral sensibilities as barbaric, and yet the Old Testament recommends just such an action to be taken (Ex. 20:3, Deut. 21:17–21). There are other similarities between the two groups. ISIS militants, for example, take young children as their wives, so too does God in the Hebrew Bible recommend the same behavior (Num. 31:17–18).

ISIS murders individuals who identify as gay, so too do certain passages in the Bible advocate for the same behavior (Lev. 20:13). ISIS militants mercilessly kill anyone (even family) who thinks to convert to another religion or who does not share their faith, and this causes many Christians to gasp in horror. Yet, the same was ordered by God in the Old Testament, even with the divine note that the murder of the family member should be done "without pity" or mercy (Deut. 13:6–9; 17:3–5; 2 Chron. 15:13). ISIS militants kill anyone who doesn't show them the proper respect, so too does the Bible say to kill anyone who is arrogant toward a priest or religious authority (Deut. 17:12).

As one YouTube video put it in their tagline, "If the Hebrews of the Old Testament had AK47s and GoPros, their footage would have looked like Islamic State (ISIS) propaganda." Another blogger refers to the books of Joshua and Judges as "the Taliban period of the Bible." Karen Armstrong rightly reminds us as Christians that "There is far more violence in the Bible than in the Qur'an."[2] And Philip Jenkins writes that:

> In terms of ordering violence and bloodshed, any simplistic claim about the superiority of the Bible to the Koran would be wildly wrong. In fact, the Bible overflows with "texts of terror," to borrow a phrase coined by the American theologian Phyllis Trible. The Bible contains far more verses praising or urging bloodshed than does the Koran, and biblical violence is often far more extreme, and marked by more indiscriminate savagery… If the founding text shapes the whole religion, then Judaism and Christianity deserve the utmost condemnation as religions of savagery… Commands to kill, to commit ethnic cleansing, to institutionalize segregation, to hate and fear other races and religions… all are in the Bible, and occur with a far greater frequency than in the Koran. At every stage, we can argue what the passages in question mean, and certainly whether they should have any relevance for later ages. But the fact remains that the words are there, and their inclusion in the scripture means that they are, literally, canonized, no less than in the Muslim scripture.[3]

Philip Kennicott continues this train of thought:

If the violence of the Islamic State often feels disconcertingly Old Testament, that's no accident. By re-enacting the appalling excesses of what we would call biblical violence in the modern world, it has issued us an invitation, a chance to return to what it posits as the basic moral condition governing all men. It is a family reunion of sorts, a chance to relive the fratricides and infanticides and genocides that give our shared religious narratives their bloody vigor, a chance to live together under the most blunt and unimaginative law ever promulgated: An eye for an eye.[4]

When one reads of how David, in order to hide his political ambitions to become King of Israel, regularly murdered entire villages (and all the women and children), a Christian's stomach should in theory churn (1 Sam. 27:1–12). Or likewise, one should feel a similar horror when one looks at the story of Numbers 31, where God orders the murder of all the Midianite men (and young boys) and any women who had already been married, but commands the Israelites to keep alive the young female children to be taken as child brides by the newly freed older Hebrew men.

"When ISIS behaves this same way in our modern world," a reader of a website asked in response to stories like this, "we call it evil. Men in both cases declared that God commanded the actions. Why do we revere Moses and condemn ISIS?" Likewise, biblical scholar Peter Enns asks: "How can Christians condemn brutal tribal warfare today when the Christian God commanded brutal tribal warfare yesterday? What kind of God are we dealing with here?"[5]

TREES AND MISPLACED PRIORITIES

Still not convinced? Look no further than Deuteronomy 20. Here's a paraphrase of *God's instructions* for his divine intention of the standard war procedure (not simply instructions for a specific period).

- When you come to a city, offer them peace. If they agree, don't kill them, but as part of that peace, take whatever you want from them and make them slaves to you *(vss. 10–11)*.

- If those people do not like your offer, you can attack them, and when God wins the battle for you, then you have two choices:
  - If the city is far away, you should kill all the men, rape all the women, kidnap the female children (to take as wives as young as twelve years) and steal everything *(vss. 12–15)*.
  - If the city is local, and God has given it to you, then you should kill everyone—men, women (pregnant or not) and children (infant or not), animals, cats and dogs, cows, sheep, everything. But do not harm the trees. Kill the people, but don't injure the trees *(vss. 16–20)*.

If you don't believe that could possibly be God's directives, take a moment to double check it in your Bible. I assure you, it's there. You've probably never heard a sermon about it before, but it's there. And contrary to how some ministers and apologists will claim that certain violent passages in the Old Testament only related to specific peoples (like the Canaanites) at specific times (such as Joshua), this passage in Deuteronomy is clear that God is giving his eternal instructions to Israel regarding how for the foreseeable future they should treat *any* enemies they eventually come across.

Peter Enns points out that physical violence and death are portrayed in Scripture, not as a last resort of sorts, but as "God's preferred means of conflict resolution." He goes on to note that:

> Why does God's word make it so hard to believe in God? Why was my faith better off before I decided to read through the Bible book by book and find a God who reminds me more of Idi Amin or Chairman Mao than Jesus? And the pressure from Christian peers and leaders to

stop "undermining" or "attacking" the Bible by asking questions like this doesn't help the problem but only makes it worse.[6]

Passages such as Deuteronomy 20 cause Christians to strangely feel uncomfortable. But perhaps more disturbing is the fact that as Chris Roberts points out, "nowhere—neither the Old Testament nor the New—do we have God saying this old way of doing things has come to an end."[7]

CONFLICTING PORTRAITS

And yet, isn't this the same God who it is also said that "his soul hates the lover of violence" (Psalm 11:5) and that he "abhors the bloodthirsty and deceitful" (5:6)? Isn't this the same God who is praised because "you are not a God who delights in wickedness; evil will not sojourn with you" (5:4)? Doesn't it say that it is "the unfaithful (who) have an appetite for violence," not the righteous (Prov. 13:2, NIV)? Doesn't it say that it is "the mouth of the wicked (which) conceals violence," and not the righteous (Prov. 10:6)? Isn't this the same God whom we pray to "protect me from the violent," not to *be violent* (Psalm 140:4)?

Isn't this the same God who we are taught wants us to "depart from evil, and do good; (to) seek peace, and pursue it" (Psalm 34:14) and who tells us through inspiration: "Do not envy the violent and do not choose any of their ways" (Prov. 3:31)? The very God who commands us to "put away violence and oppression, and do what is just and right" (Ezek. 45:9)? Isn't this the same God that Genesis 6:11 states destroyed the world by a flood for primarily one reason: that "the earth was filled with violence" (6:11). How can the God that destroyed the entire world because of violence, also be the God who orders obscene levels of violence against people throughout the Bible?

Aren't we told that among the six or seven things that God hates, one of them is "hands that shed innocent blood" (Prov. 6:17)? How can the ordered killing of children and infants be seen as anything but the shedding of innocent blood? Do we not commonly refer to the killing of the children in Bethlehem by Herod as "the massacre of the innocents"?

And most importantly, wasn't this the same God who we as Christians affirm was incarnated as Jesus, who famously told Peter and his disciples: "Put your sword back into its place; for all who take the sword will perish by the sword" (Matt. 26:52)? The same Jesus who told us to "turn the other cheek" in the face of violence (5:39), and who Peter and Paul both echo when they command Christians to "not repay evil for evil… but on the contrary, bless" (1 Peter 3:9; Rom. 12:17–18)? Are we not told that "whoever does not love does not know God, for God is love" (1 John 4:8)?

John Dominic Crossan summarizes this conundrum by pointing out that:

> The problem of the Christian Bible is that its God is portrayed both nonviolently and violently; its Christ, proclaimed as the human image of that God, is also portrayed both nonviolently and violently; and therefore Christians are called to a life of political confusion at best, or religious hypocrisy at worst. (Suspect the peace donkey, expect the warhorse).[8]

In the face of these seething contradictions, presenting equally valid portraits of either a God of Peace or Violence, Crossan asks:

> Do we choose and follow one or the other option since both are presented as the character of the biblical God? But if one Christian chooses God as nonviolent, another may—with equal validity—choose God as violent. Is the answer to my titular "How?" simply "It's your choice"? Or, alternatively, should we mix a transcendental cocktail of so many parts violence and so many parts nonviolence depending on personal taste or according to denominational tradition?[9]

THREE PROPHETS

We can see an example of this conflict between the two divine portraits in the Minor Prophets of the Old Testament who, although supposed to be the mouthpiece of the *will* of God, often disagreed violently with each other as to what that *will* would truly be. Case in point: Isaiah, Micah, and Joel.

In the book of Isaiah, we read of a miraculous, prophetic vision that Isaiah relates regarding the future coming salvation of the earth.

> They shall beat their swords into plowshares,
> and their spears into pruning hooks;
> nation shall not lift up sword against nation,
> neither shall they learn war any more.
>
> (ISAIAH 2:4)

Isaiah depicts a vision of universal peace, one in which all the peoples of the earth will receive and experience peace, what is essentially a dreamer's dream for those living in the crossroads of violent empires such as Egypt, Assyria and Babylon. Israel was always caught in the crosshairs of conflicts raging between other nations, and as such, this sort of vision must have been especially appealing to the war exhausted people simply trying to live their lives amidst such political chaos.

Yet Isaiah was not alone. Another prophetic book echoes (or perhaps quotes?) the exact same prophecy in another prediction about the same envisioned future hope. After narrating how in the future earth, the foreign nations surrounding Israel will seek to visit the God of Israel and learn his ways, Micah describes the result of their encounter with Yahweh.

> They shall beat their swords into plowshares,
> and their spears into pruning hooks;
> nation shall not lift up sword against nation,
> neither shall they learn war any more;

> but they shall all sit under their own vines
>> and under their own fig trees,
> and no one shall make them afraid.
>
> (MICAH 4:3–4)

Micah, like Isaiah, echoes the pronouncement that the God of Israel desires peace and that the future promises peace on a universal scale, even to Israel's former enemies. It's a beautiful image.

And yet, not everyone cared for it. A third prophet would later repeat the prophecy, but this time, significantly altered and theologically morphed. That prophetic voice was Joel. In his account, he does not imagine an eschatological paradise in the distant future, but imagines that he, as a prophet, could help to instigate the Day of the Lord himself in his own time. In one of his visions, he dreams that he takes it upon himself to gather together the foreign nations.

> Proclaim this among the nations:
> Prepare war, stir up the warriors.
> Let all the soldiers draw near, let them come up.
> Beat your plowshares into swords,
> and your pruning hooks into spears;
> let the weakling say, "I am a warrior."
>
> (JOEL 3:9–10)

Joel does the unthinkable, taking the prediction of peace for all peoples and reversing it into a call for war. What follows is a blood curdling description of Joel lying and convincing the nations that they can defeat God if they follow him to battle. Upon reaching their destination, Joel reveals his deception and calls out for God to kill everyone who isn't Jewish. The imagery used is of trampling grapes to create wine. The implication of Joel's prophecy is that almost the entire gentile world is wiped out and the blood of the nations flows across the land.

On the one hand, the prophets Micah and Isaiah agree that God wants a radical future vision of peace. Joel, a different prophet, rejects this, affirming that God wishes for the violent death of all "outside Zion." Perhaps Psalm 120 best describes the tension between these prophets when he writes:

> Too long have I had my dwelling among
> those who hate peace.
> I am for peace;
> but when I speak, they are for war.
>
> (PSALM 120:6–7)

What then are we to do when even God's emissaries, the prophets, cannot agree on what God's character and will is? What is a Christian to do when the God he worships is not necessarily the God who certain passages of the Bible depict or agree on? And how does this affect us in regard to how we live our lives or perceive other violent nations or groups?

To quote Crossan again, he aptly points out that,

> The tension is not between the Good Book and the bad world that is outside the book. It is between the Good Book and the bad world that are both *within* the book.[10]

As Christians, most of us already subconsciously reject biblical violence. We take our lead from Jesus, the incarnation of God on earth, who taught us to love our enemies and turn the other cheek, rather than gut them when their backs were turned. Yet, we still struggle to reject violent texts in Scripture because those scriptures attribute the violence to God. However, what if the truth was that God wasn't behind religious violence at all, even when the Bible says that he was?

SILENT ESTHER

For example, just look at the book of Esther. Esther probably seems to be an odd choice for a discussion regarding biblical violence. That's primarily because many have never read the book and particularly, of those many, most have never read the last three paragraphs. For a brief recap of one of the most Hollywood adapted Old Testament stories: a young girl hides her Jewish identity, is forced to become part of a harem, and becomes the queen of Persia, allowing her to be in a position of power that helps her to save her Jewish people from genocide. The story ends with Haman, the mastermind of the planned genocide, hanging on a pike that had been intended for Esther's uncle. That's where most of the movies end their story, about three paragraphs too early. The reason that every single adaptation of Esther does this is simple: the true ending of Esther is downright *evil*.

What many people miss out learning is that the Jews weren't just allowed to defend themselves from attacks by others (as the romanticized movies depict), but rather, the Jews were allowed to seek out that day anyone they *suspected* might wish them harm and to kill them preemptively. At the end of that day, it was reported that "the Jews struck down all their enemies with the sword, slaughtering, and destroying them, and did as they pleased to those who hated them" (Est 9:5). Not a single Jew is mentioned as having perished that day. However, the preemptive slaughter of one's enemies isn't actually the worse part. It's what comes afterward that shatters many people's nerves.

In the final closing scenes of the book, it reports that at the end of the day, Esther approached the King again with *one more* petition. Again, the King states that her petition, whatever it is, will be granted. She requests not land, nor a kingdom, but rather that "if it pleases the king, let the Jews who are in Susa be allowed tomorrow also to do according to this day's edict" (Est 9:13). And so the King allowed it.

The following day, we are told:

> The Jews who were in Susa gathered also on the fourteenth day of the month of Adar and they killed three hundred persons in Susa... Now the other Jews who were in the king's provinces also gathered to defend their lives, and gained relief from their enemies, and killed seventy-five thousand of those who hated them.
>
> (ESTHER 9:15–16)

Seventy-five thousand and three hundred dead. Let that number sink in, because that's how many Persians or non-Jews were murdered. Yes, I meant to use the word *murdered*. Esther requested that the Jews be allowed to kill anyone they even *thought* might seek them harm, but unlike the Jews who were legally allowed to defend themselves against the attacks of others, the non-Jews on this subsequent day were not allowed to defend their own lives. Should they kill a Jew in defense of their life, one who was attacking them, the action would have been illegal since the King gave authority to any Jew to kill whoever he wanted.

In short: Esther asked for state-sanctioned, Jewish-led murder. And she got it. Worse yet, this is what the Jewish celebration of Purim commemorates. It doesn't just glorify the reversal of Haman's evil plot as the films typically paint it, but gives joy for the equally evil plot of Esther. And this brings an important question to mind for all of us: just where is God amongst all of this *human* chaos?

Esther's book has often been criticized due to the fact that God appears to be a missing character within its narrative. Not only is his name never mentioned, but his presence is never expressly proven. Instead, God is *implied* throughout, with the final decision left in the hand of the reader to decide. Likewise, even the righteousness of the human characters is not affirmed outright with some such as Mordecai doubting whether Esther is even their savior at all (Est.

4:14).* These unique features of the book have often been a point of contention and were even used as a reason for possibly rejecting the book from the Canon in early discussions amongst both the Jews and Christians.

Perhaps this is not a defect of the book at all. What if it's actually one of the book's greatest strengths? Could it be that Esther shows us an example of what all Scripture is truly like? The book of Esther never attempts to attribute to God anything that occurs, especially the final vengeful scenes of bloodlust. It places the blame for everything squarely on the shoulders of the human actors, allowing God the freedom as a character to both receive praise for the good in the story and remain detached from the bad elements in it.

Could the book of Esther show us that although some biblical books, such as the book of Joshua, might claim God explicitly endorsed the slaughter of the Canaanites, the reality was closer to that of Esther? Could all of the violence that God supposedly ordered have stemmed not from God, but from humans who later *thought* God was the one who had led and inspired such things? It certainly seems possible, especially given the fact that current archaeological excavations have revealed that not only does Jericho show evidence that it did *not* fall at the hands of violent Israelites, but moreover it appears more and more likely that the Israelites actually settled the land of Canaan peacefully without any conquest at all. As such, Esther provides us an opportunity to reflect on the role God plays in the violent stories

---

* Since this sort of interpretation might be new to some people who are used to idolizing Esther as a role model, it might be helpful to gain some context. When one reads verse 14, it is helpful to keep in mind that although Mordecai urges Esther to see the King, she does not. He accuses her of trying to save her own life at the expense of the Jews and warns her that this is a failing strategy since she will die as well. In this context, Mordecai's words of "Who knows" or "Perhaps" indicate ambiguity and doubt. Mordecai does not truly believe Esther is their savior and is worried that she is not, but he remains hopeful that perhaps she can still be.

of the Bible. Could attributions of violence to God merely be that: "attributions" and not necessarily fact?

ESTABLISHING A CRITERIA

In order for this to be true, we must establish a criteria to allow us to make such an assertion. Essentially, what we must do is recognize that God is logically coherent and that his actions will, as such, not be contradictory. This means that if one part of the Bible depicts God as violent, but another depicts God as non-violent, the contradiction itself cannot be embraced (as if both are equally true), but rather, one of the two must be subservient and subsumed by the other. They cannot both be retained with equal authority, allowing both to have the same theological weight.

However, this invites a different question: how do we know that God is non-contradictory? Moreover, how would we as humans know whether something wasn't logically coherent in the first place? Perhaps, as some might argue, it only appears as if something is contradictory to us because our own logic is so deficient? Such arguments are often given by conservative Christians who seek to distance any ability for human readers of the Bible to deny inerrancy. Yet, these arguments are fundamentally flawed and disproven by the biblical texts themselves.

The very concept of saying *No!* to God (or confronting God) by rejecting something said for something else said, is only possible under two conditions: that morality is not based on a *Divine Command Theory* (God said it, thus its moral), and that as a result, morality can never be arbitrary. As we explored much earlier, if the *Divine Command Theory* was true, morality could indeed be arbitrary, allowing God to contradict himself and still remain moral. However, when this is rejected, anything arbitrary and contradictory is rejected along with it. That means that we are forced to conclude that God and morality must be logically consistent and coherent. Either they are unified, or are against each other.

Moreover, the fact that God invites humans to fight and disagree with him demonstrates that the God depicted in the Bible expects humans to be able to distinguish contradictions and reject them when tested. This means that any attempt to argue that a human cannot correctly judge divine coherency is to be rejected outright, similar to what we read of C. S. Lewis in a previous chapter. To accept the biblical testimony as explored in this book, one must reject any image of God as arbitrary or contradictory, and one must accept that human beings have sufficient ability to perceive contradictions in the divine and to accurately object to them.

Accepting this, it means that as Christians who recognize Jesus Christ as the very image and reflection of God, when we see Christ representing God as fundamentally forgiving and nonviolent, we judge the rest of Scripture based on these principles. When we see portraits of God that are at odds with the portrait of Christ, we must come to evaluate those former images in the light of Christ, and that may at times require us to deny God's involvement in horrendous acts of violence. Moses may have indeed been a human who could fail to fully comprehend God, but he was not incapable of rightly rejecting a false image of a genocidal God for a better one.

FINDING GOD

Desmond Doss of the Oscar winning movie *Hacksaw Ridge*, perhaps the most well-known Seventh-day Adventist today (second to either Ben Carson because of his failed presidential run or Ellen White herself), provides for us an example, however extreme, of what it looks like to reject violence in the Bible and God's role in it.

Doss is famous because he was a conscientious objector and one of the most celebrated soldiers of World War II. That means that although he was a deep believer in the Bible, he rejected violence to such a degree that he believed that he could not even hold a gun. Now, Doss' views are not typical for Seventh-day Adventists. Yet, some have, like Doss, taken their convictions very seriously. What makes this odd at first glance is that the Bible teaches the opposite: that violence is acceptable to God under certain circumstances, and that war can be necessary. Yet Doss, without saying it, outright rejects these texts.

At one point in the movie, he is interviewed by an officer in order to determine whether or not he is mentally unstable. He tells the officer: "I just simply believe what I believe. God says not to kill. That's one of his most important commandments." The psychiatric officer speaking to him replies: "Most people take that to mean don't commit murder. War is a completely different set of circumstances." Doss rejects this, arguing that Jesus gave a new commandment of peace. In other words, Doss chooses to have Christ set the example for what he believes about violence, not the texts of the Bible that depict God in favor of it. Whether or not he believed that God really did do and say the things that the Hebrew Bible reports (and given his background, he probably did), Doss doesn't want to consider anything other than Jesus in deciding his Christian ethics for life in the present.

In a deleted scene from the movie, Doss is asked at night by a fellow soldier: "Do you buy everything in that book?" Doss replies: "I do." Later, the solider, a graduate of Yale, says: "I studied 6,000 years of so-called civilization and all you find is empires and bloody wars. It's hard to find a just God anywhere in it." Doss nods, saying: "I understand that, I agree. It's not easy sometimes, but he's there." Doss makes a point not too far from the one Esther makes. Like the book of Esther, Doss believed we are called to see God not *through* the violent wars of his people, but in *contrast* to them. Although Doss himself would not have put it this way, we can see how what he says can benefit the arguments that this book is making: we are called to reject texts of terror in order to accept the true image of a non-violent God.

Even though we already reject the replication of violence like that seen in the Bible, I want to point out that if we are to remain true to the principles of the Bible, we must also repudiate God's own involvement in those biblical scenes. Just as Jesus rejected previous views when he credited to Moses what Deuteronomy credited to God, so too must we reject the claims of biblical texts that God ordered the extermination of children. Instead, like Jesus, we must credit such descriptions of divine acts of violence to the distorted and broken view of men. If we do not, we run the risk of fulfilling Isaiah's warning of "those who call evil good and good evil, who put darkness for light and light for darkness, who put bitter for sweet and sweet for bitter" (Isa. 5:20).

What might this look like in practice? What do we do about texts that talk about the "wrath of God" and its consequences both in biblical history and our promised future? Well, it might mean that we agree with Keith Giles, who writes in his recent book *Jesus Undefeated,* that: "The wrath of God is quite often something experienced as the fruit of one's own actions, rather than as the direct action of God against the unrighteous."[11] Or as Steve Kline asks, commenting on Psalm 18:25–27, where it states that "with the crooked you make yourself seem tortuous":

> But, for those that don't repent, is it God's wrath that will be poured out on them? Or, is it the lies and the violence of the unrepentant themselves that will come back on their own head? Throughout the Bible, we see that the pit the wicked dug they themselves fall into. Or, the snare that evil people set they get caught in themselves. And, in the depictions of Satan (for example, Goliath and Haman), he is almost always killed with his own weapon… It seems to them like

God is vengeful, spiteful, and vindictive, pouring His wrath out on them. However, in reality, it is their own lies and violence that are coming back on their own heads.[12]

Within this conception of God, it could mean that we could understand that God did not actually hand Judah into the hands of the Babylonians, but rather allowed their own bad political and societal decisions to reap the consequences such policies bring. This would explain why God is said to be angry at the Babylonians for what they did to Jerusalem, a seemingly strange idea since God was said to have sent the Babylonians to do it. Instead, we can revise our understanding of the biblical authors to recognize that God had not *sent* evil to Judah, but merely allowed for the consequences of Judah's own evil to be reaped. Thus, God did not *want* that evil to come upon them, but condemned Judah for having brought it upon themselves, and was upset when it happened. In other words, sin always and inevitably destroys itself and those attached to it, and that act of destruction does not need to come from the hand of God for it to come to pass.

If this is true then, we could also potentially apply this to the biblical descriptions of the final eschatological judgment. In this light, it could mean understanding that it is not necessarily the case that God directly inflicts violent judgment on evil humans, but rather, God allows humans to experience the consequences of the evil they harvest for themselves. If God is what is required for humans to exist, like breath is required for earthly life, then if people choose to hide from God, like one who locks themselves in an airtight room, they will die, or in the case of the judgment, cease to exist. They are effectively cutting themselves off from what they need to live, in the same way that someone who starves themselves will die. In this way, one can understand the violent imagery illustrating the judgment as perhaps reflective of contemporary attitudes of the biblical communities in their ancient warlike context, while accepting the ultimate consequences of these biblical depictions as still ultimately correct and prophetically true. Such an interpretive move would help us to retain biblical authority in balance with God's call for humans to interact with God's word, creating a truly faithful approach to Scripture.

Whether one chooses to adopt those two possible interpretations is not the point of this chapter. Rather, the goal is to simply illustrate why such attempts are needed and demanded by God's call for us to emulate Jacob and fight back against the image of a God that appears to wear the devil's mask. We, like Jacob, must fight back and affirm the blessing that we trust God wants for us, a blessing that only comes with and from our rejection of the false image of a threatening God.

14

SAYING NO TO HELL

> *"When it comes to a God we've been told is love personified, and who is perfectly merciful in all that he does, we simply cannot fathom his participation in activities which we know, deep down, are fundamentally evil and immoral... we cannot fathom a God who actively participates in, and eternally prolongs, the suffering of others."*
>
> JEFF TURNER[1]

During the Society of Biblical Literature (SBL) meetings in November of 2017, held in Boston, Massachusetts, I found time to sneak away on a train with my family to see Yale Divinity School, my longtime dream school. We had already visited Harvard earlier during our stay and were excited to see something to contrast it with. Disembarking from the train, we arrived in downtown New Haven, took an Uber, explored the sprawling campus, and fell in love with the gothic architecture and allure of the classic ivy.

Unfortunately, our train that night heading back to the meetings in Boston was canceled and so we ended up ordering an Uber driver to take us back. Over the course of our two or so hours of travel, our seemingly nice and friendly driver revealed that he was a Christian.

At first, this appeared to be a positive moment in which all four of us could bond. However, only too soon did he reveal that he staunchly believed three things: that nobody would be saved unless they were Christian, that anybody who wasn't Christian could be a good person, and everyone who wasn't Christian would burn in Hell's fires for all eternity. Needless to say, the last stretch of the ride home was torturous.

I asked if he sincerely believed that a devout Muslim woman in Iran, who was morally good, would be burned forever just because she wasn't a Christian? He was adamant not only that such a woman would burn, but that she couldn't possibly be good because nobody who wasn't a baptized Christian could possibly be anything but evil. When I pushed back on these ideas, he became more and more hostile. I tried sharing texts from the Bible that showed God had a high view of non-Israelite worship, but instead of nuancing his view, he merely rejected my quotations and informed me that he knew there was no way that the Bible could be saying the things that I said it did. As such, he said, he would ignore my verses since they were clearly a deception and lie (spoiler alert: they weren't).

What began as a pleasant ride at night, shared between Christian believers, transformed into a hostile confrontation over whether God was ultimately loving or hateful. Had someone heard us, they may well have assumed that the driver was anti-Christian, or that we each worshipped separate gods. His God sounded more like a portrait of Satan than the image of God presented by Jesus in the Gospels. And the truth is that this strange portrait of God masquerading as Satan has become far too prevalent in our modern era. The doctrine of Hell, it seems to many people, transforms Christians into worshippers of the devil, both in belief and action.

ROB BELL AND HELL

Almost nothing can stir as much controversy in some circles as the discussion of the existence and doctrine of Hell. If one has any doubts about it, all they need do is look at the story of what happened to Rob Bell in 2011 when he first published his book *Love Wins*. His church asked for his resignation and religious leaders denounced him. He was even smeared as a heretic on MSNBC. Yes, MSNBC. I know, it doesn't make sense, but it actually happened. Anyway, the point is that it brought his career as a popular Evangelical pastor to a complete end. Why was there such an uproar? In this regard, Kevin DeYoung sums up the conservative critique of Bell:

> The theology is heterodox [heretical]. The history is inaccurate. The impact on souls is devastating. And the use of Scripture is indefensible. Worst of all, *Love Wins* demeans the cross and misrepresents God's character.[2]

More to the point, Evangelicals attacked Bell's book for promoting the doctrine of "universalism," or the idea that everyone gets salvation in the end. And yet, the remarkable thing was that Bell's book wasn't even the thing that it was being attacked for. Bell never actually claimed in his book that he was a universalist, nor did he even promote Universalism, and not once did he actually deny the existence of Hell. Instead, Bell asked a large number of questions, almost endlessly, leaving a distinct impression within the readers mind that the answer to those questions likely didn't come wrapped in hellfire. But here's the point that his book illustrated: *simply asking questions can get you on the black list for many Christians.*

In response to Bell, countless Evangelical leaders have gone out of their way to spend copious amounts of effort in defending the doctrine of an eternal hellfire through numerous books and sermons. The years following the controversy have seen a wave of intense appeals for people to realize how close they are to eternal damnation. The message from Evangelicalism is clear: if you question Hell, you're not a *real* Christian (or at the very least, you're highly suspicious).

None of the controversy touched my community personally. As a Seventh-day Adventist, my denomination has actively and proudly taught since its founding that there is no such thing as an Eternal Hell. In fact, the word does not even appear within our official beliefs, even in reference to death and resurrection. We deny it so deeply that we don't even allow it to be mentioned as part of our doctrinal statements, not even to refute it.

Ellen White felt so strong about the topic, that she actually condemned the teaching as heresy and blasphemy and largely influenced the rest of my denomination to do the same. She made it clear, in opposition to what many Evangelicals teach, that one could not be a proper Christian and believe in Hell, for in her mind, to believe in Hell was to place Satan and God on the same footing and destroy the work of Christ on the cross.

> It is beyond the power of the human mind to estimate the evil which has been wrought by the heresy of eternal torment. The religion of the Bible, full of love and goodness, and abounding in compassion, is darkened by superstition and clothed with terror. When we consider in what false colors Satan has painted the character of God, can we wonder that our merciful Creator is feared, dreaded, and even hated? The appalling views of God which have spread over the world from the teachings of the pulpit have made thousands, yes, millions, of skeptics and [atheists].[3]

Many people accused Bell of being disrespectful to Evangelicals by calling Evangelical Christianity's focus on Hell "toxic." However, compared to White's straight forward denunciation of the doctrine, Bell and his book seem practically timid! Can you imagine what might have happened had Bell not simply *asked* questions, but actually accused Evangelicalism of following a heresy designed by Satan himself? Regardless of such amusing hypothetical ideas, the point is that as an Adventist, Bell's controversy was welcomed. I know many Adventist pastors who found *Love Wins* to be the best resource they knew of on the topic for their congregations.

THE ORIGINS OF HELL

So why is there this divide? And how has a doctrine so frightening become a centerpiece of the Good News for many Evangelicals in America today? How can Evangelicals claim that Jesus' cross is meaningless *unless* millions burn to death and Adventists like myself claim that Jesus' cross is meaningless *if* those millions burn for eternity? Well, to begin with, you need to have some idea of what the Bible actually teaches about these things.

Where did people get the idea of Hell from in the first place? Well, it's a bit complicated. The idea is foreign to the Old Testament. In that collection, the only thing referred to is a place called *Sheol*, which by no means is the same as what Evangelicals think of as Hell. Rather, Sheol was a word for the grave that was imagined in two ways by the Israelites: 1) as a place of eternal unconscious sleep, or 2) as a place of limited consciousness. You can see these ideas illustrated in various ways through different verses.*

---

* You might be wondering: what about the idea of resurrection? Well, that concept, as far as biblical scholars can tell, did not arise until the time of Daniel's prophecies (12:1–3) after the Exile occurred in Babylon, and only became widespread and popular close to the time of Jesus. Other parts of the Hebrew Bible refer to the concept of resurrection, but either apply it symbolically to the nation (and not individuals) or actually deny that it is possible. For example, take Job's dismal sadness when he reports that "mortals die, and are laid low; humans expire, and where are they? As waters fail from a lake, and a river wastes away and dries up, so mortals lie down and do not rise again; until the heavens are no more, they will not awake or be roused out of their sleep" (14:10–12).

The first option can be seen witnessed to in Ecclesiastes where it is written that "the dead know nothing; they have no more reward, and even the memory of them is lost. Their love and their hate and their envy have already perished; never again will they have any share in all that happens under the sun" (9:5–6). Furthermore, "there is no work or thought or knowledge or wisdom in Sheol" (9:10). Why? Because "the dust returns to the earth as it was, and the spirit returns to God who gave it" (12:7). This seems to be the sense of Psalm 115:17 when it affirms that "the dead do not praise the Lord, nor do any that go down into silence." Or take David's statement about his dead son: "But now he is dead; why should I fast? Can I bring him back again? I shall go to him, but he will not return to me."

Other places in the Hebrew Bible that are related to this view are more vague, such as Gen. 25:8 referring to Abraham being "gathered to his people" at his death. Dan. 12:2 describes the dead as "those who sleep in the dust." Job's description of Sheol perhaps helps to explain this view best:

> I would be lying down and quiet; I would be asleep; then I would be at rest with kings and counselors of the earth... There the wicked cease from troubling, and there the weary are at rest. There the prisoners are at ease together; they do not hear the voice of the taskmaster. The small and the great are there, and the slaves are free from their masters.
>
> (Job 3:13–14, 17–19)

Yet, not everyone shared that view. In Isa. 14:9–11, Sheol is imagined to have "spirits of the dead" who greet the wicked with "excitement." And most famously, in 1 Sam. 28:3–25, one writer imagines that it is possible for the spirit of a dead prophet to be aroused from his gloomy shadow existence. The ghost of Samuel even complains, "Why have you disturbed me by bringing me up?" (28:15). In Psalm

88:10–12, the poet imagines that there is some sort of afterlife existence, but nothing like we would imagine. The dead (righteous and wicked) become "shades" who live "in the darkness," do not remember God anymore, and who no longer hear or hope for God's "steadfast love." Clearly, even these Israelites lacked not only a doctrine of Hell, but even one of Heaven.

Some writers spoke poetically of more hopeful pictures. For instance, Jonah counters the Psalmist by claiming that "I cried for help from the depth of Sheol" and "you heard my voice" (Jonah 2:2). Although Jonah wasn't really dead or in Sheol, he's poetically saying that God can save anyone, even potentially those already dead (or considered as such). Similarly, Psalm 139:7 states that there is nowhere God isn't, for "if I ascend to heaven, you are there; if I make my bed in Sheol, you are there."

Clearly, the writers of the Bible did not share one agreed upon and universal portrait of what happened after death. However, what they all agreed on was that there was no punishment, no fire, and no pain for either the wicked or the righteous. The idea of a Hell was completely foreign to the Hebrew Bible.

The idea of torments in the afterlife appears to have come during the influence of Greek Hellenism. The Greeks had developed the idea of *Hades* and in the underworld of *Hades*, there was indeed eternal suffering. This idea first pops up around the third century or so BCE in Judea, beginning its development in the book of *1 Enoch*. From there, it pops up a couple more times in other pseudepigraphic/apocryphal literature. In short, the doctrine first starts raising its head in noncanonical books that later Christians deemed unauthoritative. As far as we know, the beginnings of Hell do not start in a trustworthy and widely accepted source of inspiration.

LOOKING TO JESUS

By the time of the New Testament, the Jews were increasingly divided on these issues.* Some still held to the old views of Sheol. When Jesus repeatedly claims that someone is not dead, but merely sleeping, this is similar to the older view of unconsciousness (Mark 5:35–39; Matt. 9:24; John 11:11; cf. Paul in 1 Thess. 4:15–17). On the other hand, other Jews at this time believed that the Hellenistic teachings of conscious torment were true. You can see this illustrated by the parable Jesus told of the Rich Man and Lazarus (Luke 16:19–31). Jesus himself speaks of "Hell" many times, but far more ambiguously than his contemporaries ever did, a fact all too often missed.

I could keep going with the history lesson, but I think that would be a mistake. Jesus is a perfect place to stop and gain some context. To restate what was just said: the *idea* of an eternally burning Hell is both foreign to the canonical Scriptures that Jesus was familiar with, and was already a debated idea during his lifetime that some Jews held to while others did not. When Jesus commented on Hell, it was never to *introduce* it, but to *comment* on what others already believed about it.

Why is that important? Because Jesus had a habit of working with people's presuppositions. The best example of this can be seen in his interactions with the Sadducees. Jesus knew that the Sadducees only accepted as Scripture the first five books of the Torah (and rejected

---

* When Christianity rose to prominence among Greek Gentile converts, the Hellenistic ideas of eternal torment which were already culturally familiar to them from Greek mythology became increasingly dominant in those churches. An apocryphal work known as the *Apocalypse of Peter* was written around the same time as the book of Revelation. In it, Peter is given a vision of a place called Hell where people are tortured for eternity without mercy. The book proved so popular that it was actually included as Scripture by some early Christians. Ultimately, many of our images of Hell derive from its influence.

the authority of the prophets and writings). As such, whenever the Gospels record Jesus debating the Sadducees, one can notice that Jesus never makes any of his arguments from outside the Torah. He accepts the assumptions that his discussion partners bring and works within their scope of understanding.

This insight opens up a startling question: how do we know that when Jesus discusses Hell, he is describing it as *he* believes it and not merely as *they* believed it? This is an important question. One possible test case for this would be the parable that Jesus gave of the rich man and Lazarus in Luke 16:19–31. In it, Jesus describes a poor man, named Lazarus, who used to sit outside the gates of a rich man's house. He was hungry and longed to be fed, but the rich man ignored him. Then, Lazarus died "and was carried away by the angels" immediately after death to be with Abraham. Then, at a later time, the rich man himself died.

As the rich man is "in Hades, where he was being tormented, he looked up and saw Abraham far away with Lazarus by his side" (16:23). The rich man tells Abraham to order Lazarus to serve him and come and bring him water to cool his tongue, since "I am in agony in these flames" (16:24). Abraham informs the rich man that now their roles are reversed and Lazarus no longer serves him. It ends with Abraham proclaiming that if people will not listen to the Scriptures, they won't believe someone even if they came back from the dead.

Many Evangelicals understand this parable to be a literal and nigh precise account of what the literal eternal burning and endless suffering Hell is like. For them, this is reality, and it is one they want very much to avoid experiencing personally. But is that the correct way to understand this parable? Is Jesus teaching *about* Hell or is he *using* other people's ideas about Hell to teach other important truths? The Gospel of Luke itself says that Jesus told the parable because the Pharisees "were lovers of money" (16:14).

As Ellen White once commented on it:

> In this parable Christ was meeting the people on their own ground... The Saviour knew of their ideas, and He framed His parable so as to inculcate important truths through these preconceived opinions. He held up before His hearers a mirror wherein they might see themselves in their true relation to God. He used the prevailing opinion to convey the idea He wished to make prominent to all–that no man is valued for his possessions; for all he has belongs to him only as lent by the Lord. A misuse of these gifts will place him below the poorest and most afflicted man who loves God and trusts in Him.[4]

According to this understanding, the point of the parable is not what Hell looks like, but how God judges between the rich and the poor. The imagery is merely a tool to carry the message across, whether it's literally true or not. And honestly, that makes sense. Another parable told by Jesus in Matt. 25:31–32 which describes sheep and goats being carried by angels to a throne for judgment is not usually taken to be a visually accurate description of the final judgment. It is understood to be a parable, and as a parable, more truthful in its central message than its imagery.

Another way to think about this is to ask: would Jesus have told this parable the same way if he were speaking to the Sadducees instead of the Pharisees? The Sadducees didn't believe in any afterlife. If Jesus was willing to not quote scriptures that the Sadducees didn't believe in, wouldn't it make sense that he would also not tell parables to them about things they didn't believe in? And if that's the case, that Jesus would not have told this parable about Lazarus to the Sadducees, because these images were not relatable to them, does that once again point to the idea that Jesus is merely reflecting the views of those around him rather than confirming supernatural realities?

This idea shouldn't be shocking to anybody. It's also true that this same phenomenon appears in the Hebrew Bible. For example, in the book of Job, God actually claims outright, in speech, that other foreign gods do exist. While describing the mythical sea monster Leviathan, God proclaims to Job that "any hope of capturing it will be disappointed; were not even *the gods* overwhelmed at the sight of it?" (41:9). Again, a little later, God again states that "when it raises itself up *the gods* are afraid; at the crushing *they* are beside themselves" (41:25).

Why would God speak to Job of the existence of other gods if they didn't really exist? Because Job wasn't an Israelite, wasn't a monotheist: and lived in a polytheistic land, and ultimately he likely believed that there *were* other gods out there. God hadn't come at the end of the story to try and fix Job's theological understanding of polytheism. He came to tackle other, bigger issues, but along the way, God utilized Job's mistaken beliefs in order to make larger points about more important truths.

What Jesus did in the Parable of the Rich Man and Lazarus is no different. He took prevalent ideas that existed in his time and used them to make larger points about bigger truths. But again, that opens up some important questions: if the only narrative description of Hell by Jesus is potentially not reflective of Jesus' own beliefs, what is? This is made more complicated by the fact that many of the things in the Lazarus Parable are things repeated elsewhere about Hell by Jesus. Does this suggest that much of what Jesus says on this issue is merely parabolic language?

Well, one interesting bit of evidence is the fact that a number of things that Jesus claims about Hell contradict other things he claims about it. For example, in several places Jesus describes Hell as a bright blazing fire (Mark 9:43,48; Matt. 3:12; 5:22; 13:41–42,50; 18:8–9; 25:41; Luke 16:24), *but elsewhere* describes it as outer darkness (Matt. 8:12; 22:11–13; 25:30; cf. 2 Peter 2:4,17 which describes it as "gloomy" and "utter" darkness). Jesus never mixes these metaphors together and so appears to demonstrate that these are mutually exclusive categories: either Hell is bright with flames or it is dark, gloomy and lacking fire.

One possible (and likely) explanation is that Jesus is doing what he does best: using the presuppositions of those he talks to. For example, within *1 Enoch*, the "Book of Watchers" describes the wicked dead existing in pits of darkness where some are tortured and others are left to rot in the darkness forever (*1 En.* 22:1–2, 10). Contrary to the fate of humans, only the angels are said to be burned with fire (*1 En.* 21:7, 10). We have reason to believe that at the time of Jesus, the Essenes (and likely others) appeared to believe *1 Enoch* was Scripture and would have imagined Hell in this way. Is it hard to imagine that Jesus may have been appealing to people who held this view when he spoke of Hell in terms of darkness, rather than fire?

Jesus spoke with many different Jews from different backgrounds, each with their own ideas, unique scriptures, and cultural backgrounds from which they would draw their images of Hell. The fact that Jesus' descriptions of Hell contradict each other points to the idea that perhaps his statements are conditioned by *who* he was speaking to. And recognizing this means that Jesus' words cannot simply be repeated without taking this into account.

It is interesting to note that Jesus barely speaks of Hell in either Mark or Luke, and not once in John! People often claim that Jesus spoke more about Hell than Heaven, but that's only true in the Gospel of Matthew. Given what we've seen, that tells us two things: that Matthew purposefully emphasized Hell because he believed that language spoke to his community's faith, and that Mark, Luke, and John largely avoided references to Hell because their communities didn't connect best with those images. In either case, three out of the four Gospels did not believe Hell was as important as modern

Evangelicals do. Matthew's *choice* to emphasize Hell should not be taken as a requirement for us to do the same.

How important can Jesus' audience be? This is another great question. Would those who heard Jesus describe Hell have understood him differently depending on what they already believed about Hell? The answer is yes. For example, in many places Jesus claims that those in Hell will be "weeping and gnashing their teeth." In some places, it describes this as happening in a bright fiery furnace of destruction (Matt. 8:12; 13:42; 50; 24:51), and in others Jesus describes it as occurring in the outer darkness (Matt. 8:12; 22:13; 25:30; cf. Luke 13:28).

Obviously, if you were one of the Jews who imagined a fiery Hades underworld, then the "gnashing" would be understood to be due to the severe pain of suffering. However, if you were someone who had *1 Enoch*'s vision of Hell, with pits of darkness, you would imagine that the wicked weren't gnashing their teeth in pain, but in anger and vengeance! That may not sound plausible at first glance until you realize *what* gnashing of teeth means in the Bible. The Greek word βρυγμός *(brugmos)* is used in the Greek translation of the Bible (the Septuagint) in two places: Prov. 19:9 and Sirach 51:3. In both places, the term refers to the wicked as they plot evil on the righteous. The "gnashing" is a metaphor for how they are like a lion which is enraged and seeks prey.

And honestly, it makes sense. The vision of darkness in *1 Enoch* paints a portrait of wicked people *awaiting* their judgment. Thus, Jesus' description of "gnashing" hints that they cry and get angry because they have mixed feelings about their coming trial. This is likely the inspiration for Revelation's description of Satan rousing the wicked for battle against God at the end of time. They have been gnashing their teeth for centuries!

The point is that depending on what sort of Jew you were, you would have a different vision of Hell, even when hearing Jesus say the exact same things. This is likely why Jesus switches between the different images, because of the different sorts of Jewish groups he is speaking to. In fact, only once does Jesus reference gnashing of teeth without an image to go with it. Might we potentially assume that this indicates that when he spoke on that occasion, several different Jewish groups were present and he was willing to allow each to imagine what they wanted (Matt. 24:51)? What we see again is further evidence of Jesus utilizing the beliefs of his audience for the sake of teaching.

Moreover, is the language employed about Hell even used literally or consistently to begin with? In Jesus' parable of the rich man and Lazarus, he describes a situation in which the righteous and wicked on either side of the divide can walk freely, but according to 2 Peter 2:4, Tartarus (another name for Hell) is a place of chains and immobility. Perhaps strangest, how can Jude claim that Sodom and Gomorrah's destruction is an example of "a punishment of eternal fire" (1:7)? Sodom stopped burning many centuries before Jude wrote. All of this suggests that the language many take as literal today may have been understood as something far more metaphorical.

So again, I mention what I brought up before: could much of what Jesus says reflect more on how his audience thought rather than what he believed himself? I'll let that question sit with you. The next time you're reading a "proof text" for the eternal torment of Hell, supposedly derived from the lips of the nonviolent Jesus, ask yourself whether you can be sure Jesus is teaching a theological truism or echoing contemporary theological speculations from those listening to him?

MISTAKING SATAN FOR GOD

So, where does that lead us? Most Evangelical authors approach this topic by first amassing as much evidence as they can to support the doctrine. Others attempt to poke as many holes as they can in such evidence. Neither approach solves anything. As it is, this chapter is already too long and there is no way to undertake an exhaustive study here of every facet of this topic. As such, let's tackle the underlying issues first. The biggest and most important question of which is this: how does the doctrine of Hell affect our view of God?

Ellen White stood firm on the denial of Hell primarily due to her experiences with its horrifying effects on human psychology and mental health. When she was a young child, growing up toward the end of the Second Great Awakening in the 1830s, she became terrified of the idea that God might burn her alive for all eternity.

> In my mind the justice of God eclipsed His mercy and love. I had been taught to believe in an eternally burning Hell, and the horrifying thought was ever before me that my sins were too great to be forgiven, and that I should be forever lost. The frightful descriptions that I had heard of souls in perdition sank deep into my mind. Ministers in the pulpit drew vivid pictures of the condition of the lost… While listening to these terrible descriptions, my imagination would be so wrought upon that the perspiration would start, and it was difficult to suppress a cry of anguish, for I seemed to already feel the pains of perdition… Our heavenly Father was presented before my mind as a tyrant, who delighted in the agonies of the condemned… the thought took possession of my mind that God delighted in the torture of His creatures, who were formed in His image… When I reflected that the Creator of the universe would plunge the wicked into Hell, there to burn through the ceaseless rounds of eternity, my heart sank with fear, and I despaired that so cruel and tyrannical a being would ever condescend to save me from the doom of sin… I would look upon the dumb beasts with envy, because they had no soul to be punished after death. Many times the wish arose that I had never been born… I have since thought that many inmates of insane asylums were brought there by experiences similar to my own… My sufferings of mind were intense. Sometimes for a whole night I would not dare to close my eyes, but would wait until my twin sister was fast asleep, then quietly leave my bed and kneel upon the floor, praying silently with a dumb agony that cannot be described. The horrors of an eternally burning

Hell were ever before me. I knew that it was impossible for me to live long in this state, and I dared not die and meet the terrible fate of the sinner.[5]

Remember, this is the experience of *a child* who was not yet ten years of age. It is no small truth when some atheists claim that religious doctrines in Christianity can easily become child abuse. So how did young Ellen find peace? Ultimately, by trusting Jesus as the true depiction of who God was. Seeing Jesus as a friend and not a judge is what won the little Ellen's heart back to God. But in the short term, it was a conversation with her mother that helped her to cross the divide from fear to love.

When Ellen later learned that her mother no longer believed in an eternal Hell, she was shocked. "If you believe this strange theory," she remembered telling her with a child's sincerity, "do not let anyone know of it; for I fear that sinners would gather security from this belief, and never desire to seek the Lord." Her mother's reply?

> Instead of preventing the salvation of sinners, it will be the means of winning them to Christ. If the love of God will not induce the rebel to yield, the terrors of an eternal Hell will not drive him to repentance. Besides, it does not seem a proper way to win souls to Jesus by appealing to one of the lowest attributes of the mind—abject fear. The love of Jesus attracts; it will subdue the hardest heart."[6]

Can it really be that simple? Can the love of Jesus be all that is needed? Ellen, in her later theological writings, focuses the issue of Hell on a different question: how do we understand God? Her youthful anxiety, shared by many today, centered on her understanding of God, and more specifically, his character. Was Jesus and all his loving grace the image of God's character, or was it instead something far more frightening as revealed by the fires of Hell?

For White then, the true evil of the doctrine of Hell, what drove her to fight it tooth and nail, is what it does to our understanding of who

God is. The terrible price this doctrine enacts on those who believe it is what it does to mar the character of Jesus. It is by Hell's presumed fires in our frightened imaginations that Jesus becomes morphed into Satan himself. The devil and God become one and the same.

> Thus the arch-fiend clothes with his own attributes the Creator and Benefactor of mankind. Cruelty is Satanic. God is love… Satan and his emissaries represent God as even worse than themselves… The great deceiver endeavors to shift his own horrible cruelty of character upon our heavenly Father… How repugnant to every emotion of love and mercy, and even to our sense of justice, is the doctrine that the wicked dead are tormented with fire and brimstone in an eternally burning Hell; that for the sins of a brief, earthly life they are to suffer torture as long as God shall live.[7]

That's the problem. God becomes a moral monster far worse than even the worst violent depictions contained in the Hebrew Bible. God and Satan blend together in ways that are unthinkable and, to be frank, truly blasphemous. Benjamin Corey in his recent book *Unafraid*, brilliantly opens with a modern analogy that shook me to my core when I first read it:

> On January 3, 2015, the Islamic State of Iraq and Syria (ISIS) posted one of its trademark execution videos online. ISIS fighters executed Muath al-Kasasbeh, a Jordanian pilot… [they] doused him with flammable liquid, set him on fire, and filmed his grisly death… As I watched my fellow Christians express outrage and disgust over his burning in this life, I kept thinking to myself, "You guys—you realize that you believe God is going to do this to the vast majority of people who have ever lived, *don't you?*" Think about that for a minute: if the theology of salvation and Hell that so many of us grew up with is true, the moment that Muslim pilot succumbed to the flames and died, he immediately went to a place where the flames and torture started *all over again*. According to the traditional hellfire theology, al-Kasasbeh went from twenty-two minutes of burning alive to an e-freaking-ternity of burning alive—with *no hope of even death to stop the torment*. Essentially, to affirm the hellfire theology of my youth, a

person would say that what God did to al-Kasasbeh after death is *far worse and less unmerciful than what ISIS did to him*. If the traditional theology of Hell is correct, God is like an ISIS terrorist—but like one on steroids. If it is depraved and disgusting when ISIS does it, why is it good and just when God does it? Are we really okay with a vision of God that makes him look like an ISIS terrorist who burns his enemies alive?[8]

But some might object to these analogies and arguments. Hell, some would argue, is merely a byproduct of our own sins. It reflects on our evils, but does not reveal God as somehow connected to them. However, this way of thinking about Hell is actually logically incoherent. Jeff Turner, in his recent tour-de-force *The Atheistic Theist*, best describes the true logic of the ultimate horror that is Hell:

> Now, not only must God play an active part in the torments of Hell, he must actually be the source of all of it. Hell, after all, whatever it actually is, could not have spontaneously generated out of thin air when we are dealing in a worldview where God is creator. This means that whatever you believe about Hell must also be, on some level, what you believe about God. You simply cannot separate the two. If Hell *really* is what many Christians would like us to believe it is, then it isn't just "Hell" that is horrifying, but God himself, for he created it, and anything created has to somehow reflect on the character of the creator. Some might argue that there are a great many evils in the world that do not originate in God, and so call my point moot... but Hell is never touted as being a product of "the fall" in modern Christianity, only as a place for things fallen. Hell, though, if it is to represent God's perfect justice and righteous anger towards sin, must be untouched by corruption, and therefore a perfect picture of his nature. So, again, whatever one believes about Hell, they also believe about God. There is simply no way around this.[9]

And yet, none of this matches the character of the God revealed in Scripture. None of it comes close to the image of God revealed within the incarnate Word, Jesus of Nazareth. How are we to match what

Jesus claimed to show us about God with what the doctrine of Hell claims to reveal?

In many ways, the issue at the heart of a discussion of Hell is the same issue that we have previously faced with our understanding of God's role in the violence recorded in Scripture. We are faced with rival portraits of God in Scripture and must struggle to sift through them. Turner, again, best gets to the heart of the matter when he points out that:

> If you're like most decent human beings, the thought of applauding the sight of billions of souls in torment makes you recoil in disgust, but if you cannot say that Hell is good, and if you cannot applaud the things said to be happening within it, are you *really* convinced that *God* is good? ... Think about it. When you raise your hands on Sunday mornings, and sing words like, "How Great is Our God," or, "You Are Beautiful in All of Your Ways," is it Hell that you picture?

So, what gives? Given the size of this chapter, an exhaustive examination of the doctrine is not possible. This isn't the book to turn over every stone. However, a limited search might be possible. And in my opinion, the best place to look for answers would be the book that most people believe best describes Hell: the book of Revelation.

THE OPEN POSSIBILITY

In Revelation 14, three angels declare woes and warnings on humanity. The third angel's message is directed to "those who worship the beast and its image, and receive a mark on their foreheads or on their hands" (14:9). It declares that as punishment, "they will be tormented with fire and sulfur in the presence of the holy angels and in the presence of the Lamb" (vs. 10). Most take this as a description of the future Lake of Fire. But is it? Take a close look at how it describes this torment.

> And the smoke of their torment goes up forever and ever. There is no rest day or night for those *who worship* the beast and its image and for anyone *who receives* the mark of its name.
>
> (REVELATION 14:11)

Did you notice something important? Their torment is described in the *present* tense. The torment spoken of here by the angel refers to their present lives, not their future fates. They suffer not in some future afterlife, but in the very midst of their living worship! Likewise, notice that it is the smoke generated from their torment that goes up "forever and ever," but not actually their torture itself. "There is no rest day or night" for them, but that only applies to those who live under the light of the sun and moon. Moreover, this torture is said to occur as soon as they receive the mark and worship the beast, demonstrating that this supposed text about a future otherworldly hellish torment is actually describing an earthly reality.

But doesn't Revelation also have terrible visions of violence and bloodshed that occur, aside from this text? Does not this same book describe Jesus slaughtering the Beast?

> Then I saw an angel standing in the sun, and with a loud voice he called to all the birds that fly in midheaven, "Come, gather for the great supper of God, to eat the flesh of kings, the flesh of captains, the flesh of the mighty, the flesh of horses and their riders—flesh of all, both free and slave, both small and great." Then I saw the beast and the kings of the earth with their armies gathered to make war against the rider on the horse and against his army. And the beast was captured, and with it the false prophet who had performed in its presence the signs by which he deceived those who had received the mark of the beast and those who worshiped its image. These two were thrown alive into the lake of fire that burns with sulfur. And the rest were killed by the sword of the rider on the horse, the sword that came from his mouth; and all the birds were gorged with their flesh.
>
> (REVELATION 19:17-21)

At first glance, this appears to be a literal description of a terrifying moment in the future judgment of the earth. And yet, notice that this all happens because of "the rider on the horse" and "the sword that came from his mouth." So then, what is this sword? Earlier in vs. 11, John reports that "I saw heaven opened, and there was a white horse," and "its rider is called Faithful and True, and in righteousness he judges and makes war." Then, a few verses later, John reports the following:

> He is clothed in a robe dipped in blood, and his name is called The Word of God. And the armies of heaven, wearing fine linen, white and pure, were following him on white horses. From his mouth comes a sharp sword with which to strike down the nations…
> (REVELATION 19:13–15)

The rider on the white horse is Jesus Christ, clothed with the blood of his nonviolent sacrifice on behalf of the very people he faces. The sword comes from his mouth, a symbolic way of stating that he conquers not with actual physical swords, but with the power of the Word of God! With that in mind, how should we understand the description a few verses later that "the rest were killed by the sword of the rider on the horse, the sword that came from his mouth" (19:21)? Well, to begin with, we might notice that John actually specifies that the sword he is speaking of is the same one he mentioned previously. Why though? Because the sword from the Word of God's mouth is not the same as any other sword. This is a sword that is symbolic. But, if the sword is symbolic and not literal, what does it mean to say that he "killed" the wicked with it?

However, there's an even bigger mystery to point out: none of them were said to be thrown into "the lake of fire." Only the Beast and False Prophet were thrown into that sulfuric lake. Humans weren't. Keep that in mind as we turn to look at the end of Revelation's story. According to Rev. 20:7–8, after Satan is released from his prison at the end of a thousand years, he gathers the nations of the earth "to gather them for battle."

> They marched up over the breadth of the earth and surrounded the camp of the saints and the beloved city. And fire came down from heaven and consumed them. And the devil who had deceived them was thrown into the lake of fire and sulfur, where the beast and the false prophet were, and they will be tormented day and night forever and ever.
>
> (REVELATION 20:9-10)

Unlike in Rev. 19, where the wicked are merely killed, here they are burned up or "consumed" by fire. However, is this similar to the symbolic sword as well? Keep that thought in mind as we point out one unique aspect of this text that is routinely missed: these people are "consumed," not burned forever and ever. They are killed, permanently. Only "the devil who had deceived them was thrown into the lake of fire and sulfur." Only he, the beast, and the false prophet are said to be "tormented day and night forever and ever," but *not* human beings.

Ignoring this for the time being though, we can notice that in the following verse, God raises all the dead (including the wicked that were earlier killed). John reports that "the sea gave up the dead that were in it, Death and Hades gave up the dead that were in them, and all were judged according to what they had done." Why would they need to be judged if they were already in Hell suffering for their crimes? Yet that is hardly the most confusing aspect of this vision. For in the very next verse we are told the most striking and odd thing.

> Then Death and Hades were thrown into the lake of fire. This is the second death, the lake of fire; and anyone whose name was not found written in the book of life was thrown into the lake of fire.
>
> (REVELATION 20:14-15)

According to John, up until this point only three people had actually entered the Lake of Fire (i.e. Hell): the Beast, the false prophet, and Satan himself. Now, as the righteous and the wicked are both judged, God throws Death and Hades into the fire too. Think about that for a moment. God is said to throw *Hades* into the lake of fire. Do you remember *Hades*? It's the Greek word for *Hell*. It's the word that Jesus often uses when referring to Hell. And here, at the end of John's Apocalypse, we are told that God is going to throw *Hell* into *Hell* to destroy *Hell*.

The significance of this should not be missed. By throwing Hell into the Lake of Fire, God is punishing Hell. God is sentencing Hell to the same destruction that Satan and the Beast deserved. By punishing Hell, God reveals in the book of Revelation that Hell, like Satan, is evil and condemned by God as opposite of holiness. Hell does not reveal God any more than Satan does and it is destined for God's destruction.

Not only that, but God is said to throw death itself into the Lake of Fire, along with Hell. God is going to punish and torment death itself. In short, by throwing death and Hell into the Lake of Fire, it's a very creative way of saying that God has finally fulfilled his promise in the Bible to destroy death forever (Isa. 25:8). But in order to destroy death, God must destroy Hell as well. And yet, need I repeat myself: according to John, there are only three people inside of Hell when God destroys it!

Now then, what does it mean when it says that "anyone whose name was not found written in the book of life was thrown into the lake of fire"? Well, that's tough to say, precisely because the text doesn't tell us! Although John informs us that the penalty for not being found in the book of life is the lake of fire, he never tells us that any human beings ever end up there! Not once does he confirm that a single human gets thrown in.

Instead, the next verse informs us that he saw "a new heaven and a new earth" replacing the old. As he explores what the New Jerusalem city looks like, he gives a description that should knock us off our feet, but almost all Christian readers routinely miss.

> *The nations* will walk by its light, and *the kings of the earth* will bring their glory into it. Its gates will never be shut by day—and there will be no night there. People will bring into it *the glory and the honor of the nations.*
> (REVELATION 21:24–26)

Do you recognize something odd about that description? There are two characters/groups mentioned that shouldn't be there. The first is "the nations," whom John told us accepted the mark of the Beast and all attacked the heavenly city. Remember? Fire fell from the sky and "consumed" them all. How in the world are they *now* entering the New Jerusalem and giving it *their glory*?

The second group that shouldn't seemingly be there are "the kings of the earth." In chapter 18, we were told that all "the kings of the earth" accepted the mark of the Beast and followed it (18:3). We were told by John that "the kings of the earth, who committed fornication and lived in luxury with her, will weep and wail over her when they see the smoke of her burning; they will stand far off, in fear of her torment" (18:9). In chapter 19, in the same place where it described "the nations" as attacking the heavenly city, so too did it mention that "the kings of the earth… gathered to make war against" Jesus (19:19). They were subsequently killed. So how in the world, like "the nations," have these kings suddenly come to be allowed into the New Jerusalem, and why and how are they able to "bring their glory into it"?

Part of the answer might be related to what was said in Rev. 21:2, when John reports that on either side of "the river of the water of life," there is "the tree of life… and the leaves of the tree are for *the healing of the nations.*" To remind ourselves, the tree of life is the tree from the Garden of Eden that gives immortality. It is the tree Adam and Eve were barred from because they sinned. And yet, here we read that God has provided the tree of life for *the nations*. And not only for the nations, but for *their* healing! Healing from what? The sins that they committed two chapters earlier when they fought Jesus? But if they were completely destroyed then, how are they here now? How can these nations now be eating from the fruit of the tree of life?

This is the great mystery of Revelation that so few take the time to think about. John certainly never explains this, but he does leave us hints. Does Rev. 19:15 and its description of the Word of God destroying God's enemies with a sword from his mouth point us toward a symbolic understanding of the final judgment? Does Rev. 20:14 and its description of God throwing *Hell into Hell* point us toward an answer? How can God destroy both death and Hell together, prior to judging everyone? Even if someone was found guilty, how could God judge them if he has already destroyed death itself (the punishment for sin) and Hell itself (the place of punishment)?

And ultimately, does John's silence on whether any human gets thrown into the lake of fire after the judgment point to a quite hopeful possibility? I can't help but echo my friend Keith Giles when he remarks about this passage:

> But, I would ask you to notice that it does not tell us that there *were* any whose names were not found in the book of life, nor do we see any such people being cast into the lake of fire during or after this great white throne judgment. In other words: This is an "if/then" statement, but beyond this we are not told, or shown, whether are any who meet the "if" side of the statement. Maybe you would say that this is simply me splitting hairs, but I would suggest to you that we are given such a hair and we are being invited to split it, based on the way this passage is written. If the author had wanted there to be no wiggle room, then I submit that none would have been offered. Yet, I would argue, we are handed at least a small amount of wiggle

room here, and I would gladly accept it as a measure of God's grace, no matter how small.[10]

Now, do not misunderstand what I am saying. I am not necessarily advocating Universal Salvation. I have friends who do and they know my reservations about such a doctrine. I am a strong advocate of free will, so I'm never comfortable imagining God denying Hitler his ability to ultimately reject God to the bitter end. Some of course have asked me sincerely: "Does God not desire everyone's salvation? Does God not get what God wants?" The best answer to this I know can be found by Rob Bell:

> It's not "Does God get what God wants?" but "Do we get what we want?" And the answer to that is a resounding, affirming, sure, and positive yes. Yes, we get what we want. God is that loving. If we want isolation, despair, and the right to be our own god, God graciously grants us that option… If we want hell, if we want heaven, they are ours. That's how love works. It can't be forced, manipulated, or coerced. It always leaves room for the other to decide. God says yes, we can have what we want, because love wins.[11]

So, to be clear, I am not making the claim that everyone *will be* or *must be* saved in the end. That would be quite arrogant of me since I clearly don't know the future. Only God knows what will come. I am, however, like every Christian should be if they have the heart of Christ, suggesting a *hopeful* disposition toward such an idea. John appears to be suggesting in several places within his vision that grace may be more powerful than the claim death holds on sin. A wise friend and professor of mine called this "the Open Possibility." But the possibility is undefined (and likely dependent on each individual's own choice) and so I would remind anyone that we should be cautious about asserting too much about it.

While that is clearly a discussion all on its own, this is not the place for it. The point is that, regardless of what God may do at the judgment, the book of Revelation is clear on several things: that those who worship the Beast already suffer torments in *this* life, that Hell cannot be an eternal place because it will be destroyed along with death at the judgment, that the only individuals claimed by John to be burning forever are the unholy trinity, and that lastly, even some of the leaders of the world who accepted the mark of the Beast will apparently be forgiven after the final judgment and the New Jerusalem's own glory will derive from their new salvation!

REJECTING HELL

That's a lot to take in and it's quite stunning. But for the purpose of this chapter, the greatest takeaway is perhaps this: Revelation does not imagine that the dead are burning *currently* in Hell and it doesn't imagine that Hell itself will exist after the final judgment. In my own denomination, we've historically believed in a doctrine called *annihilationism*. It basically teaches that when God judges the wicked and condemns them to death, they cease to exist. No torture. No further punishment. Just peace, for all. Instead of Hitler screaming in pain for all eternity, he is finally and forever silenced in an eternal punishment. Surprisingly, Pope Francis has, according to reports, privately expressed his own beliefs about the same thing, which has, unsurprisingly, caused shock for the Vatican and other Catholics. In a private interview conducted in 2018, Pope Francis reportedly said:

> They [who die as sinners] are not punished. Those who repent obtain God's forgiveness and take their place among the ranks of those who contemplate him, but those who do not repent and cannot be forgiven disappear. A Hell doesn't exist, the disappearance of sinning souls exists.[12]

And years before in 2015, Francis was reported to have said to the same reporter that (paraphrased):

There is no punishment [for the sinner], but the annihilation of that soul. All the others will participate in the bliss of living in the presence of the Father. The annihilated souls will not be part of that banquet; with the death of the body their journey is ended.[13]

However, as one could expect, such a teaching does not fit well with the age-old doctrines of the Catholic Church which teach of an eternal Hell. As such, the Vatican has consistently denied that the reports are accurate. However, the repeated choice of Pope Francis to continue to be interviewed by the same individual appears to undercut the claims of the Vatican. Rather, it appears possible that the current Pope holds views that he wants known, but which he is not allowed to utter publicly in any official capacity. Regardless of the internal politics at Vatican City, the point is that even the Pope currently struggles to see an eternal Hell as congruent with God's love.

It seems clear that John in Revelation has something closer in mind to *annihilationism*, if not the possibility of *reconciliation*, rather than the popular idea of an eternally burning place of torment. Whatever God is going to do, it will be merciful and not reminiscent of the Nazi gas chambers. God's future judgment will be in accordance with his Son who is the very embodiment of selfless love.

So then, we are left with only one option: *we must say no to Hell.* If the book that literally gave us the image of the lake of fire, a work said to come from a vision of Jesus himself, promises that Christ is going to destroy Hell, I can rest assured that I should join him in his future effort by saying no to any doctrine that teaches Hell as part of God's plan. No, I proudly proclaim, the very idea of Hell itself is the enemy of God, just like death, and no Christian should find themselves supporting it. If the devil is indeed "a liar and the father of all lies" (John 8:44), then Hell and its monstrous portrait of Jesus, the slain lamb of Revelation, is one of the greatest deceptions he has convinced Christianity of. It is time to reject this satanic lie, and instead proclaim the love of Christ crucified.

As Jeff Turner ends his own discussion on the topic:

> If deep down you know better, don't you think maybe God does too? If deep down you feel a burning desire to separate God from such an evil concept, maybe God burns to be separated from it as well?... Perhaps, instead of taking hell seriously and then trying to figure Jesus into, [or] out of, the equation, we should start by taking Jesus seriously, and seeing if traditional concepts of hell have any place in a world over which he is Lord.[14]

That seems like a healthy and right approach to take. And perhaps, if we can put our seemingly favorite self-destructive heresy down for even a little while, we might begin to see Christ's loving gaze on the cross, rather than our supposed fear of his retribution. Perhaps we will begin to see many things differently when the God we turn to looks less like Satan and more like Jesus.

15

SAYING NO TO EXCLUSIVITY

"I am the good shepherd. I know my own and my own know me... I have other sheep that are not of this fold."

JESUS[1]

There are around fifteen million Christians in America and twenty-five million worldwide who identify as Evangelical. Among the many widespread beliefs such Christians hold to is one that has in particular caused unnecessary pain and division both in and outside the church. What is this harmful doctrine? It is the teaching that being a Christian is the only way to find salvation, or in other words, to get to heaven.

The idea that Christianity is an exclusive religion, barring all other paths but its own to the pearly gates, is not new. Until recent times, the Catholic Church had previously held and maintained this view. At one time, it even extended this idea to state emphatically that Protestant Christians who had left the Catholic fold had also forfeited salvation, since they argued that salvation is found only in the *true* Christian church, which of course, they argued they were.

This thinking, now spread by sincere Evangelical believers across the world, leads to some very bad theology. Inevitably, if someone comes to the conclusion that a person can only be saved if they are Christian, they come to believe that everyone who dies without accepting Jesus is lost, or to use their own language, "burning in the fires of Hell."

FINDING THE WAY

Yet this idea is not foreign to the Bible. Many who espouse it do so by looking at certain biblical texts that seem to suggest that salvation is a narrow path. Or at least, those texts are used in such a way so as to suggest that idea. One of these, likely the most famous, is from the Gospel of John.

> Jesus said to him, "I am the way, and the truth, and the life. No one comes to the Father except through me."
>
> (JOHN 14:6)

This is the most quoted and referenced verse on salvation. The argument that is typically given from it is this: if Jesus says that no one can come to the Father (God) except through him (Jesus), then no other religion can find salvation since only Christianity worships Jesus.

I still remember a famous video from Oprah's cable show back in the 90s when she expressed her belief that people other than Christians would be saved. She received the same reaction that many still do from certain Evangelicals: she was quoted this text from John and told that she was calling Jesus a liar.

The logic sounds simple enough, yet perhaps it's *too simple*. Maybe because, if you poke at it, you'll notice that it's missing something crucial. So, allow me to suggest an alternative proposal for this text's meaning, one that appears to make better sense of both Jesus and the context of John's Gospel.

First of all, there are many texts and stories from the Bible that all appear to *strongly* indicate that God is in favor of salvation for all people, regardless of religious affiliation. While a couple of these will be explored in this section, there are countless others which for the sake of space cannot be explored here. While it's certainly possible that John didn't believe the same as other writers of the Bible and reflected that belief in how he told his Gospel, I'm not convinced that's true in this case.

So how else could we understand this enigmatic text from John's Gospel? How, other than an *exclusive salvation* model, could we read it? Well, surprisingly, it's not that difficult. John's Gospel, unlike the three Synoptic Gospels, portrays Jesus not simply as the Messiah, but as literally God incarnate. This is an important point. He's not the great *man* of Mark, the inspired *teacher* of Matthew, or the great *prophet* of Luke, but rather he's *God himself* in John, the last of the Gospels to be written.

So let's read that text again and really think about it in the context of John. Jesus (who is God) says that no one can come to God (Jesus) except by coming through Jesus (who is God). In other words: you can only come to Jesus through Jesus, or put the other way, *you can only come to God through God.* That sounds a bit redundant, no? Yet we must keep in mind that for John, the Son and the Father are both separate and yet one. So then, if we remember that the Jews believed in the resurrection of the dead, perhaps we can finally discover the missing key.

If Jesus is God, the logic given by John's Gospel is that *when* everyone is resurrected at the Day of Judgment, righteous and wicked alike (Rom. 5:12–21), those who are resurrected, no matter their beliefs or religious convictions prior, will ultimately only see Jesus, because after all, Jesus is God and God is the only one who will resurrect the dead.

Doesn't that make sense? Of course you can't get to God without Jesus, because Jesus is God! The statement has nothing to do with who *receives* salvation, only about who is *the one giving it*. The statement by Jesus is not intending to speak about salvation but rather to, like his other I AM statements, describe his divinity and relationship to God. In the end then, instead of limiting salvation, it isn't even talking about it. It's simply describing Jesus as the final judge of humanity. In short, it's all about Jesus, which is, after all, what *we* are supposed to be all about.

SALVATION BY CONFESSION?

A similar issue can be found in Paul's letter to the Romans, where he makes a statement that some confidently assert limits salvation only to those who are confessing Christians.

> If you confess with your lips that Jesus is LORD and believe in your heart that God raised him from the dead, you will be saved.
> (ROMANS 10:9)

This verse is often drawn upon by Evangelicals and hardline conservatives to argue that Christians are the only ones who confess Jesus and as such, will ultimately be saved. Yet, this is not what the verse actually says and in context, it doesn't even make sense to interpret it in that light.

To begin with, Paul does not state that the way to be saved is to confess. Rather, he says that those who *do* confess will be saved.

There's a big difference in the nuance of those two statements. Paul simply says that those who confess Jesus can rest assured of their salvation, but it does *not* state the reverse, that if you *do not* confess or believe in Jesus then that means you will not be saved. To read that latter meaning into this verse, as some fundamentalist interpreters do, stretches the meaning and as we will see throughout the rest of this chapter, would contradict other parts of Scripture.

Second, in context, this hardline conservative interpretation would make no sense. In the context of chapter 10 of Romans, Paul is discussing Christians. He's not discussing the larger world, only the church. Particularly, he's giving attention to the issue of some early Jewish Christians who were arguing that the law needed to be observed (including circumcision) in order to be saved. Paul argues back with them that the confession of Jesus is enough to save anyone, apart from the law.

Paul is having a discussion about Christians, within the church, with other Christians. He's not even considering those on the outside. He's discussing the merits of salvation for those who *already* believe. To twist that into something else is not just bad exegesis, it's dishonest. And with that said, we come to Malachi.

AMONG THE NATIONS

It could possibly be one of the most shocking passages in the Bible or your new favorite. Tucked away in a short work of Israel's prophetic history and obscured for hundreds of years in English translations prior to the twentieth century, three short verses hold the potential to change everything for some.

In Mal. 1:10–12, God makes a startling claim, a claim that still has the same "punch" for many that it did well over two thousand years ago. Wishing that the returned Jewish exiles would shut the doors of the newly rebuilt temple, God announces, probably much to the horror of those in Judea, that he "will not accept an offering" from them. No offerings? No sacrifices? No altar? No rams? No lambs? No forgiveness? No thanksgiving? "I have no pleasure in you," he says with a hint of disgust, before speaking the words that would prove arguably more radical than many that had been said prior in the pages of the Hebrew Bible.

> From the rising of the sun to its setting, my name is great among the nations, and in every place incense is offered to my name, and a pure offering; for my name is great among the nations, says the LORD of hosts. But you profane it...
>
> (MALACHI 1:11–12)

God's name, Yahweh, is great among the nations? In every place his name is worshiped? In every place, a pure offering is made in foreign temples that is acceptable to God; offerings are made by foreigners that are, dare we say, holy? His name is great in the pagan nations around Israel, but not in Israel itself? These are some shocking claims, no matter what your previous opinion was on the topic.

Let's unpack this, just in case you didn't quite catch the weight of Malachi's words. God proclaims in these verses that his name is great among the nations. But his name, Yahweh, is unknown outside of Israel. The nations of Egypt, Assyria, Babylonia, and all of the others that surround the Fertile Crescent do not worship Yahweh. Rather, they worship other gods. Their incense and their offerings are not offered to Yahweh, but rather to the gods of Dagon, Marduk, Isis, Ba'al, and an even larger assortment of other smaller and greater pagan deities. So what in the world is God claiming when he says that these nations offer a pure offering to him and Israel doesn't?

God's claim in Malachi is nothing short of revolutionary. He essentially claims that even though Israel's foreign neighbors do not know him by his personal name, Yahweh, and even though they are unaware of his divine will, he accepts their worship, incense, and sacrifices as "pure." When a Canaanite worships the god Ba'al and offers prayers, God announces that he accepts it as if it were directed to him.

Why on earth would God accept and honor the sacrifices and worship of pagan nations? Because, according to the verses that follow, they are *willingly* and *wholeheartedly* giving their sacrifices to their gods out of devotion, unlike the returned Exiles in Judah. God is reportedly upset that the returned Judean exiles and their descendants are no longer serving him with a true heart (Mal. 1:13–14). Instead of offering what is required, such as an unblemished lamb, they are "cheating" him and offering animals that fall short of God's requests and requirements. Essentially, they do not really wish to give their offerings. It is something that they do only because it's required. God is so upset at this, that he wishes and calls upon the Israelites to shut the temple up and worship him no more.

God is saying that he'd rather accept the worship of Egyptians sincerely honoring the god Ra, who clearly do not know him, than accept the lackluster worship of those who know his name yet consider their worship "wearisome." Not only does God say that he would rather accept the Egyptians' worship, he announces that he already is and says he no longer takes pleasure in the Israelite temple. The Greek translation of this passage, the one Jesus would have grown up hearing, is far more damning when it says that "It is not my desire to be among you" (Mal. 1:9). God is, quite literally, disowning his people.

So what gives? How come you haven't heard this passage mentioned before? If you've read through Malachi previously, how come you missed these verses during your past devotions? Well, part of the reason is that some Bible translations purposefully change the text so that it does not say what it actually says.

Yes, conspiracies are sometimes true, but not always as exciting as those that help to fuel books like *The Da Vinci Code*. Granted, it's not much of a conspiracy since no one involved is trying to hide what they did. As one can imagine, the claims made in Malachi are radical and somewhat unique. Some Bibles are produced by committees of translators that share similar convictions to those of the Evangelical community. They read Malachi's words and refuse to accept that the verses could really say what they clearly seem to be saying. And so, what does any good translator of Scripture do? They interpret the text and in so doing, change what the text says.

The King James translation, first published in 1611, was aware of the role translators play in influencing how people read Scripture. One of the particularly nice features of that old translation was that any words that the translators added to the original text they were using, words that were not originally part of the Hebrew or Greek manuscripts, were typed in italics to help readers be aware of the translator's interpretations. As such, there are a number of italics in the KJV version of this passage in Malachi. In the King James, it reads that "my name *will be* great among the nations." It says that "in every place incense *will be* offered to my name."

The KJV translators, quite essentially, turned what is an indictment against Israel into a prophecy of future indictment. They neutralized what is an otherwise radical and paradigm shifting message from God. And worse: there's no reason for them to have done it. There is nothing in the Hebrew text that would lead them to assume that it is speaking of the future. The only reason that they changed the translation is because these translators already held to a belief that the God of Israel would never say something like Malachi clearly says he does.

This is all made quite ironic because the Geneva Bible, the first true Protestant translation of the Bible into English published in 1599, retains the original present tense. In fact, in some ways, the Geneva translators attempted to make Malachi's point even more forceful than it already was. In their translation, it says that "my name is great among the Gentiles" and "my name is great among the heathen." Why am I pointing this out? To show you that the King James translators purposefully changed the translation because of personal beliefs. However, I would be pressed to note, they have not remained alone in that decision.

Modern translations such as the ESV, NIV, NASB, NET, NJB, ASV, HCSB, AMP, and NKJV follow this pattern of changing the text. They too write that the foreign nations "will" offer worship, but not always using italics like the KJV to help readers realize that the words are the translator's interpretation, not Malachi's actual words. But it should be emphasized that not all translations follow this pattern of changing the text. Others remain more faithful to the Hebrew such as the NRSV*, NLT, NAB, LEB, RSV, and GNT. Even some paraphrases, frowned upon for inaccuracies, also remain more true to the Hebrew original, such as *The Message*. So, if you haven't been using one of those translations, it's quite likely that there's a really good reason why you haven't seen this before when studying.

A PRAYER TO OSIRIS IS A PRAYER TO YHWH

The Greek translation of Malachi, found in the Septuagint, differs slightly from the Hebrew and states that God's name "has been" and "is" to Malachi's day honored by the nations. In other words, this isn't a new thing. It's been done before. Essentially, it boils down to this: God has, in the past, even when Israel's worship was acceptable,

---

* The New Revised Standard Version (NRSV) is the most trusted Bible translation available today. It is the standard Bible of choice by biblical scholars. If you are looking for a translation that is close to the Hebrew and Greek, the NRSV is a great choice. Likewise, the NAB is another good translation in this regard.

honored the worship of pagan nations. In other words, "Nothing is new under the sun."

Or better yet, to quote Malachi again: "I the LORD do not change" (Mal. 3:6). This is a famous verse, evoked by many Bible readers, which hints at the heart of God. If God could be shown to accept the worship of foreign nations at any point in history, clearly this couldn't be a new thing for God to have done. God must have been doing it all along.

We shouldn't be surprised by Malachi or the translators of the Septuagint. This truly *wasn't* a change for God. This was the kind of God he had been all along. After all, the book of Exodus had already told its readers that this had happened before.

> The Israelites groaned under their slavery, and cried out. Out of the slavery their cry for help rose up to God. God heard their groaning, and God remembered his covenant with Abraham, Isaac, and Jacob. God looked upon the Israelites, and God took notice of them.
> (EXODUS 2:23–25)

According to the beginning of the book of Exodus, after Joseph's rise to power and the peace and security that had resulted from it, the new Egyptian pharaoh turned on his descendants and enslaved the Hebrew people. This bondage lasted four hundred years and it didn't come to an end until a baby boy in a basket, floating down the Nile, was rescued by an Egyptian princess. His name was Moses, and when he grew up, he met the God of his parents, the God of those enslaved in Egypt. He met him in a burning bush.

Yet when God, through the burning bush, instructs Moses to speak on his behalf to the enslaved Israelites, Moses asks what he should answer if his people ask who this God is that sent him? He expects that they will not know this God and will inquire as to his name (Ex. 3:13). The implications of this are quite huge and I owe a debt of gratitude to my friend Andrew Jones and his Friday morning Bible study for first making this observation. Moses admits in this single verse that the Israelites have forgotten who the god of their ancestors was. Just telling them that the "God of their ancestors" cared about them wasn't specific enough. Which god? Only one? What about the others? Four hundred years of slavery had eradicated the memory, and they don't remember anymore who that god might be.

It also explains why the Israelites soon after the Exodus think it's completely natural to make an idol in the form of a golden calf (Ex. 32:1–3). Aaron, Moses' own brother and eventually a priest of Yahweh, leads the efforts. These Israelites from Egypt don't think twice about what they are doing. They had long since forgotten what kind of God Yahweh was. They didn't know how to worship him. This was now the way they understood religion.

But then, if the enslaved Israelites in Ex. 2:23 were not crying out to Yahweh to save them, since they didn't remember him anymore, who were they crying out to? Who else: other gods. It shouldn't surprise us. After all, the first law of the Ten Commandments dictates that the Israelites were to *have* no other gods. The law is given because the Israelites were already serving multiple deities. Yahweh is simply one of many at the start of the Exodus story, and to them, new at that. In fact, the book of Joshua explicitly states that this was the case (Josh. 24:14).

Aaron's own words when the golden calf is made confirm this. The people request Aaron to make gods for them (plural) and Aaron announces to the freed slaves that the "gods" (plural) saved them from Egyptian slavery (Ex. 32:4). The Israelites that Moses was born to and came to announce liberation to were worshiping Isis, Ra, Hathor, and other foreign deities.

Think about it. The logic of these Israelites kind of makes sense. Who had they cried out to? Not Yahweh. So, if they were saved, if their prayers had been answered, didn't it make sense that they would think that they should honor the gods that they had prayed to for salvation? They didn't understand yet that *only* Yahweh heard their cries. Not Isis. Not Hathor. Not Ra. Even though they were praying to foreign gods, who was hearing their cries? Only Yahweh.

Far from introducing a new and revisionist view of God, the book of Malachi presents us with an attempt to reclaim an older known truth: that God listens to the prayers of even those who do not know him. And, more importantly, he answers them.

WHOSE VOICE?

In a later work, written around two hundred years before the beginning of Christianity, a man by the name of Jesus Ben Sira wrote a large volume of Jewish wisdom. The book, known commonly as Sirach, is included in non-Protestant and Ecumenical Bibles, which is another way of saying that *most* Christians consider it canonical. Whether one accepts it as Scripture or not, Sirach offers some food for thought and certainly presents us with a portrait of how the Jewish people were thinking about such issues near the time of Jesus. The Jewish sage asks:

> "When one prays and another curses, to whose voice will the Lord listen?"
>
> (Sirach 34:29)

So as to avoid misunderstanding, "to curse" in this case, as it is in almost every case in the Bible, does not mean to use foul language. It refers to the act of calling on God to strike someone else with a curse. In other words, both of the things that Sirach mentions (prayer and curses) are forms or examples of what we would today simply consider prayer. Sirach, however, is making a distinction between these two forms of prayer and considers one as illegitimate. For him, he cannot reconcile them both as equal merely because each beseeches God.

No, Sirach is raising an interesting question. What is prayer and what kind of prayer is acceptable to or desired by God? Both actions that Sirach mentions are examples of speech or requests aimed at God. Sirach is prodding his readers, asking the question concerning what it is exactly that God is most interested in. He asks whether God will listen to a request to do harm or turn his ear to the one seeking goodwill. The question is rhetorical for Sirach. He offers no answer. He expects that those who believe in Yahweh will know him well enough to answer the question without his help.

The answer, of course, seems fairly obvious: God is interested in the prayer which is made from a heart that does not wish to curse another creation of his. On the other hand, he is not interested in a prayer which is made by one who wishes to curse another creation of his. This all adds up to form a picture of a God that Sirach implies is more interested in the heart of the person praying than the fact that they are addressing their concern to the right name of the god.

Sirach is not presenting a new and profound theological discovery to the Jewish people. The same idea had already been sung aloud in the past within the temple. In Psalm 66:18, the psalmist writes that: "If I had cherished iniquity in my heart, the Lord would not have listened." When Jerusalem was about to be taken into Exile, the prophet Jeremiah proclaimed that because their hearts were not right, they had sealed their fate. God proclaims that "when they cry out to me for help, I will not listen to them" (11:11).

C.S. Lewis shared this same idea in the final book of his book series known as "The Chronicles of Narnia." In this final book, titled "The Last Battle," the land of Narnia finds itself at odds with another nation where they serve Tash (the devil). The leader of Narnia, the lion known as Aslan (an allegorical representation of God), meets someone from there named Emeth who immediately becomes afraid.

> There came to meet me a great Lion… then I fell at his feet and thought, Surely this is the hour of death, for the lion (who is worthy of all honour) will know that I have served Tash all my days and not him… But the Glorious One bent down his golden head and touched my forehead with his tongue and said, Son thou art welcome. But I said, Alas, Lord, I am no son of thine, but the servant of Tash. He answered, Child, all the service thou hast done to Tash, I account as service done to me… I overcame my fear and questioned the Glorious One and said, Lord, is it then true, as the Ape said, that thou and Tash are one? The Lion growled so that the earth shook (but his wrath was not against me) and said, It is false. Not because he and I are one, but because we are opposites, I take to me the services which thou hast done to him, for I and he are of such different kinds that no service which is vile can be done to me, and none which is not vile can be done to him. Therefore if any man swear by Tash and keep his oath for the oath's sake, it is by me that he has truly sworn, though he know it not, and it is I who reward him. And if any man do a cruelty in my name, then though he says the name Aslan, it is Tash whom he serves and by Tash his deed is accepted. Dost thou understand, Child? I said, Lord thou knowest how much I understand. But I said also (for the truth constrained me), Yet I have been seeking Tash all my days. Beloved, said the Glorious One, unless thy desire had been for me thou wouldst not have sought so long and so truly. For all find what they truly seek.[2]

As Aslan explains it: whatever service (i.e. worship) that is good ultimately goes to Aslan, regardless of whatever Emeth or others may have intended. On the other hand, those who seek evil are ultimately serving Tash (i.e. the devil), even if they addressed their worship to Aslan (i.e. God). In short, Lewis' theological message in his children's story is that God is judging the heart that makes the prayer, not the name the prayer was directed to. This agrees with texts such as Matt. 6:12 and Eph. 4:32 that warn that if a believer does not forgive those who have wronged them, their prayers will not be heard by God. The emphasis is on the heart of the believer, not the name of the God they are praying to.

It's a good point. The Israelites worshiped foreign gods as slaves and cried out to them for salvation. They prayed with sincerity and God answered them. In Malachi, God listens to the foreign worship of other gods because those worshipping were sincere. Sirach asks his readers to ask themselves, which is God more interested in? Is he pleased the most because you are directing your prayers to him or is he more concerned with what the heart of yours is like when you ask?

THE EXODUS...OF THE PHILISTINES

There are few things that are more defining in both the biblical vision and the modern Jewish cultural memory as that of the Exodus experience. For the Israelites of the Bible, the Exodus was the ultimate moment of their history when they as a people escaped bondage and sought liberation in God, entering into a covenant with God that signified themselves as his people. This was a staple cornerstone of Israelite religion and is today the foundation of the Jewish worldview.

That said, this makes the words of a certain eighth century prophet quite glaring. Amos, a Judean farmer turned prophetic messenger, had some shocking ideas for his time. One of the most overlooked of these is a brief statement he makes about the Philistines and Aramaeans, particularly their historical relationship with the God of Israel.

> Are you not like the Ethiopians to me, O people of Israel? says the LORD. Did I not bring Israel up from the land of Egypt, and the Philistines from Caphtor and the Arabians from Kir?
>
> (AMOS 9:7)

If your jaw didn't drop from the surprise, it might only be because you didn't quite catch what that passage is saying. Amos declares that the Israelites and their Exodus from Egypt are no more special than two of their greatest antagonistic neighbors. The Philistines, Amos says, were led in their migration to Canaan from the land of Caphtor by Yahweh himself and so also, the Arameans were led by Israel's deity in their own migration from the land of Kir. Both nations were, quite to the point, often historical antagonists of Israel and both were situated on the west and east of its borders (Isa. 9:11; Ezek. 16:57). Amos' declaration, in essence, announced that at the time of Israel's migration to Canaan, Yahweh was purposefully leading two other peoples to settle in the Promised Land with them.

The message of Amos is given precisely because Israel had come to view themselves as a unique people with a unique and privileged position with God. They, like some Evangelicals today, assumed a position of religious superiority. Israel, as early as the prophet Amos' own day, believed that they knew God's limits. In contrast to this, God asserts that not only was he behind the events of the Exodus from Egypt, but he was behind the migrations of those they considered their enemies.

Although Amos' message was radical, it was not entirely unique. The same message is also later echoed by Deuteronomy 2:23, in which the author appears to say that the Philistines were settled by Yahweh in Canaan. What did it mean to say that God was leading their enemies? What did it mean for Amos to declare that Israel, while special, was not unique in even its most sacred and special historical memories of their covenantal relationship with God?

It meant that the Exodus, while special, was not unique for God. He was helping the nations around them as well, even at the same time. For some Israelites who listened to Amos, this must have sounded insane. Today, for many, it still might.

FOLLOWING OUR GODS

So what in the world are we to make of this profound message in the biblical prophets? It singlehandedly throws the claims of Evangelicals into doubt on this issue. By themselves, these verses would be enough to poke a large hole in Evangelical claims that all apart from those who accept Israel's God have no access to God in their worship. Yet, like many things in the Bible, what makes a message like this so much more powerful is realizing that it's not all that new.

As Rob Bell writes in his book *Velvet Elvis*,

> I am learning that what seems brand new is often the discovery of something that's been there all along—it just got lost somewhere and it needs to be picked up, dusted off, and reclaimed.

Or put another way, to use the words of an old and revered sage: "What has been will be again, what has been done will be done again; there is nothing new under the sun" (Eccl. 1:9). This certainly proves true when we turn to the work of another prophet: Micah.

> For all the peoples walk, each in the name of its god, but we will walk in the name of Yahweh, our God, forever and ever.
> (MICAH 4:5)

At first glance, the text doesn't strike us as especially strange. Someone might assume that it's merely a typical affirmation of Israel's choice to follow Yahweh in a world filled with rival deities. However, that would be incorrect. I was first introduced to this fact when Walter Brueggemann, during an interview at the Loma Linda University Church, pointed out what might escape most: the text above is from *a future vision* of the promised New Earth (the Restoration). It is set *after* the destruction of sin. In Christian language, it would come *after* the Second Coming of Christ. With that in mind, notice what the text doesn't say: *Not everyone is worshipping Yahweh,* even after God sets up his kingdom on earth.

The prophet, speaking of his vision of "the days to come," tells us that "many nations" will come to the temple of Yahweh. It does not even say that all of the nations will. It only says that *many* will. More interestingly, the vision does not say that they come in order to worship him. They do not come to become Israelites. Instead, they come so that "He may teach us his ways and that we may walk in his paths" (Mic. 4:2). What is that way? *Nonviolence.* In other words, *peace.* Micah prophecies that the nations, as a result of Yahweh's teachings, shall "beat their swords into plowshares, and their spears into pruning hooks." He declares that "nation shall not lift up sword against nation, neither shall they learn war anymore."

It promises that war will be a thing of the past when Yahweh rules the world. But it is within this future eschatological context that Micah tells us in vs. 5 his most shocking revelation: "For all the peoples walk, *each in the name of its god.*"

To what must have been the surprise of Micah's readers and likely modern readers as well: God allows the nations to continue worshipping their individual gods even in the coming New Creation. The nations recognize God's wisdom and seek his ways, but leave unconvinced that he is the one that they've been desiring. God, gracious as always, allows them their freedom to remain ignorant, inviting them merely to walk with him by imitating him.

Micah, in essence, reveals the divine principle that God is more interested in the foreign nations following his wisdom than whether or not they finally acknowledge that the God of Israel, Yahweh, is the only and true God. He cares more about their practices than the specific name they begin their prayers with. He cares more about their hearts than their brains. Or, as discussed in an earlier chapter, *he cares more about their orthopraxy than their orthodoxy.*

WHEN A SIN ISN'T A SIN

But wait. If the Hebrew Bible and New Testament indicate that the Jewish God wasn't discriminating against other nations and their citizens for their pagan religious convictions, then what are we to assume is God's rationale for not doing so? Does this negate God's sense of justice?

Doesn't the Hebrew Bible clearly describe a God who judges nations, peoples, and individuals for their sins and crimes? How can Yahweh simultaneously accept the offerings made to Ba'al as his own (as per Malachi), but make judgments against other nations (as per everywhere else)? How can God consider Israel's exodus no more special than the Philistines (as per Amos), yet call Israel his special chosen people? How are we to understand these confusing paradoxes?

Though the idea can be argued by implication from the Hebrew Bible, the New Testament spells out some of the underlying theological ideas that help us to understand this issue. The first is a radical definition of sin which is offered near the end of the New Testament, grouped among what are called the Catholic Epistles.

Although Martin Luther considered it a book best thrown out of the Bible, it is within the Epistle of James that we find one of the most overlooked and radical verses in either of the two Testaments.

> Anyone, then, who knows the right thing to do and fails to do it, commits sin.
>
> (JAMES 4:17)

At first glance, you may nod in agreement, utter a cursory "Amen" and then wonder why I called this verse radical. Isn't it just common sense? I would agree, but also point out what you missed. This verse can be understood not simply as pointing out what *can* be considered sin, but as an actual *description* of sin; an early Christian definition of the word.

In other words, if we were to reverse the order of thought, it would say: "Anyone who commits sin is someone who knows to do the right thing and does not do it."

Still, you might note, how is this radical? In fact, you might think that this is a great definition of sin. Yet again, I would ask you to notice James' choice of words. Sin is when "someone knows" to do the right thing. As with other earlier discussions, let that thought sink into your mind for a bit. Sin, according to James, is only sin when the person is aware that they are sinning. Sin is then, by this definition, not sin until the person sinning is aware that they are supposed to do something other than what they are doing, until they know that what they are doing is wrong.

A sin, according to James, *isn't always a sin*.

Radical.

Then again, you may have heard of this idea before. Sometimes ministers call it "sinning in ignorance." Often, when some conservative ministers announce something doctrinal, they'll follow it up with a statement that affirms something along the lines of: "and now you can no longer claim ignorance on this issue, and if you so choose to not act accordingly, you are condemned."

Yet, there's something wrong with this approach if we take a careful look at what James wrote. The person sins only if they "know." These ministers appear to be under the impression that if a person simply becomes aware that *someone else* believes what they do is a sin, than they now can be understood as "knowing they are in sin." This seems at best naïve, and at worst stupid. Knowledge doesn't work that way. It never has. These ministers have forgotten that there's a difference between what we call knowledge and conviction.

To explain: I *know* what Catholics believe. I am *aware* of their doctrinal positions and history. However, that knowledge does not mean that I am *convicted* that this knowledge is better than the beliefs that I currently hold. To put it another way, while a Christian may be *informed* by some sincere Muslim believers that the Qur'an holds the truth about God, that does not mean that they *know* (i.e. are convicted and convinced) it does, but rather, they merely have become *aware* of how certain groups of people think. It's head knowledge, but not heart knowledge. It is not their conviction that it is truth.

James is radical because it can be understood to argue that if a person is not convicted that what they are doing is a sin, then it quite simply isn't (for them). Put more simply, God's not condemning them for what they are doing.

Sometimes a sin isn't actually sin. It's a shocking idea. And yet, it's also not. Sin is defined in other places within the Bible simply as rebellion against God. To rebel, one must be aware that God held to a position that you have chosen to go against. If you are not of the belief that God holds to such a position, then you cannot be guilty of rebelling against him. Or to borrow the words of Paul, "I would not have known what sin was had it not been for the law. For I would not have known what coveting really was if the law had not said, 'You shall not covet'" (Romans 7:7). Paul had to first believe and be convicted that the law was right for him to be convicted that it was a sin to deviate from it. All James has done is taken Paul's logic a step further. Also, in Rom. 14:22–23, Paul takes this idea further still by suggesting that what defines a sin is whether someone thinks it is. In other words, we are judged primarily according to what we believe to be right, and how we live in that knowledge.

Thus, adopting James' message, we learn that God judges people not on whether they do the right things or are part of the right religion, but whether they have tried their best to live up to the truth that they know. God, in the end, has always been more interested in our heart than our mind.

THE MAJORITY WILL BE SAVED

Although the prevailing belief is that "broad is the way to destruction," John of Patmos presents a shockingly different portrait of the world's final climactic days. Which is kind of odd, since for most people, Revelation is the book of the Bible best remembered as damning everyone. Yet, in many ways, this idea couldn't further be from the truth, and the previous chapter outlined a number of reasons why.

Like many things in our lives, especially in the realm of religion, our ideas about faith are more shaped by others than our own theological growth. We have concepts and popular notions given to us that, when double checked, appear to have been nothing less than conjecture. Such, it turns out, is especially the case with the book of Revelation.

One of the major texts that give people the impression that there will be only a minority saved is a passage in chapter 7 which speaks of God's people as "the 144,000," a relatively small number not only by today's reckoning, but even by ancient standards.

> I saw another angel... saying, "Do not damage the earth or the sea or the trees, until we have marked the servants of our God with a seal on their foreheads." And I heard the number of those who were sealed, one hundred forty-four thousand, sealed out of every tribe of the people of Israel... After this I looked, and there was a great multitude that no one could count, from every nation, from all tribes and peoples and languages, standing before the throne and before the Lamb, robed in white, with palm branches in their hands.
> (REVELATION 7:2–9)

Many people have misunderstood this verse because they haven't read the text carefully enough. Most interpreters have not realized that the 144,000 and the great multitude *are one and the same*. How is that possible? Two words: literary device. One of the literary devices which John uses involves having himself *hear* one thing and then *seeing* something else.

John *hears* "a loud voice like a trumpet" but *sees* "seven golden lamp stands" (1:10). John *hears* one of the elders tell him to see that "the Lion of the tribe of Judah... has conquered," but *sees* a "lamb standing as if it had been slaughtered" (5:6). John *hears* the angel tell him "I will show you the bride, the wife of the lamb," but *sees* "the holy city Jerusalem coming down out of heaven" (21:9–10). As such, when John *hears* that there are 144,000 Jews from Israel, he is surprised to actually *see* that contrary to his expectation, there is a "great multitude" that is so big that it cannot be counted "from every nation, from all tribes and peoples and languages." The 144,000, ironically, is a symbolic number for an innumerably large multitude that are saved.

Of course, that's not the only text that people mistakenly imagine suggests that the majority are doomed. Here's another:

> So the four angels were released, who had been held ready for the hour, the day, the month, and the year, to kill a third of humankind. The number of the troops of cavalry was two hundred million.
> (REVELATION 9:15–16)

At first glance, that's terrifying. It's frightening. It's downright hair-raising! On the other hand, there's something strange going on. How many angels were *needed* to kill only 1/3 of humanity? 200,000,000 of them. So what does that in reverse mean? If you assume that each of the 200 million angels kills one and only one person, then 200 million people will be killed. But if that is only 1/3 of the population, that means over 400 million people will survive!

Ignoring the graphic imagery of John's vision, and allowing for his culturally-influenced violent language and imagery, the point is this: *only* 1/3 were judged. An astounding 2/3 were not affected and were saved. In short, the *minority* were the wicked. The *majority* were the *saved*.

But here's an even more astounding implication. John said that the number of the righteous was "a great multitude that no one could count," yet here we are told the number of the angels (200,000,000) is a countable number. Which means that the number of the redeemed *must* be even *larger* than the number of the saved 2/3 of the earth (400,000,000). In other words: far from a minority who are saved, the odds are looking far greater than expected. The great multitude is so big that it's a number that can't be counted, a number that is far in excess of four-hundred million. If we think about John's own world and time, his reported numbers would have encompassed almost everybody alive on the earth.

"But wait!" someone screams, "I *really* thought John said that the minority are the saved! Didn't he call his people at the end the 'remnant,' which would imply a small number of people?" Well, actually, no. The truth is that Revelation never even uses the word "remnant." Open your Bible and look. It's not there… unless you are using the King James Version. And that's where all the confusion started.

The text is Revelation 12:17, which says that "the dragon… went to make war with the remnant of her seed." Well, that's what it says in the King James translation. Every other translation says "with the *rest* of her children." The word in Greek, λοιπῶν *(loipown)*, means "the rest of," and can be used to denote the majority that is left over, as well as the minority. Nothing in the Greek assumes that it is a "remnant," that was simply the guess of the King James translators. With this in mind, let's look at one more passage from Revelation.

In chapter 11 we are told of "the great city" which God's two end-time witnesses will die within. For context, in Revelation, John only appears to speak of two cities. The world, which is represented by the city of Rome (prophetically called Babylon), and the New Jerusalem, the city of God (which represents the Kingdom of Jesus). So when we read of this great city in chapter 11, we are reading about what we would call "the world," in the negative sense.

According to the prophecy, when the two witnesses are resurrected after three days and a half, an earthquake occurs.

> At that moment there was a great earthquake, and a tenth of the city fell; seven thousand people were killed in the earthquake, and the rest were terrified and gave glory to the God of heaven.
> (REVELATION 11:13)

Now here's the thing to catch: how many were killed? 7,000. How much did they represent of the city's total population? 1/10. How many repented and turned their hearts to God? 9/10. In short, John says in the book most imagine as condemning the world, that 9/10 of the world's population will repent and find salvation. In a great reversal of expectations, the *majority* are saved and it is the *minority* who are lost due to unrepentance.

Revelation is, to borrow a term that one of my professors, Kendra Haloviak-Valentine, once used: it illustrates a *reverse remnant*. A small group turns their back on God and refuses to repent. The majority however do repent and are saved. In response to the repentance of "the great city," an angel blows his trumpet announcing that "the kingdom of the world *has become* the kingdom of our LORD and of his Messiah" (Rev. 11:15). The majority of the world will be saved! When was the last time that you heard that message preached?

More importantly is this though: those saved are not judged based on what religion they are part of. Salvation comes freely in John's vision to Christians and non-Christians alike. Quite the opposite of many ideas held by conservative readers today, the book of Revelation demonstrates (as do the many other verses that we looked at) that Christianity does not have a monopoly on the path to salvation. God has children in other flocks, and we need to take that into account, and celebrate it. God hasn't neglected them and never will.

LEARNING TO SAY NO

It suffices to say that although the Bible has verses that can be understood to be exclusive, the weight of Scripture does not lean in this direction and we as Christians must be aware of this so that we can, working alongside the Holy Spirit, say no both to the minority of verses that promote exclusivity, but more so to misuses of the Bible which seek to present God's character opposite of who he is. As friends of God (John 15:15), we must speak like friends, just as Moses once did (Ex. 33:11), saying no to something that mars the character of our friend.

With this issue behind us, we come near to the conclusion of this book. It is my hope that whether or not you accept my own specific approaches to wrestling with Scripture in this second half of the book, you have recognized the principles undergirding them. My sincerest hope is that by now you have seen why you *can* say no to God, and as a result, the Bible itself, even if perhaps you still struggle with discerning exactly how you yourself will articulate your own specific *no*. I am less interested in whether you agree with *how* I approach a topic, than whether you have begun to recognize the legitimacy of why we need to engage these issues, and why we shouldn't be afraid to potentially contradict parts of the Bible that stand at odds with the character of Christ. And often, we discover, that just like Calvin once said, we will find that God provides us from Scripture the means to fight those aspects of Scripture that are contrary to his character. Our victory is God's.

16
WE AREN'T ALWAYS RIGHT

"Jacob's defiant words to the stranger I take as a challenge to the Bible itself: 'I will not let you go unless you bless me.' I will not let go of the book unless it blesses me. I will struggle with it. I will not turn it over to my enemies that it curse me. Neither will I turn over to friends who wish to curse it. No, over against the cursing from either Bible-thumpers or Bible-bashers, I shall hold fast for blessing. But I am under no illusion that blessing, if it comes, will be on my terms—that I will not be changed in the process."

PHYLLIS TRIBLE[1]

Caution, however, is needed and a good dose of humility, lest we begin to imagine that there are no rules or limits to what we can fight God about. It isn't always the case that when we say no to God (or usually, the writers of the Bible), when our sense of justice rubs against his (or more accurately, theirs), that we are right. I would be failing my commission from God to not point this out. Sometimes we discover that we are wrong, we are blind, and our own sense of morality or justice is not the same as his. In short, there are times when God says *No!* to *us*.

In the book of Jonah, just such an occasion occurs. For most of us, the story is a familiar one. Jonah, an eighth century (B.C.E.) prophet, is told to proclaim judgment against the Assyrian city of Nineveh and instead of delivering the message, he runs away. Eventually, after an interesting encounter with a giant *fish*, he finally obeys God and then, after the city repents, gets angry at God when the Almighty decides to forgive them. It's an odd book, a classic children's story, and a memorable sermon starter.

What makes the story of Jonah so interesting is that he, like Abraham, knows God so well that he admits that when God ordered the destruction of Nineveh, he knew that God wouldn't follow through on his word. "I knew," says Jonah, "that you are a gracious God and merciful, slow to anger, and abounding in steadfast love, and ready to relent from punishing" (Jonah 4:2). It should, in theory, be an excellent example of faith, of God's merciful character. Except, that for Jonah, this was "why I fled." In fact, this not only was "displeasing" to Jonah, but it made him angry.

Whereas Abraham believed that God's actions against Sodom would prove God unjust if he didn't show enough mercy, Jonah believes that justice demands the level of violence that Abraham abhorred. How strange, that a prophet of God, someone who had a long history of serving the God of Israel, was so fed up with God's mercy that he fled from God.

What's really interesting is that Jonah, like Abraham and Moses, verbally fought with God over this *before* he snuck on the boat and hid from God. Although the story begins with God's order to pronounce judgment and Jonah's attempt to escape, according to Jonah's words in 4:2, he had said all of this before to God when the original mission was given to him. Jonah, like Abraham, had defied God directly and when God wasn't going to change, Jonah decided to passively resist by running away.

Jonah, however, unlike Abraham, does not succeed in changing God's mind. Rather, God pushes Jonah to overcome his own biases.

Many scholars believe that the book was likely written around the same time as the book of Ruth, shortly after the return from the Jewish Exile in Babylon. During the reforms of Nehemiah and Ezra, xenophobia and racism were rampant in the newly reconstituted Jerusalem. Though the stories of Ruth and Jonah may have been older and might also have been well-known, the authors who wrote the books we now have wrote them down for a reason at this time. Like sermons, they were to address the issues of their day and help apply old truths to present realities.

Jonah's story touches on many issues, but most prominent among them: negative relations with foreigners. Jonah's bias against foreigners is so strong, his anger toward the Assyrians so deep, that he asks God to kill him several times rather than let him live in a world ruled by a God who has such mercy on his enemies. Jonah would rather die than serve the God of Abraham. That's how deeply he believes that foreigners deserve judgment. Unlike Job or Abraham who beseech God for his mercy (which they believe is true justice), Jonah demands justice (which he believes is opposite of mercy).

And so, what does God do? God reasons with his prophet. God, like Abraham, reverses roles and begins to beseech Jonah to understand him. The story tells us that as Jonah prays for God to take his life away, God asks him: "Is it right for you to be angry?" (4:4). Jonah ignores the question and leaves the city, situating himself to the east. He sits and according to the text, waits "to see what would become of the city."

Why does he wait? Didn't God already forgive the city? What's he waiting to see? If God will change his mind again? No. He's waiting to see if the people in the city really repented. He doesn't believe that, as an old parable once said, "a leopard can change its spots." He doubts that it's possible for this city to really repent and change. Though Nineveh had the largest conversion ever recorded in the Bible due to the shortest sermon ever preached, Jonah refuses to believe it. Even though we are told that even the animals repented of their sins (a feat not recorded elsewhere), Jonah will still not believe that it is possible that the Ninevites could truly change (3:8; 4:11).

While Jonah waits, a "bush" grows over Jonah to provide him shade. This causes Jonah to grow "happy." Yet the following day, as the sun rose, God causes the bush to wither and disappear. Once again, as the sun beat down hard against Jonah, the bitter prophet proclaimed, "it is better for me to die than to live."

Finally, God returns, repeating his words from earlier: "Is it right for you to be angry about the bush?" Jonah replies back, "Yes, angry enough to die!"

> Then the LORD said, "You are concerned about the bush, for which you did not labor and which you did not grow; it came into being in a night and perished in a night. And should I not be concerned about Nineveh, that great city, in which there are more than a hundred and twenty thousand persons who do not know their right hand from their left, and also many animals?"
>
> (JONAH 4:10–11)

Like the prophet Nathan who explained David's sin of murder and adultery by way of a parable (2 Sam. 12:1–7), God now uses a bush to explain why Jonah's sense of justice is wrong. God reasons with Jonah. He doesn't simply tell him he is wrong. He welcomes and respects Jonah's objections. God wrestles with us even when we are wrong and we will never win.

We are not told whether Jonah eventually accepted God's explanation. We are not told whether Jonah ever realized the error of his ways. We are not told whether he eventually realized that though he felt God's sense of justice was wrong, it was in fact his own views that suffered from a lack of justice. We're not told, because the point of Jonah's story isn't to tell us what happened to the historical Jonah, but to challenge those today and every day who find ourselves thinking *like* Jonah.

THE CUSHITE WIFE

Another example of "getting it wrong" can be found in the first five books of the Hebrew Bible, in a story about Moses' sister and brother. According to the account preserved in the book of Numbers, Moses' siblings (Miriam and Aaron), rose up to speak against Moses because of his foreign wife.

> While they were at Hazeroth, Miriam and Aaron spoke against Moses *because of the Cushite woman whom he had married (for he had indeed married a Cushite woman)*; and they said, "Has the Lord spoken only through Moses? Has he not spoken through us also?" And the Lord heard it. Now the man Moses was very humble, more so than anyone else on the face of the earth. Suddenly the Lord said to Moses, Aaron, and Miriam, "Come out, you three, to the tent of meeting." So the three of them came out. Then the Lord came down in a pillar of cloud, and stood at the entrance of the tent, and called Aaron and Miriam; and they both came forward. And he said, "Hear my words:
>
> When there are prophets among you,
> I the Lord make myself known to them in visions;
> I speak to them in dreams.
> > Not so with my servant Moses;
> > he is entrusted with all my house.
> > With him I speak face to face—clearly, not in riddles;
> > > and he beholds the form of the Lord.
>
> Why then were you not afraid to speak against my servant Moses?" And the anger of the Lord was kindled against them, and he departed.
>
> When the cloud went away from over the tent, Miriam had become leprous, as white as snow. And Aaron turned towards Miriam and saw

that she was leprous. Then Aaron said to Moses, "Oh, my lord, do not punish us for a sin that we have so foolishly committed.

(NUMBERS 12:1–11)

The text clearly states that they confront Moses *because* of his wife. Moreover, it says that they confront him because *his wife is a foreigner*, a Cushite (potentially indicating that she is black or dark skinned). While the text tells us that the siblings of Moses spoke out because of her, it does not actually reveal *what* specifically was the reason for their outcry against Moses. The author of this story in Numbers is crystal clear that they confronted him because of his wife, *and yet*, the author quickly shifts to the consequences of the accusations, rather than expanding on the details of the uprising.

Since the author leaves such crucial details unexplained, one must look for *implications* that could reveal such things. Primarily, since the author emphasized twice that Moses' wife was a Cushite (or a foreigner), the issue at hand was likely due to her status as a foreigner. The fact that Miriam received an initial punishment may indicate that the altercation started originally with her. This then is a story about a female prophet (Miriam) who protests to Moses regarding his wife, because she is foreigner.

With this in mind, pay attention to the words of Aaron and Miriam recorded in Numbers:

...they said, "Has the LORD spoken only through Moses? Has he not spoken through us also?"

(NUMBERS 12:3)

The potential implication of the story is that Miriam and Aaron believe that it is wrong to be married to a foreigner. Moses, on the other hand, has defied this by marrying one. Thus, the prophets are split in their interpretation of God's will. Moses is open to foreign marriages (perhaps because he had been raised as an alien himself), and his siblings are against them.

Though the argument shifts to one of *authority*, the central underlying issue is that of objecting to someone based on their national origin or race. God's response is swift and his curse against Miriam should be understood as more of a reaction to her motivations about Moses' wife than with her verbal rejection of Moses' authority.

God reveals in this story that fighting him about xenophobia is a losing battle. Yahweh is open to foreigners and will not allow them to be unjustly harassed, even if by his own prophetic voices.

PETER'S ARROGANCE

Lest I only utilize the Old Testament, we have a similar story found in the New Testament as well. The Gospels of Mark and Matthew recount an incident during the ministry and life of Jesus in which the Galilean rabbi announces that he must die and Peter, one of his top disciples, physically moves his teacher to the side to tell him that this cannot be true.

> Then he began to teach them that the Son of Man must undergo great suffering, and be rejected by the elders, the chief priests, and the scribes, and be killed, and after three days rise again. He said all this quite openly. And Peter took him aside and began to rebuke him. But turning and looking at his disciples, he rebuked Peter and said, "Get behind me, Satan! For you are setting your mind not on divine things but on human things."
>
> (MARK 8:31–33)

Peter, like many Jews, had been raised with certain expectations for the Messiah. Certain verses from Scripture and specially selected texts had been rehearsed again and again to create a theological portrait of a conquering military messiah who the Jews fully expected to destroy the Roman occupation. Jesus' vision of a coming death was, to Peter, downright lunacy. For him, it might as well have been Jesus' abdication of his divine role.

It was a bold move for someone to make, perhaps unthinkable to many. Peter has the audacity to take Jesus to the side and begin instructing *him,* because what he had heard didn't agree with what he knew about God. In many ways, the formula we grew used to in the stories of the first section of the book is readily present in this story. Peter hears something that strikes against his sense of God's will and takes it upon himself to argue with God, and in so doing, call him back to his senses. Only that's not what happens. Instead, Jesus replies with the words: "Get behind me, Satan!"

Moreover, Jesus says this shocking rebuttal while looking *at the other disciples,* as if to imply that although Peter was the one who reprimanded him, he knew that all the others felt the same. Peter and the other disciples expected God to act a certain way. He believed that if Jesus, as the Messiah, didn't eradicate the Romans, then he was failing his divine purpose. What Peter didn't realize was that his vision of God, like Jonah's, was significantly defective.

Unsurprisingly, Peter's blindness followed him in his faith journey. In the book of Acts, Peter is said to be on the rooftop praying when suddenly he is given a shocking vision.

> About noon the next day, as they were on their journey and approaching the city, Peter went up on the roof to pray. He became hungry and wanted something to eat; and while it was being prepared, he fell into a trance. He saw the heaven opened and something like a large sheet coming down, being lowered to the ground by its four corners. In it were all kinds of four-footed creatures and reptiles and birds of the air. Then he heard a voice saying, "Get up, Peter; kill and eat." But Peter said, "By no means, Lord; for I have never eaten anything that is profane or unclean." The voice said to him again, a second time, "What

God has made clean, you must not call profane." This happened three times, and the thing was suddenly taken up to heaven.

(ACTS 10:9–16)

To understand what Peter found so objectionable, one need only to take a moment to read Leviticus 11, in which God is said to outline all of the specific dietary laws that he expects his people to follow. Ultimately, it's a long list of ritually unclean animals to avoid eating. As such, everything that is on the "large sheet" which Peter sees are animals that God had supposedly forbid anyone from eating. For Peter, God is telling him in his vision to disobey Scripture.

After this vision ends, Peter has a Gentile invite him to his home and he agrees to come. When he steps inside their house, he suddenly understands that God's vision had a two-fold meaning: the animals were symbolic of Gentiles. The Jews had come to believe that they couldn't associate with the Gentiles because the Gentiles were unclean in part because they ate the forbidden unclean foods. Peter now understands that all humans are clean in God's sight.

Yet the vision is not purely symbolic. It is also literal, for by accepting the symbolism and allowing himself to sit and eat with this Gentile family, Peter subjects himself willingly to *their food*. Remember, these were not the most well-off people in the world. They did not have refrigerators and could not offer Peter a kosher alternative. Whatever they fed him was likely to be not only not kosher, but unclean by the standards of Leviticus 11. So the vision is two-fold, allowing Peter to see these people as clean so that he can sit and eat with them and giving him the freedom to eat what they serve him.

Now, let us return to the issue of the vision again. Typically, most Christian pastors (at least of the conservative variety), would teach their congregations that if they feel led by the Holy Spirit to reject something in the Bible, it's not from the Holy Spirit (because, they say, it would *never* do that). Working with that premise, one would expect that Peter's insistence that he will stand by Scripture and reject the vision sounds correct. Peter appears to be the paradigmatic model of a good conservative biblical Christian.

The only problem? The book of Acts tells us that Peter is wrong to defend Scripture and that instead, he should be obeying God's new *anti-scriptural* directions. It's a tough pill to swallow for some. God commanded Peter to disobey Scripture? The answer is yes. Peter objects again and again to the divine command out of sincere faith. He objects to the voice of God because of the voice of Scripture, but in the end, he finds himself having chosen the wrong dancing partner. Peter wrestled with God and lost.

In this story, God directly refutes and ends the illegitimate fight with him. The wrestling is not allowed to continue until the morning as it did for Jacob. However, now I want to turn to three examples of those who fought God, did so for the wrong reasons but reaped lasting consequences on more than just themselves.

RETURNING TO MARY

Lest one assume that those who had previously fought God and won were *always* wise, look once more at the story of Jesus' mother. Although she won her battle against Jesus at the wedding of Cana, she later loses another according to the Gospel of Mark.

> When his family heard it, they went out to *restrain him*, for people were saying, "He has gone out of his mind."... Then his mother and his brothers came; and standing outside, they sent to him and called him. A crowd was sitting around him; and they said to him, "Your mother and your brothers and sisters are outside, asking for you." And he replied, "Who are my mother and my brothers?" And looking at those who sat around him, he said, "Here are my mother

and my brothers! Whoever does the will of God is my brother and sister and mother."

(MARK 3:21; 31–35)

This may be one of the least known stories from Mary's life (which isn't that extensive to begin with). So scandalous is the story, that both the Gospels of Matthew and Luke purposefully removed it from their two accounts. Mary, according to Mark's Gospel, leaves with Jesus' other brothers to go and "restrain him." In less vague language, they planned to physically force him to stay at their home.

It's not an image we imagine easily, but Mark gives it to us nonetheless. Mary, fearful of what she doesn't understand about Jesus, decides that while he is nearby, she and her children should restrain him and bring him home. It always seems easier to silence God than to actually wrestle with what he has to say, doesn't it?

When they approach, Jesus is surrounded by a crowd. They ask the crowd to have Jesus come to them, supposedly to just visit his family. Jesus, however, ignores them. Moreover, he rejects Mary as his mother and his brothers as his family. Can you imagine Mary's broken heart? Can you imagine Jesus'? Mary's no to Jesus ultimately causes heartbreak and a familial division.

Although Mark doesn't reveal how, Mary ends up eventually reconciling with her son, because he reveals that she is by his side during his crucifixion in Jerusalem. Perhaps she had come for the Passover, just as she had with the younger Jesus when he was twelve years old (Luke 2:40), and had reconnected with Jesus at last at *his* very last? We will never know because Mark leaves this story of reconciliation untold.

But we can know this: because Mary allowed fear and worry to concern her, she did not listen to Jesus but judged him based on what others said. She didn't wrestle with what he had to say because she was too busy trying to fight him in order to avoid hearing what he had to say!

WHO SHOULD BE KING?

While Mary and her children only caused Jesus emotional suffering in part of his ministry (somewhere between 1–3 years potentially) because of their resistance to God's ways, other examples from the Bible show the damaging effects that saying no to God *for the wrong reasons* can produce. One of the most poignant examples of this is found in 1 Samuel. Before we can explore it, though, a bit of context is needed.

Let's start with a pop quiz just like in chapter 1: Do you know who the first king the Israelites served was? If you're thinking the answer is Saul, you're wrong. While it is true that Saul was the first king of a nation called Israel and may have been the first king chosen by them, he was not, in fact, the first king the Israelites *served* while in the land of Israel. That honor goes to none other than King Cushan-rishathaim of Aram-naharaim.

I'm not making that up. Check it out for yourself in Jdgs. 3:8. He was the first foreign king who subjugated the Israelite tribes to serve him for eight years. What happened to make this possible? The biblical text tells us that the Israelites chose to start worshiping the local Canaanite gods, and God, in short, allowed Israel to be subjugated by their first Canaanite king. In short, God was not-so-subtly telling them that by worshiping other gods, he'd give them the kings that such gods inspired.

After eight years, God raises a "judge" or hero to save the Israelites and give them their freedom. Lesson learned, right? Nope. Israel got their *second* monarch to serve, King Eglon of Moab (Jdgs. 3:12–14). Instead of eight years, they served him eighteen years, before God eventually raised another "judge" or hero to save them. Unfortunately, the pattern continued. Their *third* king was King Jabin of Canaan, who they served for not eight years, not eighteen, but *twenty*. Their *fourth* monarchs were two dual-ruling kings of Midian known as

Kings Zebah and Zalmunna (Judg. 6:1–2; 8:5). Both kings were overthrown by the hero named Gideon.

In spite of the victory by Gideon, the Israelites *once more* began to do the same things. Gideon had given birth to seventy-one sons, seventy by one woman and another one by a concubine from Shechem. As the years progressed and his sons grew, they apparently continued to judge or rule over the disparate Israelites by virtue of merely being the sons of the previous judge. They also exercised their rule over those in Shechem.

One son, named Abimelech, the one born by the concubine, eventually travels to Shechem. He calls on them to make him king over them, because, as he asks: "Which is better for you, that all seventy of the sons of Jerubbaal rule over you, or that one rule over you?" (Jdgs. 9:2). According to the book of Judges, he asserted his rulership over all of Israel for three years (9:22). So what did this new monarch of Israel do? He immediately went to his father's household and murdered his sixty-nine brothers. Long story made short: he eventually gets killed by a random woman with a giant millstone dropped on his head (sort of, see Jdgs. 9:54). Consequently, what's the point of all this history? All of this served to prove a point: *human kings typically don't work out well for their subjects.*

Now, with all that backstory out of the way, we come to the book of 1 Samuel. Samuel, the last of the judges, has two sons. His sons, however, who should theoretically takeover as Israel's next two judges, are described as having "took bribes and perverted justice" (1 Sam. 8:3). In response, the people of Israel approach Samuel with a rather surprising request.

> Then all the elders of Israel gathered together and came to Samuel at Ramah, and said to him, "You are old and your sons do not follow in your ways; appoint for us, then, a king to govern us, like other nations." But the thing displeased Samuel when they said, "Give us a king to govern us." Samuel prayed to the Lord, and the Lord said to Samuel, "Listen to the voice of the people in all that they say to you; for they have

not rejected you, but *they have rejected me from being king over them. Just as they have done to me,* from the day I brought them up out of Egypt to this day, *forsaking me and serving other gods,* so also they are doing to you. Now then, listen to their voice; only—you shall solemnly warn them, and show them the ways of the king who shall reign over them."

(1 Samuel 8:4–9)

If the book of Judges only *implied* the fact that earthly kings were bad (after Israel suffered under six or so of them), God *explicitly* states now that he wanted the Israelites to have nothing to do with them. God himself was to be their king, but in spite of their experiences with previous tyrants, they still insisted on having a king so that they could be "like other nations." Samuel tells them what they should have already known from their past experiences:

> So Samuel reported all the words of the Lord to the people who were asking him for a king. He said, "These will be the ways of the king who will reign over you: he will take your sons and appoint them to his chariots and to be his horsemen, and to run before his chariots… He will take your daughters to be perfumers and cooks and bakers. He will take the best of your fields and vineyards and olive orchards and give them to his courtiers. He will take one-tenth of your grain and of your vineyards and give it to his officers and his courtiers. He will take your male and female slaves, and the best of your cattle and donkeys, and put them to his work. He will take one-tenth of your flocks, and you shall be his slaves. And in that day you will cry out because of your king, whom you have chosen for yourselves; but the Lord will not answer you in that day."

(1 Samuel 8:10–18)

Samuel's words sound dire, yet not that surprising considering the previous stories of their experiences with both foreign and domestic kings. Yet such words do nothing to persuade the people. They are bent on a model of government that they have seen fail, but which they are unwilling to be dissuaded from.

But the people refused to listen to the voice of Samuel; they said, "No! but we are determined to have a king over us, so that we also may be like other nations, and that our king may govern us and go out before us and fight our battles." When Samuel had heard all the words of the people, he repeated them in the ears of the LORD. The LORD said to Samuel, "Listen to their voice and set a king over them." Samuel then said to the people of Israel, "Each of you return home."

(1 SAMUEL 8:19–22)

This story represents an interesting case in that Israel tells God no and God grants the request, though he doesn't agree with it. In other scenarios, God "changes his mind," but in this case, he maintains that Israel is wrong, but is unwilling to fight them over it any longer. After hundreds of years of wrestling, Israel wins, but gains no blessing.

In the end, Israel ended up losing their monarchy when Babylon conquered Jerusalem in 586 BCE, sending them into Exile. Although the Maccabees started another Judean monarchy in the late second century BCE, after overthrowing Syrian forces, the king was technically illegitimate and the "dynasty" failed soon after starting. The Jewish people, as such, became a kingless people at the same time they embraced a radical monotheism. God finally got what he wanted (sole worship and non-monarchial government), but it took a long time because his people wouldn't stop fighting, and in the end he didn't get it the way that would have been best for everyone involved. The story is a strong warning that God is not only willing to provoke a human party to struggle with him, but that he is just as willing to allow a human party to be wrong if they insist on doing so.

BUILD THE WALL

Long before the current President of the United States, Donald J. Trump, became famous (and largely despised) for desiring to build a wall to keep out migrants from Mexico, another politician (equally despised by others in his time) desired to build his own wall to keep out unwanted foreigners. His name was Nehemiah and his book, recounting his political and spiritual journey is still today found in the Hebrew Bible.

For most Christians, Nehemiah is a famous nobody. He's somebody whose name is familiar and whose general timeframe has been memorized (he was after the Exile, right?), but whose book is largely ignored by pastors and unread by church goers. What makes this all the more ironic is that Nehemiah's book is the only work of the Hebrew Bible or Old Testament which is written in *the first-person*. In other words, the book reads as an autobiography *by Nehemiah himself*. He believed that his life experience was so important that others should read it, and thus it is ironic that very few do.

However, there is admittedly some justification for the book of Nehemiah's relative obscurity. The book of Nehemiah is the only purely *political* work of the Bible. Nehemiah is notable because he was neither a priest nor prophet, but rather a politician (a governor to be exact). He has no claim to special insight from God and never claims divine inspiration for his work.

Nehemiah had only one task he was given by the Persians: oversee the rebuilding of Jerusalem and specifically help to rebuild the walls *of the temple*. Nehemiah, however, believed that God must have intended for so much *more*. He was convinced that he needed to rebuild the walls around Jerusalem itself and not just merely the temple. He wanted this because he also believed that the foreigners residing in Jerusalem needed to be thrown out. This, however, was explicitly against God's will. The prophet Zechariah had prophesied that Jerusalem's walls were to remain unbuilt and that God himself would be the wall around Jerusalem. He had also prophesied that Jerusalem was to be an open door to foreigners (Zech. 2:3–5).

When Nehemiah arrived, he found that all the prophets in Jerusalem were led by a woman of God named Noadiah (Neh. 6:14). Presumably, she repeated the warnings of Zechariah to Nehemiah, attempting to dissuade him from building his wall around the city. However, Nehemiah gave no heed and in spite of not being a prophet or having a message from God, rejected God's actual messengers and built the wall regardless. Not only that, but he kicked out the foreigners, oversaw the divorce of all foreign wives, and silenced the prophets in Jerusalem who he believed were wrong.

Nehemiah said no to God by saying no to God's messengers, and since he held political power (and apparently many of the people supported him), God gave up his fight and allowed it to happen. In the end though, God got what he wanted, but not the *way* he had wanted it. Because of Nehemiah's policy of isolationism and nationalism, the Maccabean rebellion was inevitable and triggered religious views that fueled the Zealots of the first century (which ultimately led to the destruction of Jerusalem in 70 C.E.).

God couldn't get Jerusalem to be a city without walls, so he allowed them to reap the consequences of their decisions, the effect of which eventually forced Judaism and Christianity out of the city so that they would literally have no walls. Instead of allowing foreigners *into* the city, the people of the city were forced out *into* the lands of the foreigners.

Why is this important? Because it underscores that saying no to God, fighting God, *can* be dangerous business. Sometimes, we can be blinded and fight for things that are ultimately harmful to ourselves and others (both physically and spiritually) and God might, well, *give up*. God is not going to wrestle with you endlessly. There comes a point at which he declares, like with Jacob, that the morning's sun has almost risen.

THE ADVERSARY

I would be remiss to not give mention to one other famous individual in the Biblical corpus whose very job is to say *No!* to God. That divine being I speak of, is of course, the *ha-satan*. Translated as a title, it means "the Adversary" or "the Accuser," and is more often familiar to readers by either its untranslated Hebrew "Satan" or Greek "Devil."

There is no reason to delve deeply into this character's background (you might be surprised to learn that you know far less about him than you think, and what you think may in fact be false). He is mentioned numerous times in the New Testament for Christians, but is only referenced around three to four times directly in the Hebrew Bible. For Christians, he is considered evil, for Jews he is one of God's (unfallen) angels. This is not the book to attempt to explain that paradox, so I will merely mention it and move on.

In each of those three stories of the Hebrew Bible, the figure of the Adversary brings a charge against someone. However, though he is at face value humanity's adversary, his actions point not to humanity, but God himself. In the book of Job (1:6–11), for example, God declares to Satan that Job is the most righteous man on earth, a man who is blameless and upright. Satan abruptly tells God no, informing him that his love has blinded him to Job's true reality, a reality he promises to bring out of Job if allowed the power to torture him.

Again, in the visions of Zechariah (3:1–7), God appears to accept Joshua* as high priest (and the nation of Israel who he symbolically represents in the vision) but Satan appears ready to object, telling God no, arguing that he is wrong because Joshua's dirty clothes cannot

---

* This is a different Joshua than the famous one you might be thinking of. This Joshua lived after the Babylonian Exile and served as High Priest for Post-Exilic Israel during the beginning of the Second Temple period.

be acceptable. In response, God grants new clean clothing to Joshua (and the people of Israel) and rebukes Satan.

In each case, the Adversary says no to man, but in so doing, says no *to* God *about* man. Furthermore, the Adversary is not interested in fighting *for* others, but condemning others *for* God. Satan, in short, doesn't believe that Job or Israel are deserving of God's grace and so he fights God, just as did Jonah the prophet. And like Jonah, Satan is rebuked by God for fighting him for the wrong reasons.

WHAT IS THE CRITERIA?

In reviewing these many stories, we not only can learn the *fact* that God is willing to allow us to win temporarily on issues we're wrong about, but we can learn the *criteria* that God has that determines whether a situation ends up going south as it did with Israel's desire for a king or Nehemiah's arrogance.

First, we should note the *motivations* of each character in these stories. For Jonah, it was xenophobia (fear of the foreign or other) and hatred toward his enemies. For Miriam and Aaron, it was xenophobia and pride. For Nehemiah, it was xenophobia and arrogance. For Mary, it was fear and misunderstanding. For Peter, it was arrogance, a desire for vengeance, and an incorrect hermeneutic of Scripture. For ancient Israel, it was rebellion and pride.

In summary, that list comes out to be (in order of occurrence):

- Xenophobia
- Pride
- Fear
- Arrogance
- Hatred of Others (or Unmerciful Justice)

- Vengeance
- Bad Interpretations of Scripture

Those are the seven things that led these biblical characters to say no to God. What's fascinating about a list such as this, is that we see that the motivations which led to an *incorrect* fight with God are the sorts of things which are common to humans but frowned on by God in the Bible. The Bible constantly commands that people welcome the stranger and foreigner, condemns pride, rejects fear, abhors arrogance, promotes peace, and refuses justice that does not have mercy (remember the stories of Abraham and Moses?). So, what these stories of *bad* arguments with God reveal is that the people who instigated them either didn't care about what God thought, or didn't know God's character at all.

Second, we should note that in only one of these seven cases was the issue about obeying God's words. Think about that: neither Jonah, nor Miriam, nor Mary, nor Peter, nor ancient Israel had a specific word from God that they were saying no to. Rather, sometimes they were going against principles and characteristics of God that were unspoken or naturally assumed (such as Jonah) or rejecting God himself as a direct *political* ruler (like ancient Israel). Sometimes, like Mary, they were completely unaware that they were doing something wrong (simply acting out in fear and misunderstanding). However, sometimes they were like Peter whose very views were shaped and formed by Scripture, but due to incorrect interpretations, led him to say no to the new things that God was doing. Only in Nehemiah's case do we have an unequivocal rejection of God's words through the prophets, ironically, not because Nehemiah didn't believe God, but because he believed he understood God better.

This is important to note, because many Christians have grown up constantly hearing that the only reason people say no to God's word is because they do not wish to follow it. Yet according to the stories of Peter, the danger of saying no to God is when one allows their interpretations, expectations, and hermeneutical frameworks to determine what is and is not possible for God. In the case of Nehemiah, a wrong view of God's character is what leads him to reject God's own messages.

So in conclusion, what does this mean? Well, it means that the only times that the Bible records people saying no to God for the *wrong reasons* is when they are motivated in very human (but ungodly) ways. It means that the danger of saying no to God lies in saying no when you don't know his true character (which in this case is mercy and love) and may be led then to reject the very things that make God who he is.

To put this all in perspective, let's review a different list. Here are the motivations of those who fought God and won:

- Seeking Merciful Justice (Abraham, Moses, Job)
- Protecting the Innocent (Abraham)
- Rejecting Evil/Violent Acts (Moses)
- Promoting Moral Justice (Job)
- Keeping Covenant/Promises (Moses)
- Promoting Forgiveness/Mercy (Jesus)
- The Continuation of Joy (Mary)

We see here seven very different reasons for saying no to God. Why are they so different? Precisely because each of those seven things are things which we expect to be representative of who God is. We almost wonder, looking at the list, why we would need to say no to God about something like this? Isn't this who God called us to be? Yes, which is *exactly* why these biblical heroes of faith win the battles, because in the end, both they and God were on the same side *all along*.

At the end of the day (and this book), the lesson from both of those lists is this: the key to arguing successfully with God is by only being motivated to fight for reasons related to God's own character. When Abraham says, "Far be it from you," it's because he recognizes a disconnect between the character of God and the actions or words presently coming from God. Whereas when Peter "rebukes" Jesus for saying he must die, he does so because he does not understand God's character. He believes God will take vengeance on Israel's enemies, and cannot fathom that God will find a nonviolent (let alone a self-sacrificial) approach to Israel's problems.

At stake in every story is the character of God. Every time Israel fights God the *wrong way*, they do so because they don't know who God truly is. Remember, Jacob received the name of Israel because he fought *to gain a blessing*. The goal is to fight against God in order to grow more like him. In the case of ancient Israel wanting a human king, it revealed not a desire to defend God, but *an admission that they had come to view God's kingship as interchangeable with human tyrants*. Their rejection of God as king was an admission that they saw God no differently (perhaps worse) than a human king. It revealed that they did not truly know God.

In order to fight God successfully, one must do so *in faith,* not necessarily faith in God himself (as Job demonstrates), but in what God is supposed to stand for and represent: justice, mercy, love, peace, joy, etc. Starting from that standpoint, any fight with the Almighty will bear many blessings, fulfilling the name of Israel. However, should someone fight with other motivations, namely hate, xenophobia, fear, cruel justice, etc., the message of the previously overviewed stories is that God's rebuke will be stern or worse, he may allow you to temporarily win just so that you can see the consequences of such an action.

This all illustrates my final point: sometimes we will, because of our culture, our family, our background, and our worldview, say no to God when in fact we should be saying yes. We should not assume that simply because something in Scripture disagrees with us, that it means that we are the superior authority. After all, he did warn us that "my thoughts are not your thoughts, neither are your ways my ways" (Is. 55:8).

The goal then, is to have our thoughts be molded by God's, and our ways imitate his own. And how do we do that? By remembering his character. And what is that? Nothing less than the affirmation of 1 John 4:16: that "God is love, and whoever abides in love abides in God, and God abides in him." Or in other words, it is nothing less than the Good News of Jesus Christ.

Again, the point of this book is to get you thinking, speaking and hopefully, preaching about God in ways that previously, you may never have allowed yourself to even think were acceptable. If it does not translate from thought into action, I have failed. *None of this, after all, amounts to anything more than dead words on a printed page if it does not find a way to become a living reality in your soul.* That is the point of Scripture and the reason why we preach or speak theology: to give room for the Spirit to breathe life into it once more.

Yet, just as important as allowing ourselves to begin walking a path that accepts our responsibility from God to say no to certain things in Scripture, is also the responsibility of accepting in humility that there are many things in which we must allow the witness of Scripture to say no to us. The wrestling match is not one-sided and as the previous chapter showed, God has *won* as many matches as he has seemingly *lost* (though, as we've also seen, God's loss is often his greatest victory).

When God says no, we must listen and more importantly, wrestle with it. There's no denying that. However, *we might never be able to learn when to appropriately hear God's no to us, unless we first learn what he has already invited us to say no to.*

17

ADAM & EVE'S FAILURE

"It is because I still believe in God that I argue with him."

ELIE WIESEL[1]

As we conclude this book, bringing an end to this unusual journey, there remains one last issue that should be raised. If someone has read this far and fallen this deep into the rabbit hole, then surely I would be negligent not to tackle an issue that at least one reader will inevitably bring forth: doesn't the Bible explicitly tell us *not* to argue with God? Doesn't the Bible present the opposite message of resistance?

> "Woe to anyone who argues with his Maker, one earthenware pot among many! Does the clay say to its potter, 'What are you doing? Your work has no hands!' Woe to anyone who asks a father, 'Why are you begetting?' and a woman, 'Why are you giving birth?' Thus says Yahweh, the Holy One of Israel and his Maker: I am asked for signs regarding my sons, I am given orders about the work I do."
> (ISAIAH 45:9–11; NJB)

At first glance, the text of Isaiah appears straightforward. God seems to be discouraging his people from questioning him, from doing the very things that this book has argued for. As such, I suspect that some conservative readers will be tempted to cite this single text in order to argue that the entire enterprise of this work is not for the benefit of Scripture at all, but to its detriment. Although this text in Isaiah appears to be saying this, it in fact is not. The rest of the text reveals *what* it was that God was being questioned about:

> "I myself have raised him [Cyrus] in saving justice and I shall make all paths level for him. He will rebuild my city and bring my exiles home without ransom or indemnity, says Yahweh Sabaoth."
> (ISAIAH 45:13; NJB)

God is reacting to the objections of some Jews in exile who cannot believe that God would choose to use a pagan like Cyrus the Persian to save them. Their xenophobia prevents them from accepting why God could ever bless the people they consider their enemies. *This*, and not the idea of arguing itself, is what God reacts to in Isaiah 45. As we explored in the previous chapter, there are some things that we aren't supposed to resist, because our resistance demonstrates a lack of understanding about God and the limitless love God holds for all humanity.

After all, this is the same book of Isaiah which opened with the invitation from God to "let us argue it out" (1:18) and who welcomes us to "argue the matter together" (43:26). The point of Isaiah 45 is simply to acknowledge that *some* arguments (those which stem not from God's character of love) are not worth God's time and are rooted in self-interest or bigotry. It is not that we are forbidden from saying no to God, rather, it is that we are encouraged to pursue the sorts of arguments that mirror God's heart.

WE MUST CHANGE

In the book of Jonah, God sends Jonah to condemn the Ninevites. The text of Scripture is clear that God does not provide a way for the Ninevites to repent. His message to them is simple and straightforward: "Forty days more, and Nineveh shall be overthrown" (Jonah 3:4). It's a prophecy, a prediction of what will soon become their reality. There will be, seemingly, no escape for the Assyrians living within those city walls. If you were one of those in the city, what options would be left to you after God had seemingly declared his eternal will? You could probably flee the city, abandoning it. You might resign yourself to the inevitable fate of judgment. Perhaps you might do other things as well, but none of those things could change what God had declared, right?

And yet, something strange is reported: "the people of Nineveh believed God; they proclaimed a fast, and everyone, great and small, put on sackcloth." The king then ordered that the people "shall cry mightily to God" (3:8). Why? God had condemned them. God had abandoned them. God had said no to them. There was no changing God's prediction. Did they wish to make him a liar? Apparently, yes. The king believed that even though God proclaimed something, it was not necessarily the final word on the subject, for he states: "Who knows? God may relent and change his mind; he may turn from his fierce anger, so that we do not perish" (3:9).

In short, the repentance of Nineveh is performed as an act of resistance against God's supposedly hostile will. These Assyrians, faced with an image of God that wishes their destruction, essentially tell God *no* by imploring him not to destroy them as he had declared. And guess what? God stops his plan and the impossible happens: Nineveh survives, despite God promising that it wouldn't. Like Jacob resisting the divine will to destroy him, and insisting on a blessing, the Assyrians prevail against God, for the sake of a blessing from God.

The people of Nineveh not only have the greatest repentance witnessed to in the Bible, but they also demonstrate the single largest attempt, recorded in Scripture, of humans saying no to God about something he has declared. How did this work? And moreover, why did they think it *could* work? Jonah gives us a hint when he complains about this turn of events: "That is why I fled... for I knew that you are a gracious God and merciful, slow to anger, and abounding in steadfast love, and ready to relent from punishing" (Jonah 3:2). In other words, Jonah knew all along that God was playing a game. He knew this was a ruse intended for the benefit of the Assyrians.

In the book of 2 Chronicles, God reveals the reason why:

> When I shut up the heavens so that there is no rain, or command the locust to devour the land, or send pestilence among my people, if my people who are called by my name humble themselves, pray, seek my face, and turn from their wicked ways, then I will hear from heaven, and will forgive their sin and heal their land.
> (2 CHRONICLES 7:13–14)

In short, God's approach towards Israel and the nations indeed appears to be all part of the "game" or "test" that Luther wrote of: a roundabout way of getting them to say *no* to him. Although the Ninevites would act wickedly, losing sight of God and his character, God would reorient their vision of him by forcing them to confront a version of God that was hostile to them. In reality, God wasn't hostile at all. They were simply experiencing the results of their own sinful decisions. In announcing their impending doom, God positions Israel and others to implore him to change, to fulfill their name (those who fight God). Why? Because like Jacob, God wants to instill within Israel's consciousness the truth about God's character: that he wants to bless them.

The story of Nineveh illustrates for us the truth that, all too often, our own shortcomings reap negative consequences both for ourselves and society. This is usually the result of us losing sight of a clear vision of God or what God wants: morality and goodness. When this happens, God uses his mask to provoke us, and in so doing, to remind us of what we know deep down: that this God doesn't want to condemn us at all, but rather, desires to save us. When challenged by the devil's mask, God incites us to push back and reaffirm his true character. As we do, we are ourselves similarly challenged to change. We are transformed back into the image of God by fighting for the very things that God stands for.

This is why the Ninevites repent, for in resisting the threat of God's supposed curse, they recognize that their lives must change to align with God's assured blessings. If hating your neighbor causes you to find yourself without peace, and God comes to you with a judgment declaring that you will never have peace (and yet you know and believe that God wants peace), then you must stop hating your neighbor, for if this is the reason that you lack peace, repentance is simply stopping the behavior that has reaped you such terrible consequences. This is why "to repent," means "to turn around." It signifies a change in behavior and attitude. This is how the act of saying *No* can actually be a sanctifying event, as we saw earlier that Dietrich Bonhoeffer alluded to. For in order to say no correctly to God, we must affirm some *Yes* about him, and in affirming this *Yes,* we must consequently reorient ourselves to align our lives with such a *Yes*.

When we don't, we become like Jerusalem in the fifth century (B.C.E.). For though God condemned them through the prophet Jeremiah, instead of resisting God's judgment and realigning themselves to God's vision of peace, they took advantage of God. They knew that God wasn't hostile to them. They trusted that God only had their well-being in mind. And so they scoffed at his mask and denied it. They said *No*, but they failed to change in response to their affirmation of *Yes*. They failed to realize that their own wicked actions would reap the consequences, all without God's role in it. They ignored what God was trying to do through Jeremiah: provoke them to see God better and in so doing, to change themselves in the light of that increased clarity. In the end, they didn't engage with God. They simply ignored him. In denying the calling of their name, they didn't escape the judgment like their historical enemies once did.

Nineveh was ultimately saved because they said *No* to God and recognized their shortcomings, taking steps to become more like God and less like the hostile mask God wore. Jerusalem was condemned because they said *No* to God and didn't recognize their shortcomings, continuing to live in the same way that was creating their problems to begin with. As explored in the previous chapter, there is a right way to resist God that leads to salvation, and a wrong way that leads us to remain blind to the condemnation we are bringing against ourselves. Was this not what we saw occurred earlier to Israel when they wanted a king? In the end, Jerusalem denied God's mask, but failed to recognize that it was a mirror reflecting their own need to change. Let them stand as a cautious warning to all who embrace the meaning of Israel's name and calling.

We cannot simply *declare* what God is, without also transforming ourselves to *embrace* what God is. If God loves others, we cannot simply acknowledge it like some detached objective fact, but must embrace it and more importantly, incarnate it into our lives. Fighting God is not an intellectual exercise, but denotes something physical and intimate. One cannot halfheartedly battle with the Almighty. For the entire purpose of God's "game" or "test" is simply this: to cement his character and goodness in us by engaging with us hand to hand. If we truly wish to live up to Israel's name, we must be willing to engage with God with all of our heart.

REASSESSING A FAMILIAR STORY

Adam and Eve are always remembered as the biblical couple whose failure to obey God led them to unintentionally curse the human race. Or, at least, that's the way in which the story is usually told. Numerous sermons are given each week in many Evangelical churches, across the United States and elsewhere, preaching about how these two first human beings sinned because they didn't follow what God told them. If God told them not to do something, then that should have been enough to prevent all that transpired. In fact, many of these sermons go a step further and condemn Eve for even listening to the serpent in the Garden of Eden. If she truly obeyed God, they say, she would have ignored the tree and not given heed to the Serpent.

These ministers and expositors of Scripture argue that when God tells you to do something, you obey. You just do it. To listen to the serpent's words and logic, they warn, is to disobey God because it means allowing yourself to question what he told you. And questioning God, they warn again, is not possible. Often, when a Christian questions something in the Bible (Did it really happen? Is that what it originally said?), these ministers will quote the serpent's line from Gen. 3:5 as a warning to drop the question: Remember, they advise, the Serpent caused the downfall of humanity with a simple but deadly question: "Did God really say…?"

Doubt, they argue, is the undoing of everything. Adam and Eve lose it all because they *listen* to an alternative and opposing view. Had they simply obeyed God without question, these people insist, we'd still be in paradise. Of course, while this sort of thinking is widespread, it's also quite flawed. As this book has shown at length, God welcomes us to not only question what he says (1 Thess. 5:21), but to fight him about it in either an argument or even a physical wrestling match (and to even win!).

Moreover, it becomes clear that this way of understanding Genesis 2–3 is not faithful to the text itself, nor to the larger theology of the Bible. The sin of Adam and Eve cannot simply be an issue of blind obedience, since this is not what God requires from their descendants. If God does not change (Mal. 3:1), then why would we assume that God wanted blind obedience from Adam and Eve but not later from Jacob and his descendants? Would it not make more sense to assume that God treated Israel the same way in which he had treated those who came before?

I believe this is the only logical choice. And if so, then we learn a valuable truth. Adam and Eve's failure is *not* that they didn't obey God, but rather, that they didn't *fight* him. Instead of confronting God with the claims of the serpent, they accepted the accusations passively and rejected God. Instead of allowing God to refute the serpent's words, the human couple chose to let the serpent have the last word. When it told them that God didn't want them to be "like gods," they believed him.

Adam and Eve did not fight God and in not doing so, did not provide an opportunity for God to vindicate himself as he did with Abraham, Moses and the many others throughout the Bible. Adam and Eve denied God *his* voice. There was no inherent wrong in Adam and Eve looking at the tree, nor with conversing with the serpent in it. The wrong at hand was that when confronted with accusations about God's character, they didn't leave to fight God over it but merely agreed.

This reveals that the first human couple's understanding of God had some rather large defects. Their decision not to fight God stemmed from the fact that they had a poor understanding of who God was. This indicates that Adam and Eve's problem was relational and that their subsequent issues grew from that bad beginning. Unlike Abraham who, believing he *knew* God, would proclaim: "Far be it from you!" Adam and Eve hear the words of the serpent and wonder: "This doesn't sound that far from you."

The first human couple's greatest shortcoming was, in short, not having a good enough relationship with God to doubt the serpent's words, and not caring enough about God to fight him over them. And in a certain sense, God has been trying to fix that failure ever since, which explains why he named his people Israel (*those who fight God*). Throughout the Bible, he's been trying to get humanity to fight him, in the hopes that by doing so, we would learn who he truly was and imitate him.

The question that should haunt us today, as we read the Bible and debate *how to do so*, is whether or not we are ready to accept and embrace God's desire. We must ask whether we are willing to step into Jacob's shoes and fight God by the river. Will we wrestle with God to change his mind, discovering instead that we have been changed in the process? In short, are we ready to discover a way of reading the Bible that is both *radical*, but also *faithful*? Can we learn to say no to God in order to ultimately say yes to him?

If so, then all that is left to say is: *amen.*

CONCLUDING PARABLE

As you leave this book, either to reflect on it, re-read it, or perhaps burn it, may I leave you with this story. Just as this book began with a parable from theologian Peter Rollins, this work concludes with another parable, albeit far older. Originally found in the ancient collection of Jewish laws, *The Talmud*, this parable reflects the views of the Jewish rabbis living near the time of Jesus. Their story is paraphrased and rewritten here by me.

> There once was a Rabbi named Eliezer, who came to find himself in a bitter disagreement with his fellow rabbis regarding a rather minor issue of ritual purity. He had declared something clean, whereas his peers deemed it unclean. Like a snake, the sages encompassed Eliezer and using their arguments, proved it unclean. Or at least, so they thought.
>
> Rabbi Eliezer, obstinate and stubborn, refused their explanations. He in turn brought forward every possible argument in his favor, determined to be proven right. However, the other sages did not accept his views.
>
> "If the scriptures agree with me, let this carob-tree prove it!" he declared. Suddenly, the tree standing nearby appeared to be torn a hundred cubits (others swear four hundred) into the air. Eliezer gawked in surprise and smirked in satisfaction. He had received his supernatural vindication. However, the other rabbis were not impressed. "No proof regarding this issue can be brought from a carob-tree," they retorted.

Frustrated, he again raised his voice to heaven. "If," he began, "the scriptures agree with me, let the nearby stream of water prove it!" Suddenly, as before, the water began to flow backwards both to the shock and further happy surprise of Eliezer. Yet, once again, the rabbis remained unimpressed. "No proof can be brought from a stream of water," they rejoined.

Again, he declared a new challenge. "If the scriptures agree with me, let the study hall prove it!" Immediately, the walls began to fall. At the same moment, one of the rabbis, a man by the name of Yehoshua, rebuked the falling walls, asking them: "When we, as scholars, defeat each other in matters of law, what is it for you?" No sooner had he spoken, then the walls stopped falling and froze in place.

By this point, Rabbi Eliezer became distressed beyond belief. He had received supernatural proof that he was right and that they were wrong in their interpretations of Scripture. So he did what was left for him to do: he called upon God himself. "If the scriptures agree with me," he declared as loud as he could, "let it be proven from Heaven itself!" Immediately, a heavenly voice cried out, asking the rabbis, "Why do you bother Eliezer, seeing that in every place the scriptures agree with him?"

The rabbis were greatly disturbed, seeing that God had spoken to them as he had with Moses, the original law-giver. Yet, one rabbi remained unimpressed and moreover, upset. Raising his voice to the sky, instead of the previous walls, Rabbi Yehoshua spoke again, exclaiming that: "The scriptures are not in heaven!" The rabbis began to murmur amongst themselves to Eliezers confusion. They wondered what that statement truly meant. Soon, another rabbi quickly agreed with Yehoshua, noting aloud that "we must pay no attention to this heavenly voice, since God has already delivered us the scriptures with the commission to use the minds he gave us."

Rabbi Eliezer was again rejected by the rabbis and moreover, excommunicated. "There is no place amongst us for those who would call on God to prove something, rather than use the mind that God gave them in the first place to show it!" they declared. After he was banished, however, not all the rabbis felt confident that they had done right. One of them worried about whether God may have been upset to have had his own voice rejected. They had said no to God and he grappled with the guilt. Sometime later, this same rabbi was visited in a vision by the prophet Elijah who arrived from Heaven in the fiery chariot he once arose there in. Immediately, the rabbi asked him, "What did God do after that moment?" Elijah stared seriously at the rabbi and then smirked.

"He laughed and smiled," Elijah reported. "He kept saying, 'My sons have defeated me! Abraham's sons have defeated me just like Jacob!'"

(INSPIRED BY BT BABA METZIA 59A–B)

CITATIONS

A PARABLE

1. Peter Rollins, *The Orthodox Heretic: And Other Impossible Tales* (Massachusetts: Paraclete Press, 2009), 94–97.

INTRODUCTION

1. Karl Barth, *Evangelical Theology: An Introduction* (Michigan: Eerdmans, 1963), 11.

CHAPTER 1: DOUBT EVERYTHING

1. Paul Tillich, *Dynamics of Faith* (New York: HarperOne, 2009 [1957]), 25.
2. Marcus Borg, *The Heart of Christianity: Rediscovering A Life of Faith* (New York: HarperOne, 2003), 40.
3. Fritz Guy, *Thinking Theologically* (Michigan: Andrews University Press, 1999), 99–100.
4. Peter Rollins, *Insurrection: To Believe Is Human, To Doubt, Divine* (New York: Howard Books, 2011), 21.
5. Rollins, *Insurrection*, 21.
6. Ibid., 24, 29.
7. Rob Bell, *Velvet Elvis* (New York: HarperOne, 2012), ix–x.
8. Austin Fischer, "Faith in the Shadows," *Can I Say This At Church* podcast, episode #45 (October 1, 2018).
9. Peter Enns, *The Sin of Certainty: Why God Desires Our Trust More Than Our "Correct" Beliefs* (New York: HarperOne, 2015), 164.

CHAPTER 2: ABRAHAM DIDN'T BELIEVE GOD

1. Omri Boehm, *The Binding of Isaac: A Religious Model of Disobedience* (New York: T&T Clark, 2007), 45.
2. Søren Kierkegaard, *Fear and Trembling* (New York: Penguin Books, 1995 [1843]), 52.

CHAPTER 3: DID GOD SAY THAT?

1. Peter Rollins, *The Fidelity of Betrayal: Towards a Church Beyond Belief* (Paraclete Press, 2008), 34.

CHAPTER 4: SAYING NO TO GOD

1. Rollins, *Fidelity of Betrayal*, 30.
2. Ibid., 32–33.

CHAPTER 5: JOB'S LAWSUIT AGAINST GOD

1. Donniel Hartman, *Putting God Second: How to Save Religion From Itself* (Massachusetts: Beacon Press, 2016), 127.
2. Soncino translation.
3. Herzl Hefter, "Arguing with God," *The Times of Israel* (April 5, 2016).
4. Ibid.

CHAPTER 6: DID GOD SAY IT OR MOSES?

1. Richard Dawkins, *The God Delusion* (New York: Houghton Mifflin, 2008), 250.
2. Daniel L. Migliore, *Faith Seeking Understanding: An Introduction to Christian Theology* (Michigan: Eerdmans, 2014), 56.
3. Migliore, *Faith Seeking Understanding*, 57.
4. Ibid., 43.
5. Ellen White, "Objections to the Bible," Manuscript 24 (1886).
6. John Dominic Crossan, *God and Empire: Jesus Against Rome, Then and Now* (New York: HarperCollins, 2007), 95.
7. Borg, *Heart of Christianity*, 81.
8. Borg, *Convictions*, 80.
9. Ibid., 101.

10. Borg, *Heart of Christianity*, 81.
11. Leonardo Blair, "Pastor Who Says Single Christians Can Have 'Mutually Pleasurable' Sex Doesn't See the Bible As God's Infallible Word," *ChristianPost* (Aug. 23, 2016). http://www.christianpost.com/news/pastor-who-says-single-christians-can-have-mutually-pleasurable-sex-doesnt-see-bible-as-gods-infallible-word-168434/
12. Brian D. McLaren, *A New Kind of Christianity* (New York: HarperCollins, 2010), 114–115.
13. Matthew J. Distefano, *Heretic!: An LGBTQ-Affirming, Divine Violence-Denying, Christian Universalist's Responses to Some of Evangelical Christianity's Most Pressing Concerns* (California: Quoir, 2018), 56.
14. Brennan Manning, *Signature of Jesus: The Call to a Life Marked by Holy Passion and Relentless Faith* (New York: WaterBrook Multnomah, 2004), 188–189.
15. N. T. Wright, *Scripture and the Authority of God* (New York: HarperCollins, 2005), ix.
16. http://www.turningthehearts.com/nationalcity/index.php/i-m-new/beliefs
17. http://lutheranchurchescondido.com/our-beliefs/
18. http://www.greenvalleychurch.com/#/who-we-are/what-we-believe
19. http://www.cec-sd.org/ENG/aboutBelief.aspx
20. http://gracewavechurch.org/about-gracewave-church/
21. http://thecenter.co/what-we-believe/
22. http://sandalschurch.com/beliefs/
23. http://puritanchurch.com/about-2/articles-of-faith/
24. http://www.fbc-escondido.org/our-history.html
25. Kevin DeYoung, *Taking God At His Word: Why the Bible Is Knowable, Necessary, and Enough, and What That Means for You and Me* (Illinois: Crossway, 2014), 52.
26. DeYoung, *Taking God At His Word*, 87; 119.
27. Ibid., 119; 109.
28. Ibid., 78.
29. Ibid., 106; 118.
30. Ibid., 106–107.
31. http://www.atruechurch.info
32. http://www.atruechurch.info/faq.html
33. http://www.atruechurch.info/stand1.html

34. http://www.atruechurch.info/faq.html
35. Ted Olsen, "Postcard from San Diego: 'Fighting Bibliolatry' at the Evangelical Theological Society," *Christianity Today* (Nov. 14, 2007). http://www.christianitytoday.com/news/2007/november/postcard-from-san-diego-fighting-bibliolatry-at.html
36. Valerie Tarico, "In Defense of Cherry Picking the Bible," *Huffington Post*, http://www.huffingtonpost.com/valerie-tarico/in-defense-of-cherry-pick_b_7305860.html
37. Bruxy Cavey, "What's the Word on Scripture Part 2: A Case Study in Bibliolatry," *BruxyCavey.com* (Jan 1, 2012). Website is now offline. https://bruxy.com/2012/01/23/whats-the-word-on-scripture-part-2-a-case-study-in-bibliolatry/
38. John Dominic Crossan, *How to Read the Bible and Still Be a Christian* (New York: HarperOne, 2015), 35–36.

CHAPTER 7: BECOMING LIKE GOD

1. Hartman, *Putting God Second*, 135.
2. David T. Lamb, *God Behaving Badly: Is the God of the Old Testament Angry, Sexist and Racist?* (Illinois: InterVarsity Press, 2011), 145.
3. Martin Luther, "Lectures on Genesis," in *Luther's Works,* vol. 6 (Missouri: Concordia, 1970), 141.
4. Luther, "Lectures on Genesis," 130.
5. Ibid., 131.
6. John Calvin, *Commentary on Genesis*, ch. 32.
7. Karl Barth, *Church Dogmatics: The Doctrine of the Word of God*, trans. G. T. Thomson and Harold Knight, vol. 1.2 (New York: T&T Clark, 2004 [1956]), 339.
8. Dietrich Bonhoeffer, *The Collected Sermons of Dietrich Bonhoeffer*, ed. Isabel Best (Minneapolis: Fortress Press, 2012), 26.
9. Søren Kierkegaard, *Fear and Trembling* (New York: Penguin Books, 1995 [1843]), 52.
10. Ellen White, *Spiritual Gifts*, vol. 3 (Michigan: Seventh-day Adventist Publishing Assoc., 1864), 276, 278.
11. Ellen White, "Apostasy," *Youth Instructor* 49.46 (1901): 362.
12. Ellen White, *Patriarchs and Prophets* (Washington, D.C.: Review and Herald Publishing Assoc., 1890), 318.
13. C. S. Lewis, *Collected Letters* (New York: HarperCollins, 2007), 1436–1437.

CHAPTER 8: PYROTHEOLOGY

1. Darius Jankiewicz, "Hermeneutics of Slavery: A "Bible-Alone" Faith and the Problem of Human Enslavement," (Paper 135; Faculty Publications, Andrews University; 2016), 1.
2. Rollins, *Insurrection*, xii.
3. Ibid., xv.
4. Ellen White, *Gospel Workers* (Michigan: Review & Herald Publishing Assoc., 1892), 127.
5. White, *Gospel Workers*, 125.
6. Ellen White, *Counsels to Writers and Editors* (Tennessee: Southern Publishing Assoc., 1946), 35.
7. Ellen White to William H. Healey, Letter 7 (Dec. 9, 1888).
8. Rollins, *Insurrection*, xv.

CHAPTER 9: SAYING NO TO ORTHODOXY

1. Ellen White, *Counsels to Writers and Editors* (Tennessee: Southern Publishing Assoc., 1946), 35.
2. Enns, *The Sin of Certainty*, 48–49.
3. Ibid., 52.
4. Ellen White, "Love, the Need of the Church," Manuscript 24, 1892.
5. Ibid.
6. Enns, *The Sin of Certainty*, 17.
7. Ibid., 18–19.
8. Jankiewicz, "Hermeneutics of Slavery."
9. Enns, *The Sin of Certainty*, 18.
10. Ibid., 22.
11. Ibid., 22–23.
12. Ibid., 23.
13. Ibid., 53.

CHAPTER 10: SAYING NO TO PREJUDICE

1. Rollins, *Fidelity of Betrayal*, 34–35.

2. Jonathan Brown, *Misquoting Muhammad: The Challenge and Choices of Interpreting the Prophet's Legacy* (London: Oneworld Publications, 2014), 288–289.

3. Bernard Whitman, *Two Letters to the Reverend Moses Stuart: On the Subject of Religious Liberty* (Boston: Gray and Bowen, 1831), 30–42.

4. Ibid., 33–34.

5. Ibid., 35.

6. Ibid., 36.

7. Charles Hodge, "Bible Argument on Slavery," in *Cotton Is King*, ed., E. N. Elliott (Georgia: Pritchard, Abbott & Loomis, 1860), 849.

8. John Blake, "How the Bible was used to justify slavery, abolitionism," *CNN.com*, http://religion.blogs.cnn.com/2011/04/12/how-the-bible-was-used-to-justify-slavery-abolitionism/

9. Jankiewicz, "Hermeneutics of Slavery."

10. James Henley Thornwell, quoted in Eugene Genovese, "James Henley Thornwell," in *The Southern Front: History and Politics in the Cultural War* (Missouri: University of Missouri Press, 1995), 37.

11. John Henry Hopkins, *Scriptural, Ecclesiastical, and Historical View of Slavery* (New York: W. I. Pooley & Co., 1864), 16.

12. Ellen White to Alexander Ross, Letter 24 (1862).

13. Henry Van Dyke, *The Character and Influence of Abolitionism: A Sermon* (New York: D. Appleton and Company, 1860), 11.

14. Hartman, *Putting God Second*, 121.

CHAPTER 11: SAYING NO TO PATRIARCHY

1. Sarah Jobe, "A Hermeneutics of Struggle," WorkingPreacher.org (Oct 23, 2009). https://www.workingpreacher.org/craft.aspx?m=4377&post=1813

2. J. Paul Sampley, "The First Letter to the Corinthians" in *The New Interpreters Bible,* vol. 10 (Tennessee: Abingdon Press, 2002), 874. Emphasis is my own.

3. Luke Timothy Johnson, *The Anchor Bible: The First and Second Letters to Timothy* (New York: Doubleday, 2001), 203.

CHAPTER 12: SAYING NO TO HOMOPHOBIA

1. Matthew Vines, *God and the Gay Christian: The Biblical Case in Support of Same-Sex Relationships* (New York: Convergent, 2014), 15–16.

2. Jeff Miner and John Tyler Connoley, *The Children are Free: Reexamining the Biblical Evidence on Same-sex Relationships* (Indiana: Jesus Metropolitan Church, 2002), 40–42.

3. Fritz Guy, "Same-sex Love: Theological Considerations," in *Christianity and Homosexuality: Some Seventh-day Adventist Perspectives* (California: Adventist Forum, 2008), P4–53.

CHAPTER 13: SAYING NO TO DIVINE VIOLENCE

1. Distefano, *Heretic!*, 72–74

2. Andrea Bistrich, "Discovering the common grounds of world religions," interview with Karen Armstrong, Share International, Sept. 2007, pp. 19–22.

3. Philip Jenkins, "Dark Passages," *The Boston Globe*, Mar. 8, 2009.

4. Philip Kennicott, "Perspective: In ISIS horror, the old is new," *Tampa Bay Times*, http://www.tampabay.com/news/perspective/perspective-in-isis-horror-the-old-is-new/2216632

5. Enns, *The Sin of Certainty*, 122.

6. Enns, *The Sin of Certainty*, 121.

7. Chris Roberts, "Biblical Literalism and Isis" (Aug. 2014). Article is now offline as of printing. https://www.thebookofwonder.org/2014/08/biblical-literalism-isis/

8. Crossan, *How to Read the Bible*, 235.

9. Ibid., 20.

10. Ibid., 31.

11. Keith Giles, *Jesus Undefeated: Condemning the Doctrine of Eternal Conscious Torment* (California: Quoir, 2019), 148–149.

12. Steve Kline, "New Perspective On God's Wrath," *Patheos.com* (Sept. 2018): http://www.patheos.com/blogs/keithgiles/2018/09/new_perspectives_gods_wrath/

CHAPTER 14: SAYING NO TO HELL

1. Jeff Turner, *The Atheistic Theist: Why There Is No God And You Should Follow Him* (California: CreateSpace, 2016), 183.

2. Turner, *The Atheistic Theist*, 183.

3. Ellen White, *Spirit of Prophecy*, vol. 4 (1884), 356.

4. Ellen White, *Christ Object Lessons* (Washington, D.C.: Review and Herald Publishing Assoc., 1900), 263.

5. Ellen White, *Testimonies for the Church*, vol. 1 (California: Pacific Press Pub., 1868), 23–26.
6. White, *Testimonies*, 39.
7. White, *Spirit of Prophecy*, 354–355.
8. Benjamin Corey, *Unafraid: Moving Beyond Fear-Based Faith* (New York: HarperOne, 2017), 1–2.
9. Turner, *The Atheistic Theist*, 184.
10. Keith Giles, *Jesus Undefeated*, 66.
11. Rob Bell, *Love Wins: A Book About Heaven, Hell, and the Fate of Every Person Who Ever Lived* (New York: HarperOne, 2011), 116–119.
12. Pope Francis as quoted from his interview with Eugenio Scalfari, as found in Tara Isabella Burton, "Pope Francis reportedly denies the existence of hell. Vatican panics." Vox.com (March 30, 2018). https://www.vox.com/2018/3/30/17179952/pope-francis-hell-vatican-interview-scalfari-italian. For the record, the Vatican has denied the statement attributed to Francis, but the fact that Francis routinely goes to be interviewed by Scalfari weakens the Vatican's claims.
13. Pope Francis as quoted from his interview with Eugenio Scalfari, as found translated in Francesca Romana, "Exclusive translation: newest papal controversial declarations to Scalfari – Did pope defend the annihilation of souls?" *Rorate Caeli* (March 24, 2015). https://rorate-caeli.blogspot.com/2015/03/exclusive-translation-newest-papal.html
14. Turner, *The Atheistic Theist*, 201.

CHAPTER 15: SAYING NO TO EXCLUSIVITY

1. John 10:16
2. C. S. Lewis, *The Last Battle* (New York: Macmillan, Collier Books, 1956), 164–65.

CHAPTER 16: WE AREN'T ALWAYS RIGHT

1. Phyllis Trible, "Biblical Views: Wrestling with Faith," 40.5 (Sept/Oct 2014). https://members.bib-arch.org/biblical-archaeology-review/40/5/10

CHAPTER 17: ADAM & EVE'S FAILURE

1. Elie Wiesel, *And the Sea is Never Full: Memoirs, 1969* (New York: Alfred A. Knopf, 1996), 70.

ACKNOWLEDGMENTS

This book is far more than the sum of its words. After a year and a half of writing, and three years of editing, I owe much thanks to a great many people for helping to develop it to this point and time. I may have written the words down, but words by themselves do not create a book (let alone a good one!). If it takes a village to raise a child, it certainly takes many professors, countless classes, many conversations, and plenty of good friends to publish a book. I'm grateful that I had all of them in great abundance.

First and foremost, I want to give a blessing to God not just for the book, but for guiding my life and my experiences so that I could have something to say at all. Likewise, I want to thank my family. I owe so much to my amazing Mother, Virginia, for being my incredible conversation partner in life, who without, many of the insights in this work may not have been included. You dedicated me as a child to ministry and through our many discussions together you have continued to ensure that my calling remains present in my life. Particular thanks is also due to my Aunt Kathy, for whom similar conversations over many years helped to flesh out ideas and approaches to topics that otherwise wouldn't have happened. It pains me deeply that she did not live to see the finished product of those heartfelt heartaches we shared.

I also want to thank Liliia, my wonderful wife, for her tireless support and belief in me, as well as this book. Without her, I may not have stayed sane while writing it. She has been there from the first word typed to the last. Your love continues to show me new insights into God each and every day.

Likewise, certain friends of mine deserve hearty thanks for their patient feedback regarding its early drafts, among them: Cesar Baez, Andrew Goorhuis, Christopher Canon, Andrew Dykstra, Rhonda Dinwiddie, Beau Hoffman, Nathan Jennings, Ryan Becker, and T. J. Sands. Thanks is due certainly to Prof. John Razzouk of La Sierra University, who so graciously gave me the opportunity to pursue this work as my Honors Program project as a Junior, and took a risk on whether or not I would be able to pull it off. Furthermore, I would be remiss not to express my gratitude to all the professors of the H.M.S. Richards Divinity School who helped to grow and refine my understanding of faith over those five years, as well as the faculty at Yale Divinity School who have shared their influence with me at the tail-end of this project.

Equally, I am in the debt of Mark G. Karris for initially reading my book and recommending it to his publisher at Quoir, to whom this book's physical existence is entirely owed. Mark has proven to be the single most gifted and talented conceptual editor I've ever experienced, and one of the kindest people as well. And last but not least, I want to express my gratitude to my publisher, Rafael Polendo, for his enduring patience. Although accepted for publication in early 2018, it would not be until late 2019 that the manuscript finally arrived. Part of that was Mark's fault, part of that was mine, and all of it led to a much better book overall. Thank you for believing in this project.

For more information about Matthew J. Korpman,
or to contact him for speaking engagements,
please visit *www.MatthewJKorpman.com*

Many voices. One message.

Quoir is a boutique publisher
with a singular message: *Christ is all.*
Venture beyond your boundaries to discover Christ
in ways you never thought possible.

For more information, please visit
www.quoir.com